Teaching
Main Idea
Comprehension

James F. Baumann
Editor
Purdue University

Published by the
INTERNATIONAL READING ASSOCIATION
800 Barksdale Road   Box 8139
Newark, Delaware 19714

INTERNATIONAL READING ASSOCIATION

Copyright 1986 by the
International Reading Association, Inc.

Library of Congress Cataloging-in-Publication Data
Main entry under title:

Teaching main idea comprehension.

   Includes bibliographies.
   1. Reading comprehension—Addresses, essays, lectures.
2. Study. Method of—Addresses, essays, lectures.
I. Baumann, James F.
LB1050.45.T43   1986   428.4'3   85-23185
ISBN 0-87207-968-6
Second Printing, December 1986

Contents

Foreword

Even though it would be difficult to find anyone who disagreed with the contention that "reading" and "comprehending" are synonymous, it is only in recent years that researchers and practitioners have directed their thoughts and efforts to comprehension instruction. Earlier, the assumption seemed to be that if students were asked questions about the content of written text, they would somehow succeed in comprehending it. One consequence of such a posture for classroom practices was constant assessment of abilities that had never been taught. A further result was to view additional questions as the means for remedying any problems that might occur in comprehending.

Teaching Main Idea Comprehension is part of the ever increasing evidence that distinctions are finally being made between teaching comprehension and testing comprehension. The specific focus of this publication shows courage on the part of the contributors to deal with a concept that traditionally has suffered the pangs of being misunderstood; of being repeatedly but erroneously equated with topic, theme, and unstated conclusion; and of being introduced in basal reader programs both prematurely and in the wrong context — namely, in narrative text. The mistreatment explains why the first chapter in the present publication bears the title, "The Confused World of Main Idea."

What the authors cover in the eleven chapters that make up *Teaching Main Idea Comprehension* is clearly described in the Introduction. Even a quick look at the descriptions of the chapters points out that the content will be of interest and value both to researchers and to practitioners. The content might even be viewed as one response to teachers who often send me requests such as, "I know that I don't do enough with comprehension instruction. Since suggestions for teaching comprehension in my basal reader manual are both scarce and brief, is there something I can read that will help me offer more and better comprehension instruction?"

While publications such as *Teaching Main Idea Comprehension* do offer badly needed help, it is still up to teachers themselves to make sure that comprehension instruction is not assigned so much importance that the reason for providing it is forgotten. Main idea instruction, for example, is of little significance unless it is offered in a way that allows students to see its value for helping them understand and retain important content in whatever it is they either are asked to read or choose to read.

Let us keep comprehension instruction, then, from becoming an end in itself. This will require practice and application, beyond the customary workbook page and duplicated worksheet.

Dolores Durkin
University of Illinois

Introduction

At the annual meeting of the National Reading Conference in Austin, Texas, in December 1983, Jim Cunningham, Dave Moore, and I were chatting about the various presentations. I commented that a number of papers on the program dealt with the topic of main idea or importance in prose. As we counted the different papers and presenters reporting research under the rubric main idea, I realized that a volume containing state-of-the-art work on theoretical and instructional aspects of main idea comprehension would be useful to our colleagues and to practitioners. Jim and Dave agreed and, with a little brainstorming, we identified a number of prospective contributors. The result: *Teaching Main Idea Comprehension*.

The opening chapters in the monograph address definitional, theoretical, and foundation level issues in main idea comprehension. Despite their theoretical concerns, these chapters have been written with the practitioner in mind, as each contributor has taken considerable effort to discuss instructional implications. Then, the emphasis shifts completely to that of the practitioner, as later chapters focus on instructional concerns about how to teach main idea comprehension. Therefore, the word *teaching* in the title is not accidental; this volume was prepared to provide educators the most recent information about how young, developing, and skilled readers comprehend important information in written prose and how one might best teach a variety of main idea abilities to students not yet completely skilled in main idea comprehension.

In the opening chapter, James Cunningham and David Moore face the difficult task of defining what is meant by main idea. Researchers and curriculum developers often quite glibly use terms such as main idea, topic, title, topic sentence, and gist. Cunningham and Moore offer operational definitions—and rules for their use—for nine different main idea tasks and relations.

In Chapter 2, Peter Winograd and Connie Bridge review the voluminous and diverse literature on the topic of importance in prose. Winograd and Bridge succeed in synthesizing the research in an organized and comprehensible manner so researchers and practitioners will be able to draw upon the data base.

Winograd and Bridge note that by understanding "how fluent readers are able to identify the information which the author considers important, then we will be in a better position to help younger and poorer readers learn to identify important information." In the following chapter, Peter Afflerbach and Peter Johnston examine this very topic by presenting an analysis of their rich think-aloud data from expert readers as they attempted to puzzle out implicit main ideas in difficult expository texts. Afflerbach and Johnston provide an insightful analysis of the strategies and cues expert readers use when constructing main ideas, and they translate these findings into suggestions about how we might better design an instructional program in main idea comprehension.

Joanna Williams has engaged in an extensive research program designed to identify variables that influence how normally achieving children, learning disabled children, and adults comprehend the main ideas in written prose. She describes this line of research in Chapter 4 and discusses the implications of her work in building a model of expository text processing. Williams also reports the results of an interesting instructional study in which she evaluated the effectiveness of a program to teach learning disabled students to comprehend main ideas.

The shift to an institutional perspective continues as Mark Aulls discusses the principles and practices of active teaching. Aulls presents his four step, active teaching model and describes its uses and implications in providing students formal, systematic instruction in main idea skills.

The remaining chapters describe specific, empirically based instructional strategies for teaching main idea. In Chapter 6, I present a direct instruction approach for teaching main ideas that embodies findings from teacher effectiveness research. Several model lessons that exemplify the five step strategy are presented along with suggestions and an example about how a teacher might modify or adapt existing commercial materials to improve main idea instruction.

In Chapter 7, Victoria Chou Hare and Adelaide Bates Bingham offer several alternatives to the practice-only approach to main idea found so often in commercial materials. Their alternatives involve using discovery lessons and direct instruction lessons that teach students to use narrative form and expository text structure cues to determine central story elements and main ideas in informational texts.

Chapters 8 and 9 are concerned with teaching middle grade and secondary students to comprehend important information in content textbook material. Barbara Taylor describes three instructional approaches, along with underlying and validating research, for teaching students to summarize textbook passages. The strategies she presents include hierarchical summarizing, cooperative summarizing, and mapping.

Donna Alvermann recommends that various graphic organizers (visual aids that cue the relationship between superordinate and subordinate information in a passage) be used to help students identify, remember, and learn important ideas in textbook material. She describes and provides examples of three different types of graphic organizers (restructuring organizer, lookback organizer, organizer plus summarizing) as well as several extensions of graphic organizers (lesson organizers, thematic organizers).

In Chapter 10, James Flood and Diane Lapp approach teaching main idea comprehension from a composing perspective. Drawing from the emerging knowledge of reading/writing interrelationships, Flood and Lapp describe and provide an example of a four-step procedure for guiding students in composing and, hence, comprehending main ideas. Their procedure involves a prewriting stage, a theme composing stage, an elaboration on the theme stage, and an editing/rewriting stage.

The final chapter in the volume describes a main idea instructional program for low performing children, that is, students who have failed to acquire sufficient main idea comprehension skill by way of traditional, developmental instruction. Edward Kameenui presents a direct instruction approach to teaching main idea comprehension according to the Engelmann and Carnine design of instruction perspective. Kameenui provides several sample lessons which adhere to this design of instruction approach to main idea.

This monograph provides current information on theoretical and practical issues surrounding the complex task of understanding and teaching main idea comprehension. Indeed, we believe that our work will benefit classroom teachers struggling with helping students understand main ideas, curriculum developers in their quest to produce effective instructional materials on main idea, and researchers who seek to explore further the importance in prose phenomenon. We do hope that our collective efforts in *Teaching Main Idea Comprehension* will provide guidance and assistance to educators committed to teaching students the often elusive and enigmatic concept called main idea.

JFB

Contributors

Peter P. Afflerbach
Emory University
Atlanta, Georgia

Donna E. Alvermann
University of Georgia
Athens, Georgia

Mark W. Aulls
McGill University
Montreal, Quebec

James F. Baumann
Purdue University
West Lafayette, Indiana

Adelaide Bates Bingham
Beloit College
Beloit, Wisconsin

Connie A. Bridge
University of Kentucky
Lexington, Kentucky

James W. Cunningham
University of North Carolina
Chapel Hill, North Carolina

James Flood
San Diego State University
San Diego, California

Victoria Chou Hare
University of Illinois
Chicago, Illinois

Peter H. Johnston
State University of New York
Albany, New York

Edward J. Kameenui
Purdue University
West Lafayette, Indiana

Diane Lapp
San Diego State University
San Diego, California

David W. Moore
University of Northern Iowa
Cedar Falls, Iowa

Barbara Taylor
University of Minnesota
Minneapolis, Minnesota

Joanna Williams
Teachers College
Columbia University
New York, New York

Peter N. Winograd
University of Kentucky
Lexington, Kentucky

1

The Confused World of Main Idea

James W. Cunningham
David W. Moore

The term main idea *has a multiplicity of definitions within the research literature and within the domain of comprehension instruction. James Cunningham and David Moore attempt to clarify the confusion surrounding the varying conceptions and definitions of main idea by providing operational definitions for nine different terms used to denote important information in written prose. They present empirical support for their main idea classification system by reporting the responses supplied by sixth graders, preservice teachers, and inservice teachers when asked to determine the main idea of a short text. Cunningham and Moore conclude their chapter with an analysis of the various tasks used to teach and assess main idea comprehension and with several guidelines for main idea instruction.*

D uring typical recitations in 19th century schoolrooms, teachers asked students question after question until they had covered all the facts in a text. In lieu of questioning, students sometimes recalled the information verbatim from the text. The common practice was to treat all textbook information as of equal worth. In a leading professional text of its day which opposed traditional practices, McMurry (1909) pointed out that students who came through such a recitation format were "bound to picture the field of knowledge as a comparatively level plain composed of a vast aggregation of independent bits" (p. 92). McMurry and numerous others who helped notions of modern education emerge at the turn of this century frequently suggested focusing students' attention toward the important information in passages.

Helping students attend to main, or important, information seems to have become one of the accepted goals of reading instruction by the 1920s. Four elementary school courses of study that we inspected (Callahan, 1922; Course of Study, 1921; O'Hern, 1921; Reading in the St. Cloud Public Schools, 1924) included that goal stated in various ways across the grade levels. A survey of reading practices in the 1930s (Carr, 1935) revealed a widespread concern for helping students get main ideas. At present, noting main ideas and supporting details is the comprehension activity most frequently presented in four basal reader programs and most frequently recommended in five reading methods textbooks (Johnson & Barrett, 1981).

Educators have increasingly given attention to main idea comprehension, but with no concomitant increase in the clarity of what is meant by *main* or *important* ideas. The exact nature of main ideas and the teaching practices intended to help students grasp main ideas vary considerably. This variation is not a recent phenomenon. We consulted journal articles and leading textbooks from the 1920s and 1940s that dealt with main idea (see Appendix) and listed the terminology associated with that concept along with recommended teaching practices. Table 1 lists the terminology associated with main idea, and Table 2 presents the recommended teaching practices. As you can see, the diversity is striking.

Table 1

MAIN IDEA TERMINOLOGY FROM JOURNAL ARTICLES AND LEADING TEXTBOOKS
OF THE 1920s AND 1940s

Read in order to get the

general impression	outstanding point
general import	outstanding feature
general significance	
main implication	bird's eye view
central theme	kernel of the whole
central truth	heart of the passage
important element	
main point	
large view	master idea
writer's message	big idea
point of view	outstanding idea
	controlling idea
	significant idea

Cunningham and Moore

What is the passage mostly about?
What do you think is important in the passage?
What do all the facts have in common?
What do all the sentences center around?
Is the title of the passage a good one?
What is the author/passage mostly talking about?
What is the author/passage trying to say?
What is the author/passage trying to point out?
What is the author/passage trying to get across?
What is the author/passage trying to tell you?
What is the author/passage showing us?

Table 2

RECOMMENDED MAIN IDEA TEACHING PRACTICES FROM
JOURNAL ARTICLES AND LEADING TEXTBOOKS OF THE 1920s AND 1940s

---

General Recommendations

- Explain the need for selective reading.
- Challenge students to read at a high level of attention.
- Read a passage and state the main points as students follow along.
- Discourage home tutoring that drills students on verbatim memory for recitations.

Provide Appropriate Materials

- Have students read materials which contain subject matter with the greatest personal appeal.
- Provide an abundance of red-blooded silent reading material.
- Have students read materials at independent levels.
- Allow students to follow the promptings of their curiosity.
- Answer riddles, such as
     What am I?
     I am little.
     I am round.
     I grow on a tree.
     Birds like to eat me.
- Assign a long passage and provide a short period of reading time before discussing the passage.

Assign Purposeful Activities

- Make purposeful assignments.
- Remind students continually of the definite problems to be solved by reading.
- Set a purpose, check if the purpose was met, have students read section that supports their answer.
- Have students read parts from a passage that supports answers or points made during discussion.
- Direct students to locate and orally read specific parts of a passage (e.g., "Read the part that describes how the animal felt.").

Help Students Translate Text Information

Have students

- Mark most important words.
- Underline sentences that contain most important information.
- Mark important parts of a passage.
- Line out subordinate information.
- Write down the main points.
- Write headlines for news items.
- Produce a suitable main idea/topic/title/name for paragraphs/passages.
- Produce topic sentences if none are included.
- Outline passages.
- Make running notes.
- Create sentence strips that contain significant facts or episodes.
- Reproduce stories by telling/illustrating/dramatizing.
- Summarize passages.
- Write titles.

Provide Advice Regarding How to Find Main Ideas

- Examine the passage title.
- Find topic sentences.
- Note signposts such as headings and subheadings, introductory and concluding paragraphs, and words that signal relationships among ideas in a passage.
- Follow the author's organization.
- Skim.
- Concentrate.
- Preview the selection before reading.

Provide Recognition Exercises

- Select from several choices the best statement of the main idea/title/heading.
- Match main idea statements/titles/headings with paragraphs/passages.

Cunningham and Moore

A Dictionary of Reading and Related Terms (Harris & Hodges, 1981) attested to the confusion about the nature of main idea with this note: "There is little agreement on what a main idea is" (p. 188). And in a recent survey of reading professionals, 100 percent of the respondents agreed that main idea could be stated in more than one way (Ladd, 1983). Finally, on a personal level, we have found few reading educators, including ourselves until a few years ago, who were willing to conduct main idea instruction or main idea practice exercises without having the answer key nearby.

Against this backdrop, we set out to investigate the nature of main idea and main idea instruction. What follows is a report of some of our progress to date. We close with a few brief recommendations for main idea instruction.

A Summary of Our Empirical Investigations

Imagine that you selected the following passage from a piece of supplementary instructional material designed for third graders.

> Some horses are said to become "loco" or insane from eating the locoweed. They stagger around half blind and chew on tin cans or old bones—anything at all, even barbed wire. Their joints get stiff. Their coats become rough. Soon death puts an end to their misery. (Boning, 1970)

Assume that you selected this passage because it typifies the short, high interest materials that students frequently encounter during reading skills instruction and because it contains a clear topic sentence at the beginning followed by a step-by-step explanation of its subject. Imagine that you asked sixth grade students, college students who intend to be teachers, and elementary school teachers to read this passage and "decide what its main idea is." And imagine further that, instead of using a multiple-choice format so customary with such materials, you had readers write down their responses. What would you expect them to write?

We have described research like the above in two reports (Moore, Cunningham, & Rudisill, 1983; Cunningham, et al., 1984). We were curious about the types of responses good readers produced when directed to get the main idea. In order to come up with a system for classifying the responses that the readers in our studies produced, we read other readers' responses to other main idea tasks and thought about what readers might consider main or important. We identified nine types of main idea responses. The nine types, their definitions, and an example of each in response to the passage above are listed in Table 3.

Table 3

DEFINITIONS AND EXAMPLES OF NINE MAIN IDEA TASKS

Main Idea Task	Definition and Example
Gist	• A summary of the explicit contents of a passage achieved by creating generalized statements that subsume specific information and then deleting that specific (and now redundant) information. "Locoweed is poison for horses."
Interpretation	• A summary of the possible or probable implicit contents of a passage. "Horses don't always know what is good for them."
Key Word	• A word or term labeling the most important single concept in the passage. "Horses."
Selective Summary/ Selective Diagram	• A summary or diagram of the explicit contents of a passage achieved by selecting and combining the most superordinate and important words and phrases (or synonyms for them) from a passage. "Horses go crazy, get sick, and die after eating locoweed."
Theme	• A generalization about life, the world, or the universe that the passage as a whole develops, implies, or illustrates but which is not topic or key word specific. "Animal owners have a great responsibility for their charges."
Title	• The given name of the passage. [Not applicable for "locoweed" passage.]
Topic	• A phrase labeling the subject of a passage without revealing specific content from the passage. "What happens when horses eat locoweed."
Topic Issue	• A single word, term, or phrase labeling a conceptual context for the passage. "Dangerous plants."

Cunningham and Moore

Topic Sentence/	
Thesis Sentence	• The single sentence in a paragraph or passage which tells most completely what the paragraph or passage as a whole states or is about. "Some horses are said to become 'loco' or insane from eating locoweed."
Other	• Any response that cannot be classified as one of the other main idea types. These would include all literal and critical responses.

As you can see, the nine types all emphasize important, rather than trivial, information from the passage. For instance, a key word *(horses)* and a theme *(animal owners have great responsibility for their charges)* both emphasize the prominent ideas of the passage—neither one mentions what loco horses chew on or what their coats become. However, key words and themes differ in that one consists of a single term labeling the most important concept, and the other is a generalization about life derived from the passage. Our point here is that different types of main ideas are legitimate.

In addition, as you can see in the nine types listed in Table 3, the term *main idea* does not appear. We concluded that *main idea* has been used so many ways that giving it one more meaning would only add to the confusion. Instead, we choose to use *main idea* as the general, umbrella term to encompass the nine specific types listed here. We agree with Pearson (1981) that "the term main idea is but a main idea for a polyglot of tasks and relations among ideas" (p.124).

Which types of main idea responses occur most frequently when readers are asked to produce a main idea? Table 4 presents the percentage of main idea statements for each type produced by the sixth graders, would-be teachers, and teachers who participated in our studies. As Table 4 shows, readers produce diverse responses. Although individual readers tended to produce the same type of response consistently for each passage (e.g., a reader who produced a gist for one passage tended to produce a gist for all passages), there were striking differences between readers. Topics were produced most frequently, but five other main idea types were also produced a substantial number of times. The readers in our studies held various notions about what they should produce when directed to get the main idea.

Table 4
Percent of Subjects' Main Idea Statements in Each Category

Subjects	Gist	Interpretation	Key Word	Selective Summary/ Diagram	Theme	Topic	Topic Issue	Topic Sentence	Other
Teachers	17.2	2.3	0.0	5.5	0.0	64.8	5.5	3.1	1.6
Would-Be Teachers	17.9	0.5	0.0	26.0	0.0	49.5	1.5	3.1	1.5
Sixth Graders	7.6	2.5	3.2	9.6	0.0	38.2	2.5	24.2	12.1

From Cunningham, Graham, Moore, and Moore, 1984.

Determining Right and Wrong Main Idea Responses

It now makes sense to discuss whether a particular main idea response is right or wrong. After all, readers frequently aim at the main idea of a passage but miss the mark. Note that we do not attempt to decide which of the nine types of main idea responses are correct or incorrect; we assume that each type can be defended because each one identifies important information from a particular perspective. Thus, we evaluate readers' responses by determining which type of main idea response it seems to be and then determining if the particular response is an acceptable member of its type. Of course, all other responses, by definition, are considered incorrect. The following is a sample of how we would evaluate the correctness of various main idea responses which we obtained from readers while conducting our studies.

"Locoweed." (sixth grader)

Locoweed seems to be a statement of a Key Word. However, it cannot receive full credit as an acceptable main idea response because *horses* is the more appropriate Key Word in the passage. *Locoweed* might receive half credit because it is the second most important word in the passage.

"They talk about what horses can do." (sixth grader)

This response cannot receive full credit as an acceptable Topic because the statement, *What horses can do,* does not clearly label the subject of the passage. Horses can do countless things, so this statement is too broad to be an acceptable Topic. Additionally, this statement is not a good Topic

Cunningham and Moore

Issue because it does not delineate a clear conceptual context for the passage. One cannot, for example, imagine the passage appearing as a paragraph in a longer selection that deals with "what horses can do." An acceptable Topic Issue might have been *poisonous plants, dangers to horses,* or *problems for ranchers.* The passage contains information that is more specific than what horses "can do"—the passage describes what happens to horses if they eat a particular plant.

"The effect of locoweed on horses." (teacher)

This statement would receive full credit as a Topic because it states the specific subject of the passage. It reports the fact that *horses* is primarily what the passage is about, and it further reports the fact that *the effect of locoweed* narrows the discussion about *horses.*

"Maybe they shouldn't make the stuff that kills them. Horses want to live as much as people do." (sixth grader)

This response appears to be an attempted Interpretation. It cannot receive full credit because the statement assumes that locoweed is manufactured and that assumption is false and should be known to be false by an average or above average sixth grader. Half credit might be given for the insight that horses should not be allowed to eat locoweed, which the passage implies.

"Some horses go insane from eating the locoweed." (teacher)

The topic sentence of the passage, *Some horses are said to become "loco" or insane from eating the locoweed,* is reflected almost totally by this response. This response is synonymous with the topic sentence of the passage; consequently, it is an acceptable Topic Sentence.

"Horses die from eating locoweed." (teacher)

This statement goes into more detail than is needed for it to be a Topic. Additionally, it takes the most important words from the passage and combines them to form a summary. As a result, it is a good Selective Summary of the passage, although, to be perfect, the word *some* should have started the response.

"How harmful the locoweed can be to horses." (teacher)

This is a perfect gist statement. It contains accurate, general information about the impact locoweed has on horses. This statement provides too much information to be a Topic, and it is too generalized to be a Selective Summary.

A Broad View of Main Idea: Main Idea Tasks

This section presents a broad view of the concept of main idea. In this section, we move from an analysis of readers' responses when directed only to "get the main idea" to an analysis of different possible main idea tasks. We believe that an appropriate goal of main idea instruction in a K-6 or K-8 reading curriculum is to teach students to respond completely and correctly to a variety of main idea tasks. Our purpose here is to supply enough information so that teachers and publishers can analyze their reading lessons and determine whether a balanced program of main idea instruction is being pursued.

Tasks are the basic units of instructional programs (Doyle, 1983). A reading comprehension task is defined by what students do before, during, and after reading a passage. Tasks differ from responses because tasks define the immediate conditions in school that lead students to produce their responses. Tasks make up the work that students perform; they are the same thing as school assignments. Much research indicates that the same readers reading the same passage will produce different responses when given different types of comprehension tasks.

To help clarify the nature of main idea tasks so that educators can insure balanced instruction, we developed a set of guidelines in question form. To answer these questions about a comprehension task, you need to have a copy of the passage which students read, you would have to know the directions students were given before reading, and you would have to know the actual activity conducted during and after reading.

Question #1: What regulates readers' attention?

All main idea tasks require readers to attend to some information more than to other information. Readers pay attention to certain information in a passage because of one or both of two reasons: 1) the directions given before reading made the information relatively important, or 2) the author of the text made the information relatively important in writing the text. Stated differently, readers' purposes for reading as well as writers' presentations of information serve to regulate readers' attention.

Think about the reading passage presented earlier. The author emphasized the idea that some horses who eat locoweed die. Readers who allow the writer to regulate their attention come away with some form of that emphasis as the main idea. However, a reader with a specific purpose in mind might have a different set of ideas. If a reader's purpose for reading were to compile information about the symptoms of illnesses that horses might demonstrate, then that reader would ignore the author's emphasis and pay attention to the specifics about horses staggering around, chewing on unusual materials, and getting stiff joints and rough coats. In other words, either the reader or the writer can determine main or important information.

The role of purpose in regulating readers' attention toward particular information in a text has been recognized in the professional literature since the beginning of this century. The research report by Judd and Buswell (1922) provided considerable support for this view. By the 1940s the role of purpose in determining comprehension made up part of the accepted knowledge base of the reading field. For example, Betts (1946) reported that "In short, comprehension is controlled to a large degree by the purpose of the activity" (p. 95). Gates (1947) clearly recognized the role of purpose in regulating readers' attention toward main ideas:

> There is a distinction between reading merely to note the main ideas given in a passage and reading to select the materials related to some particular need. Thus a pupil may read a selection merely to report the main ideas or he may read to note the main ideas which can be applied to his purpose. (p. 462)

Note that the types of main idea responses presented earlier are ones that came from following the writer's presentation of ideas. Subjects in the studies were directed to "Read each passage and decide what its main idea is." This purpose actually is somewhat vague; it does not focus readers on any specific information. Readers with a concrete problem to solve such as "What is the ocean floor like?" or "Why did the Roman Empire fall?" have a definite purpose that drives them to specific information. A purpose such as "What is the main idea of this passage?" leads readers to depend on writers' presentations of information in determining importance. Thus, types of main idea responses such as Gist, Topic, and Theme necessarily are based on a writer's organization rather than on an organization imposed by a reader.

A second important point is that in order to be a main idea task, a comprehension task must require attention to some specific facts and ideas, rather than allowing all facts and ideas to be fair game. If either no directions or misleading directions are given before students begin reading, and if the correct response to the task is not information that the author made prominent, then no main idea task has occurred. To illustrate, if a teacher directs students to "Read in order to learn how the children in this story solved their problem," but then, after the reading, only asks students other questions, there was no real main idea task.

Question #2: To what degree are generalizations included in the response?

Some main idea tasks require readers to come up with brief statements that cover an entire passage; other tasks call for long statements that include subordinate information. In other words, some tasks call for readers to produce a short, general statement that encompasses the whole passage (e.g., Key Word, Topic, Topic Issue), and other tasks require supporting information to flesh out the whole (e.g., Selective Summary or Diagram). The primary distinction here is between getting *the* main idea (singular) and getting main *ideas* (plural).

Main idea tasks vary according to the amount of generalizations expected in the final response. For example, one teacher might be satisfied with the term *plants* as an answer to the question "What is the passage about?" Another teacher might want students to include in their response subordinate generalizations such as "The passage is about three kinds of plants: fruits, vegetables, and grains." Still another teacher might want *fruits* classified between *citrus* and *noncitrus,* and so on. As you can see, *fruit* is a generalization for *citrus* and *noncitrus,* yet at the same time, *fruit* can be combined with other items to form the generalization, *plants.*

The question, then, is "How detailed should readers be when including generalizations in their main idea responses?" For instance, producing titles for passages employs only a high level generalization, while producing outlines employs generalizations at high and low levels. Titles are short, yet they stand for the whole passage; outlines include a title, but they go on and include main headings and subheadings which more fully detail the information contained in the passage. In our opinion, activities that include identifying generalizations at different levels, such as outlining, summarizing, and notetaking, should be included as part of main idea instruction. Identifying subordinate generalizations such as *citrus* and *noncitrus* seems clearly within the family of main idea tasks.

Question #3: To what degree is invention required?

One can produce a Title, a Key Word, a Topic Sentence, or a Selective Summary or Diagram by pulling information and terminology directly from a text. But producing a Topic or a Gist requires some generation of ideas beyond the information given, and producing a Topic Issue, Theme, or an Interpretation often requires a great deal of generation of new information. This generation of new information is called invention. Invention frequently

Cunningham and Moore

requires some ingenious thinking because readers are called upon to create, rather than locate, ideas. Invention calls for readers to come up with their own statements of the ideas that underlie a passage.

In order to determine to what degree invention is required in a comprehension task, compare the expected response to the text. Ask yourself if the reader could have created the correct response by selecting words (or synonyms for them) from the text and combining them. If such a combination satisfies the demands of the task, the main idea response requires no invention. If readers need to produce information and terminology not found in the text, then invention is required.

Question #4: To what degree is language expression required?

Comprehension tasks frequently require students to choose between possibly correct responses. True–false and multiple–choice formats, for example, require students to select one answer from some possibilities. Obviously, these tasks require very little language expression. Students can complete them by simply circling or marking out items. Other tasks, however, require students to compose language either orally or in writing. To be sure, the degree to which composition is required in a language expression task can vary considerably. A Key Word or a Topic statement requires only a small amount of language expression; a Gist, Theme, or Interpretation might require a great deal.

Question #5: What is the form of the task directive?

Whenever a main idea task is given to students, it will be expressed in one of two language forms.

Generic, high technical. The teacher will use general, technical terms that the students are expected to understand, such as "topic," "gist," and "interpretation." This terminology is supposed to cue the reader to produce a response that could correctly bear the label of the technical term used.

Generic, low technical. The teacher will use general but commonly used words and phrases. "Tell me what it was about" is an example of such a directive.

The difference between high technical and low technical generic language relative to main idea tasks is fine grained. No absolute scale exists for distinguishing one from the other. Although making the distinction between specific high and low technical generic terminology is difficult, we know that such a distinction exists. To illustrate, a colleague went to a fifth grade class in September and asked the students to summarize a short passage as part of an evaluation project. About half of the students turned in papers with a message indicating that they did not know what *summarize* meant. The next day, asking the same students to write down what they thought a friend should know about the passage in order to pass a test about it, she obtained complete papers from everyone.

Question #6: Where does the comprehension task originate?

The comprehension task originates either in the comprehender or somewhere else. By "somewhere else" we mean that the task originates in the teacher, in a test, in a piece of instructional material, or in a situation such as an assigned project. In order to determine where comprehension tasks originate, we analyze whether the particulars of the task are specified beforehand by the reader or someone else. For instance, if a teacher has set aside time for sustained, silent reading followed by a few minutes when students are free to share what they have read that day, the reading is not voluntary, but the comprehension task originates in the comprehender.

Progressive educators of the 1920s and 1930s argued strongly for tasks originating in the comprehender. Such tasks were termed "purposeful." For instance, Zirbes (1932) claimed that

> There is a vast difference between purposeful reading and assigned reading. The teacher who begins by saying, "Now I want you to do thus and so," is not getting purposeful reading. We must guide the reader to set up purposes for himself. (p. 6)

Recommended Main Idea Instruction

In the ideal main idea instructional program, as we see it, students would be expected by the end of some grade, say sixth or eighth, to produce each of the nine types of main idea responses presented here. Students would be expected to produce responses that in each case were correct examples of their type, given that students had adequate prior knowledge and literal comprehension of the text. In addition, following our broad view of main idea instruction, students would be expected to 1) gather information according to preset purposes for reading as well as according to an author's organization, 2) form generalizations that represented an entire passage as well as aspects of a passage, 3) compose responses as well as select appropriate ones, 4) understand appropriate high technical as well as low technical main idea terms, and 5) originate purposes for reading as well as follow others' purposes for reading.

Getting the main idea would not be seen as a single skill that students should master at each grade level. Instead, main idea would be seen as a strand of the reading curriculum that covered several related areas. Main idea tasks would be woven together so that students became quite sophisticated in their ability to attend to what is important when reading.

In closing, our analysis of the confused world of main idea leads us to some additional guidelines about main idea instruction which we believe deserve consideration. These guidelines are based largely on our opinions— although we like to think that they are informed opinions. The other chapters in this monograph have much to say about the effectiveness of instructional practices, so our recommendations here are brief:

1. Help students develop consistent, clear understandings of the types of main idea responses. Several types of responses fall under the category of main idea, so students require distinct, stable concepts and names for those types. For instance, students need to know if *getting the main idea* means producing a Theme, a Gist, or a Topic Sentence. These three types, and others, can be perfectly appropriate responses to a passage. They are just different, and students need a handle on their differences as well as their similarities.

2. Help students produce various main idea responses through faded instruction. In one of our studies (Moore & Cunningham, 1984), we faded instruction through a three stage teaching process that produced striking results in students' performancee with various types of main idea responses. Using independent level reading materials, a specific main idea type is first presented and explained. Second, students select that type from several choices, and their selections are discussed. Third, students independently produce that type of response and receive feedback. This form of instruction currently is missing in basal reader instruction (see Hare & Milligan, 1984).

3. Help students differentiate between information that is important because of a writer's presentation and information that is important because of the student's purpose. Reading to follow an author's organization is a valuable skill; reading to locate information relative to a particular need also is a valuable skill. Sometimes an author's presentation of information matches the information a student needs, but sometimes students need to ferret out information. Thus, project type activities deserve emphasis.

4. Help students gradually refine their performance with main ideas. Move from simple to complex reading materials, from short to long materials, and from relatively simple main idea responses (e.g., Key Word, Topic Sentence) to complex responses (e.g., Gist, Theme). Along this same line, be sensitive to differences between main ideas that fit narrative materials, such as short stories, novels, and plays, as opposed to expository materials, such as the informational writing found in the content areas.

References

Betts, E.A. *Foundations of reading instruction*. New York: American Book, 1946.

Boning, R.A. *Specific skill series: Drawing conclusions, book C*. Baldwin, NY: Barnell Loft, 1970.

Callahan, J. *A course of study for the elementary schools of Wisconsin*. Madison, WI: Democrat Printing, 1922.

Carr, W.G. *Better reading instruction: A survey of research and successful practice*, Research Bulletin of the National Education Association, Vol. 13, No. 5. Washington, DC: National Education Association, 1935.

Course of study, Baltimore County Public Schools, Grades 1-8—English. Baltimore, MD: Warwick and York, 1921.

Cunningham, J.W., Graham, M.F., Moore, D.W., and Moore, S.A. Teachers' and would-be teachers' conceptions of the main idea. In J.A. Niles and L.A. Harris (Eds.), *Changing perspectives on research in reading/language processing and instruction*. Thirty-third yearbook of the National Reading Conference. Rochester, NY: National Reading Conference, 1984, 75-79.

Doyle, W. Academic work. *Review of Educational Research*, 1983, *53*, 159-199.

Gates, A.I. *The improvement of reading*, third edition. New York: Macmillan, 1947.

Hare, V.C., and Milligan, B. Main idea identification: Instructional explanations in four basal reader series. *Journal of Reading Behavior*, 1984, *16*, 189-204.

Harris, T.L., and Hodges, R.E. (Eds.). *A dictionary of reading and related terms*. Newark, DE: International Reading Association, 1981.

Johnson, D.D., and Barrett, T.C. Prose comprehension: A descriptive analysis of instructional practices. In C.M. Santa and B.L. Hayes (Eds.), *Children's prose comprehension: Research and practice*. Newark, DE: International Reading Association, 1981, 72-102.

Judd, C.H., and Buswell, G.T. *Silent reading: A study of the various types*. Supplementary Educational Monographs, No. 23. Chicago: University of Chicago Press, 1922.

Ladd, E. South Carolina Council of the International Reading Association study on main idea. *IRA speaks: Newsletter of South Carolina Council of International Reading Association*, 1983, 1 (5). (Available from Richard Culyer, Coker College, Hartsville, SC 29550.)

McMurry, F. *How to study, and teaching how to study*. Boston: Houghton Mifflin, 1909.

Moore, D.W., Cunningham. J.W., and Rudisill, N.J. Readers' conceptions of the main idea. In J.A. Niles and L.A. Harris (Eds.), *Searches for meaning in reading/language processing and instruction*. Thirty-second yearbook of the National Reading Conference. Rochester, NY: National Reading Conference, 1983, 202-206.

Moore, D.W., and Cunningham, J.W. Task clarity and sixth grade students' main idea statements. In J.A. Niles and L.A. Harris (Eds.), *Changing perspectives in research on reading/language processing and instruction*. Thirty-third yearbook of the National Reading Conference. Rochester, NY: National Reading Conference, 1984, 90-94.

O'Hern, J.P. The development of a chart for attainments in reading. *Journal of Educational Research*, 1921, *3*, 180-194.

Pearson, P.D. A retrospective reaction to prose comprehension. In C.M. Santa and B.L. Hayes (Eds.), *Children's prose comprehension: Research and practice*. Newark, DE: International Reading Association, 1981, 117-132.

Reading in the St. Cloud Public Schools, Grades 1-6. St. Cloud, MN: St. Cloud Board of Education, 1924.

Zirbes, L. Present practices in teaching reading as they affect child development. In A. Temple (Ed.), *A better beginning in reading for young children*. Bulletin of the Association for Childhood Education. Washington, DC: Association for Childhood Education, 1932, 2-7.

Appendix

Some Publications from the 1920s and 1940s that Treat Main Idea Instruction

Anderson, C.J., and Davidson, I. *Reading objectives*. Chicago: Laurel Books, 1925.

Anderson, C.J., and Merton, E. Remedial work in silent reading. *Elementary School Journal*, 1921, *21*, 336-348.

Betts, E.A. *Foundations of reading instruction*. New York: American Book, 1946.

Bond, G.L., and Bond, E. *Developmental reading in high school*. New York: Macmillan, 1941.

Gates, A.I. *The improvement of reading*, third edition. New York: Macmillan, 1947.

Gist, A.S., and King, W.A. *The teaching and supervision of reading*. New York: Charles Scribner's Sons, 1927.

Harris, A.J. *How to increase reading ability*, second edition. New York: Longman, 1947.

Lyman, R.L. The teaching of assimilative reading in the junior high school. *School Review*, 1920, *28*, 600-610.

Lyman, R.L. *The mind at work*. Chicago: Scott, Foresman, 1924.

Merton, E. The discovery and correction of reading difficulties. In J.L. Bracken (Ed.), *The problem of the elementary school principal in the light of the testing movement*. Bulletin of the Department of Elementary School Principals, Second Yearbook. Washington, DC: Department of Elementary School Principals of the National Education Association of the United States, 1923, 346-363.

Rhodes, E.N. Technique of teaching silent reading. *Elementary School Journal*, 1922, *33*, 296-302.

Shepherd, E. Some silent reading lessons in junior high school English. *School Review*, 1921, *29*, 206-215.

Smith, N.B. *One hundred ways of teaching silent reading for all grades*. Yonkers-on-Hudson, NY: World Book, 1925.

Stone, C.R. *Silent and oral reading*. Boston: Houghton Mifflin, 1926.

Wheat, H.G. *The teaching of reading*. Boston: Ginn, 1923.

Whipple, G.M. (Ed.). *Report of the National Committee on Reading*. Twenty-fourth yearbook of the National Society for the Study of Education, Part 1. Bloomington, IL: Public Schools, 1925.

Yoakam, G.A. *Reading and study*. New York: Macmillan, 1928.

2

The Comprehension of Important Information in Written Prose

Peter N. Winograd
Connie A. Bridge

This chapter reviews the literature on main idea. Peter Winograd and Connie Bridge use a broad conception of main idea—Important Information in Written Prose—and rightly so, for their review encompasses research from a variety of perspectives and sources. After pointing out the lack of precision in defining important information across numerous studies, the authors discuss some of the methodological issues involved in studying important information in prose before turning to the research on how fluent readers identify and process important information. Winograd and Bridge next examine the research on developmental and individual differences in the comprehension of important information, focusing more on research with young and developing readers. The authors conclude with a discussion of the implications of the vast store of research on importance in prose for instruction in main idea and for future research efforts in this area.

In this chapter we review research dealing with the comprehension of important information in written prose in order to help teachers better understand this complex aspect of reading comprehension. A comprehensive review of all the literature pertaining to the comprehension of important information in written prose is beyond the scope of this chapter. Those who wish to achieve a more complete overview should also refer to Baker and Stein (1981), Baumann (1982), Goetz and Armbruster (1980), McConkie (1977), Reder (1980), Shimmerlik (1978), and the other chapters in this volume.

We have organized the chapter around a series of questions, the answers to which should be of value to teachers. First, we will examine what is meant by *important information*. Next, we will look at some of the methodological issues involved in the research that examines the comprehension of important information in written prose. The information in this second section will emphasize some of the methodological difficulties and limitations of translating research findings into classroom practice. Third, we will examine how fluent readers identify and use important information. If we know how fluent readers identify important information, then we will be better able to help younger and poorer readers learn to do so. The fourth question will focus on how developmental and individual differences affect the comprehension of important information. The fifth question will address the issue of how to help less fluent readers better comprehend important information. The sixth and last question will be concerned with identifying some issues for future research.

What Is Meant by the Term "Important Information"?

As Moore and Cunningham have indicated in Chapter 1, a great deal of ambiguity surrounds what is meant by important information. Rather than repeat their discussion, we will emphasize some essential points for understanding the literature reviewed here.

First, the terms used to describe important information lack clarity: Main Idea, Gist, Summary, Main Points, Superordinate Propositions, Plot, Theme, Topic Sentence, Text Structure, Macrostructure, and Schematic Superstructures. Not only does this terminology vary in the research literature, it also varies in basal readers (Winograd & Brennan, 1983) and in children's perceptions of main idea (Moore, Cunningham, & Rudisill, 1983). Although many of these terms share common elements in their definitions, some important differences must be considered. Moreover, the same term may mean different things for different kinds of written prose. Aulls (1978), for example, argues that major differences are involved in identifying main ideas in expository texts and narrative texts. In narrative text, the most important information tells what happened in the story and why. In expository text, the most important information may be the author's thesis or argument and the information that supports this thesis.

Determining importance of information in text is further complicated by the fact that the relative importance of information within the same text varies from reader to reader and from situation to situation depending upon the reader's purpose. This has been experimentally manipulated to demonstrate that, depending upon the reader's perspective, different parts of a text are selectively recalled as important (Anderson, et al., 1977; Pichert & Anderson, 1977).

van Dijk (1979) distinguishes between *textually important* and *contextually important* information. Textually important information is considered important by the author, and well written text is usually organized to communicate this importance to the reader (Clements, 1976; van Dijk, 1979). Textually important information is what teachers generally have in mind when they ask their students to get the main idea, central content, or the gist of a passage.

In contrast, contextually important information is considered important by the reader for any number of personal reasons including interest, background experience, or idiosyncratic purpose for reading (see Cunningham and Moore's "Question No. 1" in Chapter 1). A reader skimming a chapter to find information related to a report is searching for contextually important information.

Obviously, textual importance and contextual importance may coincide, but they also may differ. Researchers (van Dijk, 1979; Winograd, 1984) theorize that fluent readers are flexible in their use of both textual and contextual criteria so that, depending on their purpose, they can determine what is important in a text. Throughout this chapter, unless otherwise specified, importance refers to *textual importance*—those ideas that the author considers central to the text.

The ambiguity surrounding the terminology used to describe important information and the important distinction between textual and contextual importance should emphasize the necessity for examining how different researchers define the term *important information* before drawing conclusions based upon their findings. We can reconcile many of the conflicting results reported in the literature by realizing that, although researchers were using similar labels, they were examining fundamentally different constructs.

What Are Some of the Methodological Issues in the Study of Important Information in Written Prose?

In addition to the confusion surrounding the term important information, a number of other problems are inherent in the study of how important information is comprehended in written prose. The researcher must decide what kind of written prose to examine, how to identify the important

Winograd and Bridge

information, and how to assess comprehension of that important information.

Selecting the Kind of Written Prose and Identifying Its Important Elements

Consider first the interrelated questions of what kind of text to use and how to identify its important elements. For the most part, the research on importance in written prose has involved either single paragraphs (usually expository in nature), short narrative, or short expository passages. These distinctions gloss over some of the real difficulties in classifying connected discourse (Brewer, 1980; Spiro & Taylor, 1980), but they are useful for organizing the literature in a reasonable manner.

Those researchers who have examined importance at the paragraph level have usually focused on the topic sentence as the statement that summarizes the main point of the paragraph (e.g., Aulls, 1975; Bridge, et al., 1984; Danner, 1976; Kieras, 1978). Some researchers have asked subjects to recognize or generate a main idea sentence as a means of assessing their ability to comprehend the main point of the paragraph (Bridge, et al., 1984; Danner, 1976). In other studies, the placement of the topic sentence within the paragraph has been manipulated to determine the effect on main idea comprehension (Flood, 1978; Kieras, 1978).

The methods that researchers have used to identify the important information in longer narrative or expository passages can be classified under two broad headings: 1) readers' ratings of perceived importance (Brown & Smiley, 1977, 1978; Johnson, 1970; Pichert, 1979; Thomas & Bridge, 1980; Winograd, 1984) and 2) more formal analyses of the text structure or content (Kintsch, 1974; Meyer, 1975; Omanson, 1982; Rumelhart, 1977; Stein & Glenn, 1979).

The method developed by Johnson (1970) is a good example of how to determine the most important information in a text using subjects' ratings. First, a group of fluent readers divides the passage into pausal units, that is, those points at which a speaker would pause. Next, another group of fluent readers rates the importance of each pausal unit to the theme of the passage on a four point scale. This is accomplished by having the readers eliminate the one-quarter of the units which they consider least important, and then repeating the procedure twice more until only one-quarter of the pausal units is left. Those pausal units that are eliminated first are the least important; those left at the end are the most important. Although this method of identifying importance lacks a theoretical basis, it and other approaches (e.g., Winograd, 1984) which used readers' ratings do provide a relatively simple and systematic way of identifying importance (Baker & Stein, 1981; Piché & Slater, 1983).

A number of researchers have attempted to develop theoretical rationales for defining what is important in narrative texts. Stein and Glenn (1979), Mandler and Johnson (1977), and others developed story grammars as models of the internal structure of simple stories and used them to identify the important information. The Stein and Glenn (1979) story grammar, for example, consists of six categories arranged in a logical sequence. The story begins with the *setting*, which introduces the characters and gives information about where and when the story takes place. The *initiating event* results in a problem to be solved or a goal to be attained. The *internal response* category describes the protagonist's thoughts and reactions to the initiating events and his or her plans for subsequent behavior. The *attempt* describes the protagonist's efforts to solve the problem or attain the goal. The successful or unsuccessful results of the protagonist's attempts are classified as the *consequence*. The last of the six categories, the *reaction*, includes the protagonist's reactions to the consequence. A number of studies (e.g., Glenn, 1978; Stein & Glenn, 1979) have indicated that story grammars can be extremely useful in predicting which elements of a story subjects will recall. These studies reveal that readers recall the categories of Setting, Initiating Events, and Consequences more often, followed by Attempts, while they remember the categories of Internal Responses and Reactions less often.

Omanson (1982) and others (e.g., Schank & Ableson, 1977) developed methods of analysis which use knowledge of social actions to identify the causal chain of events in narratives. Omanson's method, for example, differs from the story grammar approach in the classification of the story events and states. According to Omanson's analysis, the content of narratives can be classified as central, supporting, or distracting. *Central content* is part of the purposeful causal sequence of actions and events that make up the plot of the narrative. *Supportive* content adds detail to the central content. Such content, for example, might describe the main characters or the setting. Any content that is neither central nor supportive is classified as *distracting*. Examples of distracting content include descriptions of events that do not involve the main characters or descriptions of minor characters. Omanson's research has indicated that this approach to analyzing narratives is also useful in predicting which parts of a story subjects will recall. As one would expect, central content is recalled more often and judged as more important than supportive or distracting content.

The work on story grammars and on causal chains has resulted in testable theories about why some portions of narratives are considered more important and recalled more often than others. Several researchers (e.g., Kintsch, 1974; Meyer, 1975; Meyer & McConkie, 1973) have also developed methods for analyzing expository passages. Meyer's work (1975) has been extremely influential and thus will be used as an example. Her technique for analyzing texts results in a hierarchically arranged tree structure called the content structure. The content structure displays how the content words from the passage are related to one another. More important, the content structure shows which ideas in the passage are superordinate and which are subordinate. Finally, Meyer's method enables one to classify many of the basic organizational structures found in texts. These basic organizational structures include 1) *description*, specifying the characteristics or attributes of an object, person, animal, or event; 2) *enumeration*, listing the facts, details, or components related to a given topic; 3) *sequence*, presenting a series of related events in chronological order; and 4) *comparison-contrast*, comparing two or more events, objects, or people in terms of their likenesses and differences.

The development of these various text analysis systems has stimulated a great deal of productive research. Perhaps one of the most important results of this research is an increased appreciation for the complexity of written prose.

Assessing the Comprehension of Important Information

Recall that the third methodological problem faced by researchers interested in the comprehension of important information in written prose is the method of assessment (Baker & Stein, 1981; McConkie, 1977). A wide variety of methodologies have been used including free recall (Brown & Smiley, 1978), multiple-choice questions (Meyer, 1977), cued recall (Wilhite, 1984), cloze tasks (Whaley, 1981), story production (Whaley, 1981), summary tasks (Brown & Day, 1983; Garner, 1982; Winograd, 1984), think-aloud tasks (Afflerbach & Johnston, Chapter 3 this volume), title selection tasks (Williams, Taylor, & Ganger, 1981), error detection tasks (Englert & Hiebert, 1984; Williams, Taylor, & Ganger, 1981), and rating tasks (Brown & Smiley, 1977; Winograd, 1984). There are advantages and disadvantages to each of these methodologies, and different methodologies may yield different results (Baumann, 1982). To complicate matters even further, there are usually significant differences in how different researchers use the same methodology. For example, some studies have had the subjects write a one sentence summary (e.g., Williams, Taylor, & Ganger, 1981) while other studies have had the subjects produce summaries of sixty words or more (e.g., Day, 1980; Winograd, 1984).

The relationship between the type of assessment of main idea comprehension and the type of task the reader was asked to perform while reading is also important (Bridge, et al., 1984; Dee-Lucas & Divesta, 1980; Taylor & Beach, 1984; Tenenbaum, 1977). For example, Bridge, et al. (1984) found that students who generated a topic sentence after reading each paragraph performed better in a free recall measure, while students who selected a main idea sentence from a pair of sentences performed better on a recognition task.

Taylor and Beach (1984) also found facilitative effects for a generation task that required seventh graders to produce a hierarchical summary of social studies texts as compared to a group which answered and discussed questions about the text and a control group which received no special instruction. Comprehension was assessed by a free recall measure and a short answer test. On the free recall test, the summary generation group was superior to the other two groups on unfamiliar material while both generation and question groups were superior to the control group on familiar material. On the short answer test, both generation and question groups were superior to controls on both familiar and unfamiliar topics. Thus, the facilitative effects of tasks varied according to the degree of familiarity with the topic and the means of comprehension assessment.

The preceding discussion on the methodological problems faced by researchers is meant to alert teachers to the importance of examining the kinds of texts and tasks used in prose research as well as the type of information focused on in the assessment task. General statements drawn from the research literature dealing with the comprehension of important information in written prose must be tempered with specific references to the kinds of texts that were read and the kinds of tasks that were performed both during and after reading.

How Do Fluent Readers Identify the Important Information?

This is one of the central questions in current comprehension research (Stein & Trabasso, 1981; van Dijk, 1979). The answers can provide the basis for understanding how to help younger or poorer readers. Research has consistenly found that fluent readers are more apt to remember super-ordinate ideas than they are to remember subordinate ideas. Regardless of the system used to identify the important ideas—ratings of structural importance (Johnson, 1970), a complex analysis of the hierarchical structure using staging rules (Clements, 1976; Grimes, 1975), or other systems of identifying hierarchical relationships between ideas (Kintsch & van Dijk, 1978; Meyer, 1975; Waters, 1983)—fluent readers tend to recall the important information in a text. Indeed, readers more frequently recalled a paragraph when it was embedded in a passage in which it was important, than when the same paragraph was embedded in a passage in which it was of lesser importance to the meaning of the passage as a whole (Britton, et al., 1979; Meyer, 1975).

How do fluent readers identify the important ideas in text? Two possibilities exist although they are not mutually exclusive. The first is that authors provide cues in the text which mark or accentuate the ideas they deem important. The second possibility is that as readers gain experience with various text types and develop background knowledge about various topics, they develop the ability to differentiate the salient information from the less salient information. Most likely it is a combination of the two possibilities: As readers mature, they increase their knowledge of the world and of text structure and also become more efficient at identifying the methods authors use to mark important information.

Consider first the possibility that authors provide cues in the text which mark those ideas the author considers important. van Dijk (1979) provides a tentative list of these cues, which he calls "relevance signals." Some of these relevance signals include 1) graphical: type size, italics, underlining; 2) syntactical: word order, topicalization; 3) lexical: words like *important, relevant, the subject is, the conclusion is;* 4) semantic: thematic words and sentences, summarizing or introductory sentences, repetition; 5) schematic/superstructural: story grammars, narrative schema, expository text structures.

Research has examined the effect of each of these relevance signals on comprehension (see van Dijk & Kintsch, 1983, for a review of this literature). Of particular relevance to teachers, however, is the research related to topicalization and to text superstructures.

Topicalization

Topicalization refers to authors' use of the *initial mention convention,* in which the first sentence in a paragraph is a topic sentence that introduces the overall theme of the paragraph (Kieras, 1978). Research has indicated

that learners have difficulty comprehending and recalling paragraphs in which the topic sentence is not presented at the beginning of the passage (Bridge, et al., 1984; Flood, 1978; Kieras, 1978). Kieras, for example, showed that passages with summary sentences in the final position produced poorer comprehension, longer reading time, and less recall of passage content than passages with summary sentences in the initial position. A second set of studies (Kieras, 1980) using more naturalistic expository material (*Scientific American* passages) showed that subjects were more accurate in paraphrasing the main idea or in selecting an appropriate title if the topic sentence occurred in initial position than if the same sentence occurred in a different position. Additionally, Baumann (1986) found that when science textbook selections were rewritten so that main ideas were stated explicitly at the beginnings of passages and paragraphs, fifth grade students were more successful constructing main ideas than similar students who read the original versions of the same passages.

Several authors have offered theoretical explanations regarding the important role that initial topic sentences play in text comprehension. Kintsch and van Dijk's text processing model (1978) provides a preliminary explanation for the importance of topic sentences. This model was used in a text comprehension simulation (Miller & Kintsch, 1980) which demonstrated that the failure to present a superordinate proposition in initial position leads to inappropriate processing of the text's meaning. Miller and Kintsch interpreted this finding in terms of a leading edge strategy, which assumes that important propositions are remembered better because they are processed more frequently. The superordinate proposition receives additional processing as each new proposition is connected to it. In passages which violate the initial mention convention, comprehension may be disrupted when a reader fails to locate a related superordinate proposition with which subordinate statements can be connected.

Some research has been undertaken in order to learn how readers might be taught to overcome an author's violation of the initial mention convention. Bridge, et al. (1984) found that when subjects performed meaningful tasks following reading, the disruptive effects of a violation of the initial mention convention were reduced significantly.

Subjects' ability to overcome the disadvantage of reading paragraphs in which a main idea sentence is not explicitly stated in an initial position is important in view of several studies of explicit main idea statements in reading materials. Braddock (1974) evaluated adult expository materials and found that main ideas are directly stated in only 30 percent of all paragraphs and appear as the initial sentence in only 13 percent of the paragraphs. Baumann and Serra (1984) examined second, fourth, sixth, and eighth grade social studies textbooks and found that only 44 percent of the paragraphs contained explicit main ideas and only 27 percent of all paragraphs opened with an explicit main idea sentence. These findings are supported by other research on children's content area textbooks. Anderson, Armbruster, and Kantor (1980), Armbruster and Anderson (1981), and Bransford (1981) have recently observed that many of the texts children encounter in school are not clearly written. Thus it seems important to teach students how to overcome the disadvantages of reading paragraphs without explicit main idea statements, since frequently they will be required to comprehend such materials.

Text Superstructure

Another set of relevance signals which has received considerable attention is that known as schematic superstructures (van Dijk, 1979; van Dijk & Kintsch, 1983). Schematic superstructures refer to how the text is organized at the global level such as time sequence in narratives and thesis and support in expository texts (van Dijk & Kintsch, 1983).

Consider first how fluent readers identify important information in narrative passages. A considerable amount of research and debate has focused on this topic (Omanson, 1982; Nezworski, Stein, & Trabasso, 1982; Stein & Trabasso, 1981). The essence of the debate centered on whether the reader's knowledge of the text structure or knowledge of social actions played a more important role in the comprehension of narratives (van Dijk & Kintsch, 1983). Recently, however, both sides have appeared to reach a consensus on how fluent readers understand narrative texts (Omanson, 1982; Stein, 1982; Stein & Trabasso, 1981).

The first point of agreement is that stories are concerned with human actions and the underlying properties of those actions including motivations, intentions, plans, and goals (Bower, 1978, Bruce, 1978, 1980; van Dijk & Kintsch, 1983). Readers understand narratives when they can identify the motivations, intentions, and plans of the main characters (Bower, 1978). The ability to identify and account for the actions of the characters in stories is, according to Bower (1978) and others (Bruce, 1980; Schank & Abelson, 1977; Stein, 1982), the same ability that is used to understand everyday social interactions. This is an important point, and we will return to it later in our discussion of how younger readers differ from older readers.

The second point of agreement is that the events and action sequences in stories may become conventionalized (van Dijk & Kintsch, 1983); that is, stories do share a common structure which, to use van Dijk and Kintsch's terminology, consists of a setting, a complication, and a resolution. Readers use their knowledge of this structure to help them predict, understand, and retrieve important information in narratives (Stein, 1982; van Dijk & Kintsch, 1983; Whaley, 1981).

Consider next how fluent readers are able to identify important information in expository passages. This, too, is a major area of research, although expository text has received less attention than narrative text. Nevetheless, researchers have offered tentative hypotheses as to how fluent readers process expository texts. Meyer (Meyer, 1979; Meyer, Brandt, & Bluth, 1980) has suggested that fluent readers approach expository texts with some knowledge of how such texts are usually organized. Moreover, one of the strategies that fluent readers have in their repertoire is that of finding and using the text structure to help organize the information in the text. For example, a fluent reader who is reading an article about the problems of preventing oil spills from supertankers will search for some textual organization that will organize into a coherent whole the information contained in the text. In the case of the supertanker passage, the reader may recognize the organizational pattern as one of problem-solution and thus anticipate that the author will soon discuss possible solutions to oil spills.

The tentative nature of the explanations offered in this section on how fluent readers identify the important information in written prose reflects the uncertainty in the research literature. Significant research has been initiated on this issue but, obviously, a great deal more needs to be completed.

How Do Developmental and Individual Differences Affect the Comprehension of Important Information?

One of the findings the early researchers in the area of text comprehension frequently reported was that most adult subjects remembered certain portions of a text while almost no one remembered other portions (Goetz & Armbruster, 1980). When researchers examined the nature of most commonly recalled portions of the text, they noted that these portions were the most important. Intrigued by these findings, several researchers began to study children's recall to see if their patterns of recall matched those of adults (Brown & Smiley, 1977; Johnson, 1978; Mandler & Johnson, 1977; Stein & Glenn, 1979).

A number of studies yielded evidence that even young readers possess expectations regarding the types of events that are likely to occur in narratives (e.g., Stein & Glenn, 1978; Whaley, 1981; Yussen, et al., 1979). Stories that are well structured and adhere to these expectations are better remembered than stories which fail to adhere (Brennan, Bridge, & Winograd, in press; Stein & Nezworski, 1978).

However, young children differ from older children and adults in a number of ways. McConaughy (1980), for example, found that children's summaries of stories focused on the literal information of actions and events but seldom spontaneously included inferences about cause and effect sequences and the motivations of characters. While adults used a social inference schema, children employed a simple description schema. She suggests that children and adults assign hierarchical importance to various story categories differently: Adults assign more importance to psychological cause while children focus on physical cause. Their limited social experiences may account for this difference.

Young children appear to have better developed awareness of narrative text structure than expository structure. Bridge and Tierney (1981) found that third grade children were better able to recall a well structured narrative than an expository passage. Additional evidence comes from Boljonis and Kaye (1980) who found that fourth grade children were better able to recall information presented in a narrative text than the same information presented in an expository text. Baumann (1981), Dunn, Matthews, and Bieger (1979), and Taylor (1980) also found that elementary children had difficulty identifying important information when reading expository texts.

Englert and Hiebert (1984) investigated high and low ability third and sixth grade children's awareness of four types of expository text structures (sequence, comparison-contrast, description, and enumeration). They found that high ability youngsters were better able to identify text structures of all types; furthermore, developmental differences appeared in that third graders were best able to identify sequence structures and had much difficulty with description and comparison-contrast. Sixth graders, on the other hand, had developed some ability to deal with all four text types, although their scores indicated that they had not acquired full knowledge of these structures. From least to most difficult for these youngsters were sequence, enumeration, description, and comparison-contrast. While Meyer and Freedle (1980) had found that adult subjects performing a free recall task demonstrated high ability to deal with comparison-contrast text structures, even the sixth graders in the Englert and Hiebert study found this structure difficult to comprehend.

Because the children in the Englert and Hiebert study probably had not received specific instructions in identifying text structures, we can surmise that knowledge of organizational patterns develops rapidly and more or less spontaneously during the upper elementary years probably through increased experience in reading expository material in content area textbooks. Before third grade, children are exposed primarily to narrative texts and may not have had much experience with the ways that authors organize expository materials.

A particularly interesting finding has emerged from the literature concerning the differences between children's ability to recall important information and their ability to identify important information. A number of studies have produced evidence to support the contention that young children's ability to recall important information in texts may be based on tacit or intuitive knowledge (Brown & Smiley, 1977). In other words, the young child may not have a conscious awareness of the reasons why some information is more important than other information.

In the Brown and Smiley study (1977), for example, children in grades three, five, seven, and university students completed two experimental tasks designed to assess their sensitivity to important information in written prose. One of the tasks involved rating the pausal units (Johnson, 1970) in the story in terms of their thematic importance, while the other involved recalling the stories after listening to them. Analysis of the rating data revealed that the third and fifth grade children (but not the seventh grade and university students) had difficulty in differentiating the pausal units in terms of relative importance. In contrast, analysis of the recall data revealed that the important elements were recalled more often than the unimportant elements by all age groups. Findings such as these indicate that helping children develop the ability to identify and use important information in text may be necessary since the ability to focus on the important information is prerequisite for the type of study reading that children are expected to do in school (Baker & Brown, 1980; Brown & Smiley, 1977).

In many of the studies in which children successfully demonstrated an understanding of main ideas, they listened to the passages (Brown & Smiley, 1977; Christie & Schumacher, 1975; Danner, 1976; Meyer, 1977; Waters, 1978). On the other hand, children had difficulty distinguishing important information when they read the texts. Prosodic cues such as stress, pitch, and intonation, present during listening, possibly helped mark the important ideas (Kleiman, Winograd, & Humphrey, 1979). Hildyard and Olson (1978) found that elementary children were more apt to recall main ideas after hearing texts while they recalled more details after reading texts.

In addition to examining how younger and older readers differ in the comprehension of important information in written prose, research has also focused on how good and poor readers differ in this regard. A number of studies have produced evidence that good readers are more sensitive to the important information in text than are poor readers (Bridge, et al., 1984; Eamon, 1978-1979; Englert & Hiebert, 1984; Fitzgerald, 1984; Hansen, 1978; McGee, 1982; Meyer, Brandt, & Bluth, 1980; Smiley, et al., 1977; Taylor, 1980; Winograd, 1984; Wong, 1979). Consider, as an example, the study reported by Winograd that examined several hypotheses about why some students have difficulty in summarizing expository texts. During part of the study, eighth grade good and poor readers and adults rated the relative importance of each of the sentences within a series of expository passages. Results indicated that good readers were better judges of importance than were poor readers. The correlation between what the good readers and adults considered important was .71; the correlation between what the poor readers and the adults considered important was .46. Moreover, when these data were included in a series of multiple regression analyses, results indicated that sensitivity to importance accounted for a significant proportion of the variance in the children's reading comprehension even after IQ and decoding ability had been taken into account. Winograd interpreted these results as evidence that sensitivity to importance is a crucial difference between eighth grade good and poor readers.

Text and task variations must be taken into account when considering the differences between good and poor readers. Not all of the studies that have focused on good and poor reader differences have found them (e.g., Meyer, 1977; Perfetti & Lesgold, 1977; Taylor & Williams, 1983). For example, Tierney, Bridge, and Cera (1978-1979) did not find ability differences when children were reading expository texts but did find differences in narrative texts (Bridge & Tierney, 1981). In another study (Taylor & Williams, 1983), learning disabled children reading at the third grade level (but whose mean age was 12.9 years) and normal fourth and sixth grade children read short expository passages and then selected an appropriate title and wrote a summary sentence. The results indicated that the learning disabled children and the normal children did not differ on these tasks. In their discussion, Taylor and Williams commented on possible reasons why their results differed from those obtained by others working with learning disabled readers.

It is interesting to note that Wong (1979) found differences in sensitivity to text between LD and nondisabled readers when both groups were exposed to a presentation procedure similar to our reading-with-listening procedure. Wong used age peers and grade appropriate materials, as is often done. In our study, we might well have found differences between types of readers if we had increased the difficulty of the materials and compared our LD readers to age peers who were more proficient readers. (Taylor & Williams, 1983, p. 749)

We can summarize much of the research on developmental and individual differences in the comprehension of important information in prose by highlighting several findings that may be useful for teachers. First, younger readers, like older readers, tend to recall more of the important information than the unimportant information from a text. Second, although younger readers tend to recall the most important information in a text, their ability to do so appears to depend on tacit or intuitive knowledge; that is, they have difficulty explicity identifying this information or in explaining their reasons for recalling the important information. Third, younger readers probably are less sensitive to the relevance signals authors use to mark textually important information and have less social experience and world knowledge to apply to the task of judging importance. Fourth, the ability to identify and use important information in text seems to be an essential difference between good and poor readers. Fifth, as we have stressed throughout this chapter, the differences between younger and older readers and between good and poor readers vary depending upon the type of text and the nature of the task performed during and after reading.

How Can Readers Be Helped to Identify the Important Information in Written Prose?

From an educational perspective, we are most interested in helping readers learn to identify the important ideas in a text. We are encouraged that research findings indicate that certain types of tasks and training procedures help readers focus on important information and thus improve comprehension (e.g., Adams, Carnine, & Gersten, 1982; Barnett, 1984; Bartlett, 1978; Baumann, 1984; Brooks & Dansereau, 1983; Brown & Day, 1983; Brown & Palincsar, 1982; Cunningham, 1982; Fitzgerald & Spiegel, 1983; Gordon & Braun, 1983; Loman & Mayer, 1983; McDonald, 1978; Memory, 1983; Palincsar & Brown, 1983; Palmere, et al., 1983; Taylor, 1982; Taylor & Beach, 1984; Taylor & Berkowitz, 1980; Wong & Jones, 1982).

Generative tasks, in particular, can improve the comprehension of children and adults. Indeed, several studies have shown that both comprehension and memory improve when subjects generate summary sentences about stimulus paragraphs (Dee-Lucas & DiVesta, 1980; Doctorow, Wittrock, & Marks, 1978; Taylor & Beach, 1984; Taylor & Berkowitz, 1980). For example, Taylor and Berkowitz found that sixth graders who generated a one sentence summary for each paragraph of a social studies passage recalled more total information and more main ideas than did subjects who either answered interpolated questions or simply read the material. Doctorow, Wittrock, and Marks showed that children's comprehension and recall for stories were facilitated by either paragraph headings or instructions to generate summary statements. Moreover, the generation instructions were especially helpful for low ability readers. In another study (Bridge, et al., 1984), less fluent adult readers performed as well as the good readers on a free recall posttest when they generated a main idea sentence for each paragraph during reading.

Researchers (Bridge, et al., 1984; Dee-Lucas & DeVesta, 1980; Doctorow, Wittrock, & Marks, 1978) hypothesize that generative tasks may be especially helpful for poor readers who either do not possess or do not spontaneously use effective comprehension strategies, while good readers may spontaneously integrate the contents of a passage and construct the main idea for themselves regardless of processing instructions. However, even good readers recalled fewer main ideas after performing the least demanding processing task of rating comprehensibility than when they were required to generate a main idea sentence (Bridge, et al., 1984). Furthermore, generative tasks that require the formulation of a main idea appear to offer support for readers' efforts to meet the demands of comprehending texts in which explicit main ideas often are not provided.

Free recall or summarization, another type of generative task, has also proved a successful comprehension training strategy (Gambrell, Pfeiffer, & Wilson, 1984; Morrow, 1983). Morrow taught kindergartners to retell orally presented stories and found significant gains in comprehension on untaught stories for the retelling group compared to the control group which drew a picture about the story. After eight individual retelling sessions coupled with question prompts for omitted information, children who participated in the retellings had better total comprehension as well as higher scores on traditional questions and on questions designed to tap story structure.

Gambrell, Pfeiffer, and Wilson compared the effects of retellings and illustrating on fourth graders' comprehension and recall of four expository passages. Students in the retelling groups were told to read the passages and decide what the important ideas were. They were then given a blank outline on which to fill in the important ideas and two supporting details. Students completed the outline with no instruction in how to identify important information and with no teacher correction or feedback. Then the children were assigned partners and took turns retelling "all the important ideas from the story" to each other. The illustration group followed the same procedure except that they illustrated "all the important ideas from the story" rather than retelling. The retelling group had significantly better long and short term free recall and recall on a twenty item test over an untrained passage.

Bridge and Sawyer (1984) reported facilitative effects when they trained second graders to locate the answers to questions that tapped important information and to engage in retellings. Thus, both practice in retellings alone and retellings coupled with questions focusing on important information appear to facilitate children's listening and reading comprehension of important ideas.

Palinscar and Brown (1983) have also reported success in training poor comprehenders at the junior high level to improve their comprehension of important information through use of comprehension enhancing activities including predicting, clarifying, self directed summarizing, and questioning. The procedure was similar in many ways to the direct instruction training in response guidance used by Meichenbaum and Asarnow (1979) in which junior high students were trained to use the following self directions:

> Well, I've learned three things to keep in mind before I read a story and while I read it. One is to ask myself what the main idea of the story is. What is the story about? A second is to learn important details of the story as I go along. The order of the main events or their sequence is an especially important detail. A third is to get to know how the characters feel and why. So, get the main idea, watch sequences, and learn how the characters feel and why. (p. 17)

Palincsar and Brown also employed a variation of the reciprocal questioning strategy (ReQuest) originally introduced by Manzo (1969) and a simplified version of the Brown and Day (1983) summarization procedure to provide a framework for the teacher to model the comprehension processes involved in summarizing and self-questioning. In three different studies, Palincsar and Brown found improvement in ability to answer comprehension questions and in ability to verbalize and control comprehension of important information. They also noted transfer of these behaviors to other classroom tasks and to standardized tests. They attributed the success of this training to the direct instruction provided in how to use comprehension monitoring activities during reading accompanied by explanations of why these activities work and why they are necessary in daily reading tasks.

In addition to the use of generative tasks and direct instruction in activities which foster comprehension, various authors have suggested that children be taught to recognize text organizational patterns as a means of improving reading comprehension (e.g., Allington & Strange, 1980; Readence, Bean, & Baldwin, 1981; Vacca, 1981). Without an understanding of these organizational patterns, students may have difficulty judging the relative importance of ideas in the text. Although little research has been done in teaching children to recognize and employ expository text structures, several studies (Alvermann, 1982; Boothby & Alvermann, 1984; Englert & Lichter, 1982; and Taylor & Beach, 1984) indicate that such instruction may prove helpful.

Englert and Lichter (1982), for example, used an organizational strategy to teach reading and writing skills to sixth grade learning disabled students. They taught the children to use an analogy (the slices of a pie making a whole) to help in learning to locate the main idea and the proofs, examples, and other information supporting the main idea. They suggested varying the text structures of practice passages so students can learn to summarize texts using various types of organizational structures (i.e., problem/solution, antecedent/consequence, description, comparison/contrast, and collection).

The few studies reviewed in this section are meant to provide the reader with a brief introduction to some of the ways students can be helped to comprehend the important information in written prose. An impressive body of literature is beginning to accumulate on this subject; Chapters 6 through 11 of this volume offer specific instructional techniques.

What Are Some of the Future Issues in the Study of Important Information in Written Prose?

Since the ability to comprehend important information in written prose is central to comprehension in general, research in this area will continue along many dimensions. Three lines of research, however, are particularly relevant to practioners.

Toward a Better Understanding of Texts

First, researchers will continue to develop more sophisticated, complete, and accurate methods for analyzing and classifying written prose (Beach & Appleman, 1984; Brewer & Lichtenstein, 1980; Bruce, 1978, 1980; Calfee & Curley, 1984; Lichtenstein & Brewer, 1980; Spiro & Taylor, 1980). Spiro and Taylor, for example, criticize the current approach of classifying texts as either narrative or expository. They point out that disagreement exists on what constitutes an expository text versus a narrative text. Moreover, texts rarely appear in pure types. Characteristics that are considered typical to narratives are often found in expository texts, and characteristics considered typical to exposition are often found in narratives. Perhaps their most telling criticism, however, is that current text classifications ignore many important dimensions of textual differences including the form of the linguistic expressions used (complex syntax, figurative language), the type of content (abstract, concrete), the purpose for which the text was written (entertainment, persuasion), and how the text information will be used later (temporarily to complete a task, memorized for a test).

The development of more accurate and complete text classification systems will enable researchers to understand better how fluent readers identify and use important information. Such systems will also afford researchers more insight into which text factors and dimensions are most troublesome for younger or poorer readers (Johnston, 1983).

Toward Better Instructional Materials

Second, researchers will continue to examine how to improve the instructional materials which are used to teach children how to comprehend important information (Beck, Omanson, & McKeown, 1982; Brennan, Bridge, & Winograd, in press; Winograd & Brennan, 1983). Improving these instructional materials is extremely important because of their powerful influence on what is taught (e.g., Shannon, 1983). Moreover, although getting the main idea is the most common comprehension task mentioned in many of the commercial teaching materials (Johnson & Barrett, 1981), there is a serious lack of understanding on how best to develop children's ability to read for important information in a systematic and effective manner (Winograd & Brennan, 1983).

Evidence that instructional materials need to be improved comes from the study reported by Winograd and Brennan. They examined the teacher's manuals of two basal series for grades one, three, five, and eight in order to see how the manuals defined the term *main idea,* and what kinds of instructional tasks were used to teach children how to identify the main idea. Their initial examination revealed some ambiguity in how main idea and topic were defined and used. To clarify the distinction, Winograd and Brennan compared the definitions presented in the teacher's manuals with the following definitions developed by Aulls (1978, pp. 92-93): "The *topic* of a paragraph signals to the reader the subject of the discourse....The *main idea* of a paragraph signals to the reader the most important statement the writer has presented to explain the topic." One of the basal series did not distinguish between topic and main idea until the third grade and presented main idea first. In contrast, the other series distinguished between topic and main idea in the first grade and presented topic first. Although the sequencing and the timing of instruction differed between the series, both distinguished between the main idea and topic of a passage. However, the distinctions were often blurred even after the differences had been presented.

In addition to the differences in how the basal manuals introduced and defined main idea, Winograd and Brennan (1983) found substantial differences in the practice exercises used to teach main idea. Results indicated no systematic pattern with regard to 1) whether children responded by recognizing or generating the appropriate answers, 2) the kinds of texts that were used, 3) whether the main idea was explicit or implicit, or 4) where explicit main ideas were in the text. For example, in one basal series all of the first grade exercises required the children to select the correct answer, while in the other series over 80 percent of the first grade exercises required the children to generate the correct response. The practice exercises also differed in the type of texts. Both series favored narrative passages in the first grade and expository passages in later grades. One series, however, shifted back to narrative in the eighth grade. One of the series also used other kinds of materials, notably pictures and poetry in the early grades and poetry in the upper grades. Finally, a surprising number of the main idea passages did not have a main idea explicitly stated in the passage. Moreover, when the main idea was explicitly stated, its location varied greatly. Only about half of the explicitly stated main ideas in the first grade exercises were located in the first sentence.

The study by Winograd and Brennan (1983) was descriptive in nature. Other research, however, indicates that children's comprehension improves when basal stories are rewritten to adhere to story grammars (Brennan, Bridge, & Winograd, in press) or to highlight central story content (Beck, Omanson, & McKeown, 1982). Brennan, Bridge, and Winograd asked thirty-two second grade children to read poorly formed versions and well formed versions of two stories. The poorly formed versions were original basal passages which did not adhere to the organizational rules delineated in the Stein and Glenn (1979) story grammar. The well formed versions were developed from the vocabulary of the original basal passages and did conform to the organizational rules of the story grammar. Results indicated that the second grade children recalled significantly more information after reading the well formed versions and that they recalled this information significantly more often in correct sequence. We should not interpret the results of this study to mean that all stories should be rewritten to conform to the rules of story grammars, but the knowledge of how stories are usually organized should be used to select honestly written stories to include in instructional materials (Bruce & Rubin, 1981).

Toward a Better Understanding of Reading Comprehension

The third, but most essential, problem that remains to be studied is still that of *how* readers assign importance to information when reading. Although current research has provided evidence that certain tasks and training strategies lead to better comprehension, we still give readers help in performing what Palincsar and Brown (1983, p. 3) refer to as "comprehension-fostering activities" rather than explicit instructions about how to comprehend because "we are still far from a detailed task analysis of reading comprehension."

Our inability to specify the cognitive processes of readers while comprehending text is a major reason why little comprehension instruction occurs in classrooms (Durkin, 1978-1979) and why basal reader manuals provide numerous instructions directing students to identify main ideas but few instructions in what a main idea is and how to identify it (Hare & Milligan, 1984; Jenkins & Pany, 1980).

Durkin observed third to sixth grade classrooms to determine how much and what type of comprehension instruction was being provided in reading, social studies, and science lessons. She found that less than 1 percent of the time was spent on comprehension instruction but considerable time was spent on comprehension assessment and written exercises. Durkin's definition (1981, p. 518) of reading comprehension, that is, teachers doing something "to help children acquire the ability to understand, or work out, the meaning of connected text," has been criticized on a number of grounds. Heap (1982), for example, argued that Durkin's coding scheme forced teachers' behaviors into a unifunctional scheme, when, in fact, teachers' behaviors can serve many functions at once. A teacher might ask a student a question that simultaneously recaptures the student's wandering attention, assesses the student's current understanding, and helps the student learn about some aspect of the text critical to future comprehension. Another criticism was leveled by Hodges (1980) who argued that Durkin's definition was overly narrow because it failed to include such behaviors as preparation for instruction, motivation, assessing performance, and providing feedback. In reanalyzing Durkin's data using a broader definition of comprehension instruction, Hodges found that teachers spent 23 percent of their time in comprehension instruction.

Despite its limitations, Durkin's study does emphasize the need for more adequate comprehension instruction in classrooms. Durkin's definition of helping children to acquire the ability to "work out" the meaning of text implies that the teacher needs an understanding of the processes involved in comprehending text or at least an awareness of comprehension fostering activities. With the current state of our knowledge, we still are unable to specify what is involved in the comprehension process.

The dilemma is apparent in basal reading materials as well as in classroom instruction. Durkin (1981), Hare and Milligan (1984), and Jenkins and Pany (1980) concur that the instructions in basal reader manuals primarily involve questioning students to see if they comprehended information rather than teaching students how to comprehend.

Consider the data gathered by Hare and Milligan on the kinds of instructions related to main ideas given in the teacher's manuals of four basal reading series. They began their study by drawing a distinction between those instructions which directed pupils to identify main ideas and those instructions which explained to pupils what a main idea is and how to identify it. An example of a directive would be "Choose a main idea for the story"; an example of an explanation would be "To find the main idea, locate the one sentence that the others tell about."

Their results revealed a number of interesting findings. First, the four basal series provided similar types of main idea directives and explanations. Second, directives were more common than explanations. Seventy percent of the 541 instructions reviewed were directives. Third, within the directive category, the majority of the instructions were of the type "Choose a main idea for the story (paragraph, etc.)." The next most common directive required the children to "Generate a main idea for the story (paragraph, etc.)." Fourth, within the explanation category, most of the instruction focused on how to identify the main idea. Hare and Milligan noted that most of the explanatory comments asked students to use their best guess to figure out the main idea rather than offering specific suggestions as to how one separates important ideas from less important ones. Other explanations (in descending frequency) dealt with what a main idea is, where it can be found, and why finding the main idea is an important skill. Two of the 164 explanatory comments instructed pupils how to evaluate the accuracy of a main idea once they had identified it.

Based upon these analyses of basal reader manual suggestions for main idea instruction, Durkin's conclusion (1981, p. 515) may be correct: "Like the teachers, the manuals give far more attention to assessment and practice than to direct, explicit instruction." Even the research that has been labeled as direct instruction in comprehension (e.g., Adams, Carnine, & Gersten, 1982; Meichenbaum & Asarnow, 1979; Palincsar & Brown, 1983) has actually provided guided practice performing comprehension monitoring and comprehension fostering activities (Winograd & Hare, in press). Note the self-directions that Meichenbaum and Asarnow (1979, p. 17) taught students to use: "Ask myself what the main idea of the story is" and "Learn important details." Such self-monitoring alone would probably be inadequate for students who could not assign importance. Palincsar and Brown (1983) went beyond such training in that they modeled and provided guided practice in predicting, arousing prior knowledge, questioning, and stopping to recall main points before proceeding through a passage. Even so, the modeling statements such as, "I would summarize by saying" or "Remember, a summary is a shortened version, it doesn't include detail," still do not tell *how* to summarize or to identify the unneccessary detail.

Thus, the greatest need for further research apparently is to determine the steps in the process which fluent readers use to assign importance. Think aloud procedures, such as those used by Afflerbach and Johnston (see Chapter 3, this volume), may prove helpful. Until the process is more explicitly defined, teachers should find it helpful to use the comprehension fostering activities described earlier in this chapter and elsewhere in this book.

Summary

In this chapter we have described some of the difficulties involved in defining importance in prose and in assessing readers' comprehension of important information. We then attempted to summarize the research regarding what is known about the manner in which fluent readers identify important information and the difficulties that younger and poorer readers have in judging importance. Finally, we have described some tasks and instructional strategies that teachers can use to enhance readers' comprehension of important information.

At the risk of oversimplification, we will summarize as follows: The task of determining importance varies from narrative to expository text, from reader to reader for the same text, and within the same reader for the same text depending upon purpose and context. Nevertheless, good readers appear to be more skillful than younger and poorer readers at using various textual cues to identify what the author deemed important. Certain generative tasks, adjunct aids, and direct instruction strategies have been used successfully to enhance comprehension of important information. Further research is needed to learn more about the nature of written prose in general, and the nature of the written prose most suited for reading instruction in particular. In addition, research is needed to learn more about the process by which fluent readers identify important information, and how to help less fluent readers acquire this skill.

References

Adams, A., Carnine, D., and Gersten, R. Instructional strategies for studying content area texts in the intermediate grades. *Reading Research Quarterly,* 1982, *18,* 27-55.

Allington, R.L., and Strange, M. *Learning through reading in content areas.* Lexington, MA: Heath, 1980.

Alvermann, D.E. Restructuring text facilities written recall of main ideas. *Journal of Reading,* 1982, *25,* 754-758.

Anderson, R.C., Reynolds, R.E., Schallert, D.L., and Goetz, E.T. Frameworks for comprehending discourse. *American Educational Research Journal,* 1977, *14,* 367-382.

Anderson, T.H., Armbruster, B.B., and Kantor, R.N. *How clearly witten are children's textbooks? Or, of bladderworts and alfa.* Reading Education Report No. 16. Champaign, IL: University of Illinois, Center for the Study of Reading, 1980.

Armbruster, B.B., and Anderson, T.H. *Content area textbooks,* Reading Education Report No. 23. Champaign, IL: University of Illinois, Center for the Study of Reading, 1981.

Aulls, M.W. *Developmental and remedial reading in the middle grades.* Boston: Allyn and Bacon, 1978.

Aulls, M.W. Expository paragraph properties that influence literal recall. *Journal of Reading Behavior,* 1975, *7,* 391-400.

Baker, L., and Brown, A.L. *Metacognitive skills in reading,* Technical Report No. 188. Champaign, IL: University of Illinois, Center for the Study of Reading, 1980.

Baker, L., and Stein, N.L. Development of prose comprehension skill. In C.M. Santa and B.L. Hayes (Eds.), *Children's prose comprehension: Research and practice.* Newark, DE: International Reading Association, 1981, 7-43.

Barnett, J.E. Facilitating retention through instruction about text structure. *Journal of Reading Behavior*, 1984, *16*, 1-14.

Bartlett, B.J. *Top-level structure as an organizational strategy of recall of classroom text.* Unpublished doctoral dissertation, Arizona State University, 1978.

Baumann, J.F. Effect of ideational prominence on children's reading comprehension of expository prose. *Journal of Reading Behavior*, 1981, *13*, 49-56.

Baumann, J.F. Research on children's main idea comprehension: A problem of ecological validity. *Reading Psychology*, 1982, *3*, 167-177.

Baumann, J.F. The effectiveness of a direct instruction paradigm for teaching main idea comprehension. *Reading Research Quarterly*, 1984, *20*, 93-115.

Baumann, J.F. Effect of rewritten content passages on middle grade students' comprehension of main ideas: Making the inconsiderate considerate. *Journal of Reading Behavior*, 1986.

Baumann, J.F. and Serra, J.K. The frequency and placement of main ideas in children's social studies textbooks: A modified replication of Braddock's research on topic sentences. *Journal of Reading Behavior*, 1984, *16*, 27-40.

Beach, R., and Appleman, D. Reading strategies for expository and literary text types. In A. C. Purves and O. Niles (Eds.), *Becoming readers in a complex society*. Chicago, IL: National Society for the Study of Education, 1984, 115-143.

Beck, I.L., Omanson, R.C., and McKeown, M.G. An instructional redesign of reading lessons: Effects on comprehension. *Reading Research Quarterly*, 1982, *17*, 462-481.

Boljonis, A., and Kaye, D. *Differences in fourth graders' recalls of written prose as an effect of the type and level of structure present in the text.* Paper presented at the National Reading Conference, San Diego, December 1980.

Boothby, P.R., and Alvermann, D.E. A classroom training study: The effects of graphic organizer instruction on fourth graders' comprehension. *Reading World*, 1984, *23*, 325-339.

Bower, G.H. Experiments on story comprehension and recall. *Discourse Processes*, 1978 *1*, 211-231.

Braddock, R. The frequency and placement of topic sentences in expository prose. *Research in the Teaching of English*, 1974, *8*, 287-302.

Bransford, J. *Reading and learning.* Paper presented at the meeting of the College Reading Association, Louisville, Kentucky, October 1981.

Brennan, A.D., Bridge, C.A., and Winograd, P.N. The effects of structural variation on children's recall of basal reader stories. *Reading Research Quarterly*, in press.

Brewer, W.F. Literary theory, rhetoric, stylistics: Implications for psychology. In R.J. Spiro, B.C. Bruce, and W.F. Brewer (Eds.), *Theoretical issues in reading comprehension*. Hillside, NJ: Erlbaum, 1980, 221-243.

Brewer, W.F., and Lichtenstein, E.H. *Event schemas, story schemas, and story grammars.* Technical Report No. 197. Champaign, IL: University of Illinois, Center for the Study of Reading, 1980.

Bridge, C.A., Belmore, S.M., Moskow, S.P., Cohen, S.S., and Matthews, P.D. Topicalization and memory for main ideas in prose. *Journal of Reading Behavior*, 1984, *16*, 61-80.

Bridge, C.A., and Sawyer, C. *Documenting the relationship between changes in student reading behaviors and instructional interventions in the clinic.* Paper presented at the College Reading Association, Washington, DC, October 1984.

Bridge, C.A., and Tierney, R.J. The inferential operations of children across text with narrative and expository tendencies. *Journal of Reading Behavior*, 1981, *13*, 201-214.

Britton, B.K., Meyer, B.J.F., Simpson, R., Holdredge, T.S., and Curry, C. Effects of the organization of text on memory: Tests of two implications of a selective attention hypothesis. *Journal of Experimental Psychology: Human Learning and Memory*, 1979, *5*, 496-506.

Brooks, L.W., and Dansereau, D.F. Effects of structural schema training and text organization on expository prose processing. *Journal of Educational Psychology*, 1983, *75*, 811-820.

Brown, A.L., and Day, J.D., Macrorules for summarizing texts: The development of expertise. *Journal of Verbal Learning and Verbal Behavior*, 1983, *22*, 1-14.

Brown, A.L., and Palincsar, A.M. Inducing strategic learning from texts by means of informed, self-control training. *Topics in Learning and Learning Disabilities*, 1982, *2*, 1-17.

Brown, A.L., and Smiley, S.S. Rating the importance of structural units of prose passages: A problem of metacognitive development. *Child Development*, 1977, *48*, 1-8.

Brown, A.L., and Smiley, S.S. The development of strategies for studying texts. *Child Development*, 1978, *49*, 1076-1088.

Bruce, B. Analysis of interacting plans as a guide to the understanding of story structure. *Poetics*, 1980, *9*, 295-311.

Bruce, B. *What makes a good story?* Reading Education Report No. 5. Champaign, IL: University of Illinois, Center for the Study of Reading, 1978.

Bruce, B., and Rubin, A. Jobs you shouldn't count on readability formulas to do. In A. Davidson, R. Lutz, and A. Roalef (Eds.), *Text readability*, Proceedings of the March 1980 Conference. Technical Report No. 213. Champaign, IL: University of Illinois, Center for the Study of Reading, 1981.

Calfee, R.C., and Curley, R. Structures of prose in content areas. In J. Flood (Ed.), *Understanding comprehension*. Newark, DE: International Reading Association, 1984, 161-180.

Christie, D.J., and Schumacher, G.M. Developmental trends in the abstraction and recall of relevant versus irrelevant thematic information from connected verbal materials. *Child Development*, 1975, *46*, 598-602.

Clements, P. *The effects of staging on recall from prose*. Unpublished doctoral dissertation, Cornell University, 1976.

Cunningham, J. Generating interactions between schemata and text. In J.A. Niles and L.A. Harris (Eds.), *New inquiries in reading: Research and instruction*. Thirty-first yearbook of the National Reading Conference. Rochester, NY: National Reading Conference, 1982, 42-47.

Danner, F.W. Children's understanding of intersentence organization in the recall of short descriptive passages. *Journal of Educational Psychology*, 1976, *68*, 174-183.

Day, J.D. *Teaching summarization skills: A comparison of training methods*. Unpublished doctoral dissertation, University of Illinois, 1980.

Dee-Lucas, D., and DiVesta, J.J. Learner generated organizational aids: Effects on learning from text. *Journal of Educational Psychology*, 1980, *72*, 304-311.

Doctorow, M., Wittrock, M.C., and Marks, C. Generative processes in reading comprehension. *Journal of Educational Psychology*, 1978, *70*, 109-118.

Dunn, B.R., Matthews, S.R. II, and Bieger, G. *Individual differences in the recall of lower level textual information*. Technical Report No. 150. Champaign, IL: University of Illinois, Center for the Study of Reading, 1979.

Durkin, D. Reading comprehension instruction in five basal reader series. *Reading Research Quarterly*, 1981, *16*, 515-544.

Durkin, D. What classroom observations reveal about reading comprehension instruction. *Reading Research Quarterly,* 1978-1979, *14,* 481-533.

Eamon, D.B. Selection and recall of topical information in prose by better and poorer readers. *Reading Research Quarterly,* 1978-1979, *14,* 244-257.

Englert, C.S., and Hiebert, E.H. Children's developing awareness of text structures in expository materials. *Journal of Educational Psychology,* 1984, *76,* 65-74.

Englert, C.S., and Lichter, A. Using statement pie to teach reading and writing skills. *Teaching Exceptional Children,* 1982, *14,* 164-170.

Fitzgerald, J. The relationship between reading ability and expectations for story structures. *Discourse Processes,* 1984, *7,* 21-41.

Fitzgerald, J., and Spiegel, D.L. Enhancing children's reading comprehension through instruction in narrative structure. *Journal of Reading Behavior,* 1983, *15,* 1-17.

Flood, J.E. The influence of first sentences on reader expectations within prose passages. *Reading World,* 1978, *18,* 306-315.

Gambrell, L.B., Pfeiffer, W.R., and Wilson, R.M. *The effects of retelling upon reading comprehension and recall of text information.* Unpublished manuscript, University of Maryland, 1984.

Garner, R. Efficient text summarization: Costs and benefits. *Journal of Educational Research,* 1982, *75,* 275-279.

Glenn, C.G. The role of episodic structure and of story length in children's recall of simple stories. *Journal of Verbal Learning and Verbal Behavior,* 1978, *17,* 229-247.

Goetz, E.T., and Armbruster, B.B. Psychological correlates of text structure. In R.J. Spiro, B.C. Bruce, and W.F. Brewer (Eds.), *Theoretical issues in reading comprehension.* Hillsdale, NJ: Erlbaum, 1980, 201-220.

Gordon, C., and Braun, C. Using story schema as an aid to reading and writing. *Reading Teacher,* 1983, *37,* 116-121.

Grimes, J.E. *The thread of discourse.* The Hague: Mouton, 1975.

Hansen, C.L. Story retelling used with average and learning disabled readers as a measure of reading comprehension. *Learning Disabilities Quarterly,* 1978, *1,* 62-69.

Hare, V.C., and Milligan, B. Main idea identification instructional explanations in four basal reader series. *Journal of Reading Behavior,* 1984, *16,* 189-204.

Heap, J.L. Understanding classroom events: A critique of Durkin, with an alternative. *Journal of Reading Behavior,* 1982, *14,* 391-411.

Hildyard, A., and Olsen, D.R. Memory and inferences in the comprehension of oral and written discourse. *Discourse Processes,* 1978, *1,* 91-117.

Hodges, C. Commentary: Toward a broader definition of comprehension instruction. *Reading Research Quarterly,* 1980, *15,* 290-306.

Jenkins, J.R., and Pany, D. Teaching reading comprehension in the middle grades. In R.J. Spiro, B.C. Bruce, and W.F. Brewer (Eds.), *Theoretical issues in reading comprehension.* Hillsdale, NJ: Erlbaum, 1980, 555-574.

Johnson, D., and Barrett, T. Prose comprehension: A descriptive analysis of instructional practices. In C.M. Santa and B.L. Hayes (Eds.), *Children's prose comprehension: Research and practice.* Newark, DE: International Reading Association, 1981, 72-102.

Johnson, N.S. *A structural analysis of the development of story recall and summarization.* Unpublished doctoral dissertation, University of California at San Diego, 1978.

Johnson, R.E. Recall of prose as a function of the structural importance of the linguistic units. *Journal of Verbal Learning and Verbal Behavior,* 1970, *9,* 12-20.

Johnston, P. *Reading comprehension assessment: A cognitive basis.* Newark, DE: International Reading Association, 1983.

Kieras, D.E. Good and bad structure in simple paragraphs: Effects on apparent theme, reading time, and recall. *Journal of Verbal Learning and Verbal Behavior,* 1978, *17,* 13-28.

Kieras, D.E. Problems of reference in text comprehension. In M. Just and P. Carpenter (Eds.), *Cognitive processes in comprehension.* Hillsdale, NJ: Erlbaum, 1980, 249-268.

Kintsch, W. *The representation of meaning in memory.* Hillsdale, NJ: Erlbaum, 1974.

Kintsch, W., and van Dijk, T.A. Toward a model of discourse comprehension and production. *Psychological Review,* 1978, *85,* 363-394.

Kleiman, G.M., Winograd, P., and Humphrey, M. *Prosody and children's parsing of sentences,* Technical Report No. 123. Champaign, IL: University of Illinois, Center for the Study of Reading, 1979.

Lichtenstein, E.H., and Brewer, W.F. Memory of goal directed events. *Cognitive Psychology,* 1980, *12,* 412-445.

Loman, N.L., and Mayer, R.E. Signaling techniques that increase the understandability of expository prose. *Journal of Educational Psychology,* 1983, *75,* 402-412.

Mandler, J.M., and Johnson, N.S. Rememberance of things parsed: Story structure and recall. *Cognitive Psychology,* 1977, *9,* 111-151.

Manzo, A. The ReQuest procedure. *Journal of Reading,* 1969, *2,* 123-126.

McConaughy, S.H. Using story structure in the classroom. *Language Arts,* 1980, *57,* 157-165.

McConkie, G.W. Learning from text. In L.S. Shulman (Ed.), *Review of research in education.* Itasca, IL: F.E. Peacock, 1977, 3-48.

McDonald, G.E. *The effects of instruction in the use of an abstract structural schema as an aid to comprehension and recall of written discourse.* Unpublished doctoral dissertation, Virginia Polytechnic Institute and State University, 1978.

McGee, L.M. Awareness of text structure: Effects on children's recall of expository text. *Reading Research Quarterly,* 1982, *17,* 581-590.

Meichenbaum, D., and Asarnow, J. Cognitive-behavioral modification and metacognitive development: Implications for the classroom. In P.C. Kendall and S.D. Hollon (Eds.) *Cognitive-behavioral interventions: Theory, research, and procedures.* New York: Academic Press, 1979, 11-35.

Memory, D.M. Main idea prequestions as adjunct aids with good and low average middle grade readers. *Journal of Reading Behavior,* 1983, *15,* 37-48.

Meyer, B.J. Organizational patterns in prose and their use in reading. In M.L. Kamil and A.J. Moe (Eds.), *Reading research: Studies and applications.* Twenty-eighth yearbook of the National Reading Conference. Clemson, SC: National Reading Conference, 1979, 109-117.

Meyer, B.J. *The organization of prose and its effects on memory.* Amsterdam: North-Holland Publishing, 1975.

Meyer, B.J. The structure of prose: Effects on learning and memory and implications for educational practice. In R.C. Anderson, R.J. Spiro, and W.E. Montague (Eds.), *Schooling and the acquisition of knowledge.* Hillsdale, NJ: Erlbaum, 1977, 179-200.

Meyer, B.J., Brandt, D.M., and Bluth, G.J. Use of top level structure in text: Key for reading comprehension of ninth grade students. *Reading Research Quarterly,* 1980, *16,* 72-103.

Meyer, B.J., and Freedle, R.O. *Effects of discourse type on recall.* Princeton, NJ: Educational Testing Service, 1980.

Meyer, B.J., and McConkie, G.W. What is recalled after hearing a passage? *Journal of Educational Psychology,* 1973, *65,* 109-117.

Miller, J.R., and Kintsch, W. Readability and recall of short prose passages: A theoretical analysis. *Journal of Experimental Psychology: Human Learning and Memory,* 1980, *6,* 335-354.

Moore, D.W., Cunningham, J.W., and Rudisill, N.J. Readers' conception of the main idea. In J.A. Niles and L.A. Harris (Eds.), *Searches for meaning in reading/language processing and instruction.* Thirty-second yearbook of the National Reading Conference. Rochester, NY: National Reading Conference, 1983, 202-206.

Morrow, L.M. *Effects of story retelling on young children's comprehension and sense of story structure.* Paper presented at the National Reading Conference, Austin, Texas, December 1983.

Nezworski, M.T., Stein, N.L., and Trabasso, T. Story structure versus content effects on children's recall of evaluative inferences. *Journal of Verbal Learning and Verbal Behavior,* 1982, *21,* 196-206.

Omanson, R.C. An analysis of narratives: Identifying central, supportive, and distracting content. *Discourse Processes,* 1982, *5,* 195-224.

Palincsar, A.S., and Brown, A.L. *Reciprocal teaching of comprehension monitoring activities.* Technical Report No. 269. Champaign, IL: University of Illinois, Center for the Study of Reading, 1983.

Palmere, M., Benton, S.L., Glover, J.A., and Ronning, R.R. Elaboration and recall of main ideas in prose. *Journal of Educational Psychology,* 1983, *75,* 898-907.

Perfetti, C.A., and Lesgold, A.M. Discourse comprehension and sources of individual differences. In M.A. Just and P.A. Carpenter (Eds.), *Cognitive processes in comprehension.* Hillsdale, NJ: Erlbaum, 1977, 141-183.

Piché, G.L., and Slater, W.H. Predicting learning from texts: A comparison of two procedures. *Journal of Reading Behavior,* 1983, *15,* 43-57.

Pichert, J.W. *Sensitivity to what is important in prose.* Technical Report No. 149. Champaign, IL: University of Illinois, Center for the Study of Reading, 1979.

Pichert, J.W., and Anderson, R.C. Taking different perspectives on a story. *Journal of Educational Psychology,* 1977, *69,* 309-315.

Readence, J.E., Bean, T.W., and Baldwin, R.S. *Content area reading: An integrated approach.* Dubuque, IA: Kendall/Hunt, 1981.

Reder, L.M. The role of elaboration in the comprehension and retention of prose: A critical review. *Review of Educational Research,* 1980, *50,* 5-53.

Rumelhart, D.E. Understanding and summarizing brief stories. In D. LaBerge and J. Samuels (Eds.), *Basic processes in reading: Perception and comprehension.* Hillsdale, NJ: Erlbaum, 1977, 265-303.

Schank, R.C., and Abelson, R. *Scripts, plans, goals, and understanding.* Hillsdale, NJ: Erlbaum, 1977.

Shannon, P. The use of commercial reading materials in American elementary schools. *Reading Research Quarterly,* 1983, *19,* 68-85.

Shimmerlik, S.M. Organization theory and memory for prose: A review of the literature. *Review of Educational Research,* 1978, *48,* 103-120.

Smiley, S.S., Oakley, D.D., Worthen, D., Campione, J.C., and Brown, A.L. Recall of thematically relevant material by adolescent good and poor readers as a function of written versus oral presentation. *Journal of Educational Psychology,* 1977, *69,* 381-387.

Spiro, R.J., and Taylor, B.M. *On investigating children's transition from narrative to expository discourse: The multidimensional nature of psychological text classification.* Technical Report No. 195. Champaign, IL: University of Illinois, Center for the Study of Reading, 1980.

Stein, N.L. What's in a story: Interpreting the interpretations of story grammars. *Discourse Processes,* 1982, *5,* 319-335.

Stein, N.L., and Glenn, C.G. An analysis of story comprehension in elementary school children. In R.D. Freedle (Ed.), *Advances in discourse processes, volume 2: New directions in discourse processing.* Norwood, NJ: Ablex, 1979, 53-120.

Stein, N.L., and Nezworski, T. The effects of organization and instructional set on story memory. *Discourse Processes,* 1978, *1,* 177-193.

Stein, N.L., and Trabasso, T. *What's in a story: An approach to comprehension and instruction.* Technical Report No. 200. Champaign, IL: University of Illinois, Center for the Study of Reading, 1981.

Taylor, B.M. Children's memory for expository texts after reading. *Reading Research Quarterly,* 1980, *15,* 399-411.

Taylor, B.M. Text structure and children's comprehension and memory for expository material. *Journal of Educational Psychology,* 1982, *74,* 323-340.

Taylor, B.M., and Beach, R.W. The effects of text structure instruction on middle grade students' comprehension and production of expository text. *Reading Research Quarterly,* 1984, *14,* 134-146.

Taylor, B.M., and Berkowitz, S. Facilitating children's comprehension of content material. In M.L. Kamil and A.J. Moe (Eds.), *Perspectives on reading research and instruction.* Twenty-ninth yearbook of the National Reading Conference. Washington, DC: National Reading Conference, 1980, 64-68.

Taylor, M.B., and Williams, J.P. Comprehension of learning disabled readers: Task and text variations. *Journal of Educational Psychology,* 1983, *75,* 743-751.

Tenenbaum, A.B. Task-dependent effects of organization and context upon comprehension of prose. *Journal of Educational Psychology,* 1977, *69,* 528-536.

Thomas, S., and Bridge, C. A comparison of subjects' cloze scores and their ability to employ macrostructure operations in the generation of summaries. In M.L. Kamil and A.J. Moe (Eds.), *Perspectives on reading research and instruction.* Twenty-ninth yearbook of the National Reading Conference. Washington, DC: National Reading Conference, 1980, 69-77.

Tierney, R., Bridge, C., and Cera, M. The discourse processing operations of children. *Reading Research Quarterly,* 1978-1979, *14,* 539-597.

Vacca, R.T. *Content area reading.* Boston MA: Little, Brown, 1981.

van Dijk, T.A. Relevance assignment in discourse comprehension. *Discourse Processes,* 1979, *2,* 113-126.

van Dijk, T.A., and Kintsch, W. *Strategies of discourse comprehension.* New York: Academic Press, 1983.

Waters, H.S. Superordinate-subordinate structure in prose passages and the importance of propositions. *Journal of Experimental Psychology: Learning, Memory, and Cognition,* 1983, *9,* 294-299.

Waters, H.S. Superordinate-subordinate structure in semantic memory: The roles of comprehension and retrieval processes. *Journal of Verbal Learning and Verbal Behavior,* 1978, *17,* 587-597.

Whaley, J.F. Readers' expectations for story structure. *Reading Research Quarterly,* 1981, *17,* 90-114.

Wilhite, S.C. Hierarchical importance of prepassage questions: Effects on cued recall. *Journal of Reading Behavior,* 1984, *16,* 41-59.

Williams, J.P., Taylor, M.B., and Ganger, S. Text variations at the level of the individual sentence and the comprehension of simple expository paragraphs. *Journal of Educational Psychology,* 1981, *73,* 851-865.

Winograd, P. Strategic difficulties in summarizing texts. *Reading Research Quarterly,* 1984, *19,* 404-425.

Winograd, P., and Brennan, S. Main idea instruction in the basal readers. In J.A. Niles and L.A. Harris (Eds.), *Searches for meaning in reading/language processing and instruction.* Thirty-second yearbook of the National Reading Conference. Rochester, NY: National Reading Conference, 1983, 80-86.

Winograd, P., and Hare, V.C. Direct instruction of reading comprehension strategies: The nature of teacher explanation. In E. Goetz, P. Alexander, and C. Weinstein (Eds.), *Learning and study strategies: Issues in assessment, instruction, and evaluation.* New York: Academic Press, in press.

Wong, B. Increasing retention of main ideas through questioning strategies. *Learning Disabilities Quarterly,* 1979, *2,* 42-47.

Wong, B., and Jones, W. Increasing metacomprehension in learning disabled and normally achieving students through self-questioning training. *Learning Disabilities Quarterly,* 1982, *5,* 228-240.

Yussen, S.R., Matthews, S.R., Buss, R.R., and Kane, P. *Developmental change in judging important and critical elements of stories.* Technical Report No. 524. Madison, WI: University of Wisconsin, Wisconsin Research and Development Center for Individualized Schooling, 1979.

3

What Do Expert Readers Do When the Main Idea Is Not Explicit?

Peter P. Afflerbach

Peter H. Johnston

This chapter examines the issue of how expert readers—adult, fluent readers—are able to extract or construct the main idea of texts when none is explicitly stated. Afflerbach and Johnston used a method called think aloud, in which expert readers verbalized their mental processes while attempting to construct main ideas for generally difficult texts. They discuss the general strategies expert readers used to construct main ideas before, during, and after reading; the various cues the expert readers used to assign importance, such as knowledge based cues and text based cues; how the experts managed their limited memory resources during main idea construction; and how the affective dimension interacted with readers' main idea construction and related processes. Afflerbach and Johnston discuss the implications for research and practice of their findings in each of these areas.

This chapter will describe how expert readers *construct* main ideas when the text does not contain an explicit main idea statement. We will not be concerned with how readers *select* explicit main idea statements, as this is discussed elsewhere in the volume (see Chapters 4, 5, 6, and 11). We have derived our description from our analysis of expert readers thinking aloud while they read difficult text. Our hope is that this description of experts' main idea construction processes is rich enough to help teachers to 1) understand the process better, and 2) provide explicit instruction in the strategies used by very competent readers.

The initial impetus for our research on main idea construction came from work done in the area of summarizing text. Brown and Day's analyses (1983) of the summarization task involved an examination of mature readers' thinking out loud while summarizing. Interestingly, their findings agreed with a theoretical model of comprehension presented by Kintsch and van

Dijk (1978). Futhermore, the findings have profound instructional implications, in that younger and less able readers were trained to use the same procedures used by experts with excellent results. Both theoretical and think aloud analyses suggest that expert readers use the following rules to summarize text.

1. *Deletion Rule*. Delete unnecessary (trivial and redundant) material.
2. *Superordinate Rule*. Substitute a superordinate term or event for a list of items or actions.
3. *Construction Rules*. Select a main idea statement for the text (selection rule); if none is present, construct one.

Although instruction based upon these rules is dramatically effective in improving nonexperts' summaries (Brown & Day, 1983), we felt that some problems remained. First, the deletion rule requires the reader to decide which pieces of information are important. Since less able readers have difficulty with this task (Winograd, 1984), we need to develop appropriate instruction, based on further research. Second, readers will note that the third rule is that if no main idea is stated, the reader should construct one. For many young and less able readers this suggestion is not very helpful, since constructing a main idea is exactly the task they find most difficult. Thus, we wanted to know whether the construction process could be broken down into more manageable components.

Our problem, then, was to find out how expert readers (professors and graduate students) construct main ideas. In their investigation, Brown and Day reported little on how main ideas are constructed. Research generally suggests that when mental processes are used often, they become automated (LaBerge & Samuels, 1974; Shiffrin & Schneider, 1977). The processes become more efficient, but they also become inaccessible to conscious awareness (Ericsson & Simon, 1984). Thus, effective readers, having automated their main idea construction processes, would not be able to report on them as they thought out loud while reading.

Fortunately, a solution to the problem of learning about experts' main idea construction processes exists. Research such as that by Edfelt (1960) shows that as the reading task gets harder, more silent speech occurs. This suggests that the processes deautomate when the going gets tough and become available for the reader to report on. Brown and Day's experts were reading texts of fifth grade readability, so it is not surprising that processes were not reported. In order to investigate expert readers' main idea construction processes, we had them think aloud while reading difficult

Afflerbach and Johnston

material which deautomated their processes because of its unfamiliarity or convoluted style. (Readers wishing more on this methodology might read Afflerbach & Johnston, 1984.)

The rest of this chapter describes some of the findings from two different think aloud studies. In these studies, expert readers talked into tape recorders, reporting the processes they were using while constructing main idea statements.

The texts were excerpts from articles in a wide variety of professional journals. Topics included the effects of jet travel on circadian rhythms, the divorce of humanities from other social sciences, the muscle spindle controversy, British historical painting, the evolution of American Indian arrowhead styles, and the organic origins of petroleum. In short, we used texts with topics unfamiliar to most of our expert readers. Our readers were given the following directions:

> We would like you to think aloud (into the tape recorder), expressing the processes you use in trying to arrive at statements of understanding which include a main idea statement for each paragraph and a final main idea statement at the end of each selection.
>
> We are interested in the processes involved in constructing a main idea statement, so please be sure to include all that you can in terms of verbalizing the processes. Also, for main ideas, try to avoid very general statements like "It's about fish" or "It has to do with science" for final summary statements. (You can include such statements as they occur spontaneously in "thinking aloud.")
>
> Note: Some of the passages have been constructed in a manner which should make them very difficult to summarize — we intended this. So don't worry if a passage seems particularly dense or obscure, for it probably is!

We will use selected samples verbatim from the think aloud protocols to illustrate our points. These examples have a further function. Collins and Smith (1982) and Palincsar (1984) have built a strong argument for teachers modeling reading strategies, that is, thinking out loud as a means of reading comprehension instruction. Thus, these think aloud examples provide concrete illustrations of exactly the kinds of processes we need to model for children, at least if we want children to behave as mature readers.

When reading this chapter, please bear in mind that we collected data from expert readers' reading texts which were generally difficult and lacked explicit main ideas. Indeed, our interest in readers' main idea construction processes necessitated the removal of the few explicit main idea statements, or topic sentences, originally present in the texts. This insured that we would engage main idea *construction,* rather than *selection,* processes.

It might be argued that by removing topic sentences we put the reader at a disadvantage and created atypical texts. However, Baumann and Serra (1984) found that only 27 percent of short passages in social studies texts in grades two, four, six, and eight contain topic sentences, or explicit main idea statements. Additionally, only 44 percent of the paragraphs in such texts have explicit main idea statements. We also suspect that the text difficulty faced by our experts constitutes a reasonable reflection of the content text difficulty faced daily by many students.

In describing the main idea construction processes of expert readers, we will first describe the general strategies they used in the construction process. Second, since a major part of constructing a main idea is deciding what is important, we will discuss the cues and strategies used to assign importance. The third section will describe readers' management of their limited memory resources during this complex mental activity. In the fourth section we will describe important and related affective aspects of the reading process. A brief discussion of the instructional implications will follow each section, and a summary will conclude the chapter.

General Approaches to Main Idea Construction

Our expert readers attempted to construct main idea statements in roughly three places which might be characterized as before, during, and after reading. Our discussion will consequently follow this division. Examples of the different approaches are presented in Table 1 and are referred to as needed.

Table 1

GENERAL APPROACHES TO MAIN IDEA CONSTRUCTION

Before Reading
    Hypothesis Generation
        (1.1)
                "...what I understand here is that...things are changing...and that probably...I'll probably read something new about the sedimentary organic compounds...."

Afflerbach and Johnston

(1.2)

"...this tells me...it's going to be about...traits...identified...it's about—uh...(reads: "even contemporary cultures in the Northeast")...it's about past cultures...."

(1.3)

"...so I'm told...in the beginning sentence that this...would...would possibly be about...these...changes in views...uhm...this tells me it's a historical article...and...uhm...I'll be looking to hear...uh—an explanation of...developments through time...in—in a particular discipline...."

(1.4)

"...for the next...sentence or paragraph I'm expecting to read something about archeology...and...I expect also from...this sentence... that it's got to do with...historical archeology...this may not be true... but I expect that...."

(Reads next sentence)

"...OK (laughs)...this next sentence is proving me wrong...obviously it's got to do with...prehistorical people...archeology...."

(1.5)

"...I thought they were gonna talk about something real interesting... about different economic foc—foci...uhm...but they...they instead they just've gone and give...some information...on point styles...uh— that's conjectural at best...but it's a possibility...maybe it's directing us to what...they're gonna talk about...."

During Reading

Crunching

(1-6)

"...and right now I'm just staring blankly at the page...trying to gather ...probably not...well—I'm not reading anything new...and I think I'm just cycling these things around to see if anything seems reasonable...."

(1.7)

"...all right...now I'm just muddling...sort of blank...sort of gray... letting things fall back...."

After Reading

Listing

(1.8)

"...the big point that they wanted to make...they...took 'em about ten seconds to get back into it...and I'm looking for...again...key words...buried sediment...bacterial activity...partial transformation ...and biochemical metabolites...."

("How are you choosing those words?")

"...uh...my choice is based...on what's gonna tip me off...the material is already in my mind...I can get the material there...what I need is key words to help...bring it back out...."

What Do Expert Readers Do?   53

(1.9)

"...OK...just searching through that little pile of grist...uh...these two guys...I guess later than Bessou and Pages...and they're doing something more on these...nerve endings...doing some sort of experiment...."

Topic/Comment

(1.10)

"...you have a spindle (topic)...you can attach a...to a particular spindle you can attach microelectrodes to it (topic and comment)...and you can register stimulation (refined comment) to that spindle...."

(1.11)

"...he is...talking about the—uh...reason for the appearance of the broadpoint and source...of the—uh appearance of the broadpoint (topic)...
uh—and there are two possible sources...one is trait diffusion... (comment)."

Draft and Revise

(1.12)

"...it's giving two frames of reference for how much...uhm...how much change biochemicals and petroleum have to go through...and the first one is that the — the greater part of the chemicals in petroleum don't go through much of a change at all...on the other hand...the...the — there are a few...uh — chemicals contained in petroleum that go through a great deal of change...and so it seems that while...for — uh the vast part of petroleum it doesn't have to go through much of a biochemical change...a part of it does...so apparently there's a case to be made for both sides...."

(1.13)

"...they...talk about their...their traits and how they relate to the... resident groups as they call them...and — uh...and this piece of data which...indicates a capping of the narrow-stemmed point levels...in these particular areas...so they're talking about the...integration of some people—broadpoint users—within...a particular area...."

Main Idea Construction Before Reading

The first approach to main idea construction involves generating a hypothesis of the main idea of a passage, and then trying to verify or refine the prediction. The generation of hypotheses was facilitated by various forms of prior knowledge, such as readers' familiarity with a word or phrase (see examples 1.1, 1.2), or genre of article (see example 1.3). This is a forward planning strategy, for the reader generates the hypothesis in anticipation of what will be encountered in the text. After generating initial hypotheses, readers continued through the text refining or confirming with subsequent text information (see example 1.4). In some instances, an initial hypothesis is off the mark and requires replacement or substantial modification (see example 1.5).

In general, hypothesizing a main idea before reading the entire text was a fruitful strategy. Expert readers often skimmed through the text, keyed on particular words or phrases, and used them to call up appropriate knowledge structures (schemata). Hypotheses were generated based on these schemata, and the accuracy of these hypotheses was then judged against subsequent reading. The principle behind the use of this strategy might be characterized as "If you think you can predict with reasonable accuracy what will be in the text, then do so, and simply use the text to check whether you are correct and which bits are different."

Main Idea Construction During Reading

A second observed approach was what we call crunching, which often occurred *during* the reading of the text. By crunching, readers reduced text information into more manageable kernels of important information. One method of crunching involved a quite passive role for the reader. Here, the reader waited for an automatic process to act on the information already in working memory (see examples, 1.6, 1.7). The result of the crunching process was a kernel of important information, which the reader might use as a main idea statement.

As opposed to the strategy of hypothesizing an initial main idea *before* reading the text, crunching occurred *during* the reading. Because we found that the process was automated, we can give little suggestion as to how it might be improved. However, we can suggest instruction that might aid the strategies leading up to and contributing to an efficient use of the crunching process. As these involved monitoring of the reader's memory system, we will discuss them later in the section on reader's memory management strategies.

Constructing a Main Idea After Reading

What did our readers do when they had completed reading a paragraph or text and did not have a main idea statement? They generally used two approaches.

Their first approach was to try again to use the automated crunching process, but to give it a helpful hand. After reading a paragraph of text, readers simply skimmed what they had read, listed the important elements, and waited for a main idea to be automatically constructed from the pre-digested information (see examples 1.8, 1.9). We called this strategy listing, and it seemed to be very effective.

Often, after reading a paragraph (and on very difficult text even after using the listening strategy), readers were only half way toward a main idea statement. One of these half way points was when readers would find themselves able to state a topic, such as "It's about biorhythms," but unable to qualify it with a comment. Frequently, a reader would rerun the listing strategy to find a comment (see examples 1.10, 1.11). A second half way point was when readers would be able to state a rough draft of a main idea, which they knew was not quite right. The response to this situation was to revise the draft while scanning the paragraph, until the main idea statement felt right (see examples 1.12, 1.13).

Thus we have two two-stage strategies which a reader can deliberately use to reduce the working memory burden in constructing difficult main idea statements. We call these strategies *topic/comment* and *draft and revise*.

Instructional Implications for Teaching Main Idea Skills

We have identified the strategies expert readers used to construct main ideas and have noted when and where these strategies occurred. We would now like to discuss the implications of these findings for the classroom.

The first approach to main idea construction was hypothesis generation and testing. We feel that the training of such a skill would particularly benefit less able readers. The hypothesis generation approach is a component of recent effective approaches to reading comprehension instruction (Brown, Palincsar, & Armbruster, 1984; Brown & Palincsar, 1982), and the strategy of hypothesizing a main idea statement at the beginning of a text may be easy to teach. Accurate hypothesis generation, however, is largely dependent on readers' prior knowledge of text content or text structure. Thus, if no words, phrases (and appropriate schemata), or text structures are familiar to the reader, generating an initial hypothesis may be both costly and inefficient because of its inaccuracy. Students need to know when not to apply such strategies.

We have noted that the crunching strategy depended on an automatic mental process. Consequently, we cannot suggest how it might be improved. When our readers used the listing strategy, they did report on several

Afflerbach and Johnston

processes immediately before listing. In the active case of listing, readers skimmed text for related words and concepts. Thus, being able to skim text for related words, ideas, or concepts seems to be a valuable skill, and we feel that teaching students to do this is a good practice. Note that readers can also use such a skill in either initial hypothesis generation or the draft and revise, topic/comment strategies. This strategy does, however, require the ability to determine important and related words and concepts, a topic addressed later in this chapter.

Generally, our readers performed the drafting and revising strategy *after* reading a paragraph or larger portion of text. They did this in two ways, one being the topic/comment strategy. We did not find any instance of our readers using the topic/comment strategy proactively—that is, in anticipation of a main idea—unless we consider initial hypothesis generation and testing as such. This might be a valuable strategy to teach. Should the initial hypothesis testing strategy be unfeasible due to little or no prior knowledge for the text, the reader can skim or scan the text to derive a topic and then continue reading the text to determine a comment to add to the topic. This strategy can serve to break down what appears to be an unsolvable problem into more manageable pieces.

The second strategy requires the reader to pose a main idea statement at the end of reading and then revise while rereading or scanning. Like the topic/comment strategy, this strategy serves to make the main idea construction process more manageable. Thus, we feel that it might be valuable to teach students to read through the text once and then state a main idea, keeping in mind that they might need to revise it.

We have noted three strategies for constructing main idea statements (hypothesizing a main idea, listing, drafting and revising), and when they tended to occur: before, during, and after reading. We feel that teaching students to use these strategies effectively would be worthwhile. Our think aloud protocols yielded explicit sequences of how these construction strategies are executed; thus, they could be used to model the strategies for children.

Expert readers do more than perform a single strategy to derive a main idea statement. Rather, they have to perform many related strategies to get to the point where they can construct a main idea statement. As we noted at the outset, deciding which pieces of information are more important than others plays a crucial role. In the following section, we will discuss how our readers decided what was important in text, in a sense providing grist for the main idea construction mill.

Assigning Importance in Text

In order to construct a main idea statement, readers continually make decisions about relative importance. Our readers used three types of cues to help determine what was important in text. These cues were contextual knowledge based cues, such as words or phrases; text based cues, such as text structure; and readers' beliefs about the authors and authors' intentions. Additionally, our readers reported strategies indicating flexibility in assigning importance to different parts of text. Table 2 contains specific examples of the importance assignment strategies that we discuss.

Table 2

IMPORTANCE IN TEXT

Contextual Knowledge Based Cues

Familiar Words and Phrases

(2.1)

"...I'm identifying the words that I really know...for example...contemporary cultures in the northeast...."

(2.2)

"...array is a very familiar word...because of my work...uh—array...the minute I saw the word 'array' it—ah...it caused—uh...remembrances of...th—the...in other words...again—I read the word...and...some...filing mechanism went off in my head...so I went through the...I said...'Ah! I recognized that word'...."

(2.3)

"...'carbon-14 readings' rings a bell because of my work...and it shows...that they're talking about aging...."

(2.4)

"...right there I would tend to think of—y'know...Darwin's theory...survival of the fittest...so you have a survival here...a merger...y'know—where...with a narrow stemmed point tradition with the broadpoints...so it's like a chemical reaction almost...you...react—y'know...for years and years they were separate...y'know—it's like say you have...it's like what I was saying before...you have one billion atoms or something...eventually #1 will collide with #5,280...at some time...just like this...."

Unfamiliar Words and Phrases

(2.5)

"...now you can go two ways with some of these words...right now I'm inclined to think that 'Podsnappian' is not...you're not really

Afflerbach and Johnston

gonna have to know...becasuse he throws in things like 'grandeur' and 'impatience' to explain why he's dismissing these other things...."

(2.6)

"...I don't understand very well this word...but...my guess right now...is that it's—it's many things put together somehow...so—what I'll try to do...probably is try to understand this word...I'll expect to understand it after reading...the rest of the text...because...it's obvious that the word is very important...."

Degrees of Importance

(2.7)

"...'if not exclusively' I just throw out...that's just making the sentence longer...uhm...and 'suggested' to some is just...is just extra too...so I'm trying to get rid of these things that are...pare it down...uhm...OK...so...the whole first part of this sentence is...was...I've pared off...so it's just—I wanna know what fossil organic matter consists largely of...."

Text Structure Cues

(2.8)

"...OK...y—I always see—y'know...words...or just the word 'point'...'broadpoint'...'Sqibnocket point'...so...I'm just...trying to understand what that means...."

(Later in the same paragraph the reader noted)

"...there's that word 'points' again...."

(2.9)

"...suddenly something just clicked...that is the words 'narrow' and 'broad'...and now we have a narrow broad...so he's—he's suddenly...which should have been—seemed to me obvious in the beginning...with the terms—with the key words 'narrow' and 'broad'...uhm...uhm...'narrow stemmed'...as he calls it...so I wonder if they're talking about stems...of some sort...because now it's broad...broadpoint versus narrow stem...but I think he's talking about the same thing...."

(2.10)

"...the piece does seem to have a pretty straight continuity...based on...y'know...the second paragraph leads off with 'Later'...so you figure in the first paragraph he's talking about something in the first place...."

(2.11)

"...'broadpoint users'...though...is an undefined term...so I don't know what the broadpoint users actually means...but I know how it fits in in the sentence...."

(2.12)

"...I don't know what these words mean...but I—I'm not trying to understand them very well because I know...that...what I do understand is that they just don't bear importance to the...the text itself because they're only examples...."

(2.13)

"...basically I'm remembering what was in the first paragraph...and remembering...uhm...what I'd said the important parts of that paragraph were...and tying that in together with the information that I've gotten from this...from this paragraph...."

(2.14)

"...it—it poses a particular...sense of interest...because in science that's what you do—and that's what I do...uh—you always try to link...uh—well first you link...first there's a question...first there's a problem...as we call it...and then there's a solution and then there's how to find out...so...this is...they're stating a problem...from what they know...there should be a problem...and that is...how these people...are making out...."

The Writer As Determinant of Importance

(2.15)

"...what I'm thinking at this point is that...although they think one thing is occurring...there's other things that could be responsible for it...and I got that because they say that...uhm...uhm...'a preferred explanation nonetheless'...to me they're not saying this is uh...it's a good reason...but...."

(2.16)

"...so there's two interpretations there...I don't know that it's the primary testament...I disagree...it's not...it does not address the different economic focus at all...it says nothing about that...it's a supposition...just a history—nothing to do with the process...so...I would disagree...."

Strategies Related to Importance Assignment

(2.17)

"...the first paragraph I read...I was trying to understand every word...in order to see what was going on later on...and the difference now...is that...I understand what is going on...but I'm not...I'm not giving it importance because I know that I won't remember it...and it doesn't bear on the understanding of the text...."

(2.18)

"...and what I'll try to do when I finish this text...is probably try to remember two sentences...that there's a controversy...and I'll try to remember that what...the conclusion is...and not remember the whole controversy because I know positively well that I'll never remember it...so I'm not...I shouldn't even waste my time...trying to remember every detail...because I won't...."

(2.19)

> "...trouble with the word 'intrusive'...kind of gets put in...speaking of parcels...it kind of gets put in a buffer...that—uh...awaits work...y'know—you put it there and you say 'OK—remember that word and see if you can use context to figure it out'...."

Contextual, Knowledge Based Cues

Readers' knowledge related to the text topic figured greatly in the strategies they used to assign importance. Familiarity of the text topic had a marked effect on what different readers deemed important. In more familiar texts, readers often skimmed to pick out important words or phrases. The readers often appeared to integrate these words or phrases easily with relevant prior knowledge. Thus, the important words and phrases activated schemata that helped readers interpret the text. Readers then used these words and phrases to construct the main idea statement (see example 2.1).

In unfamiliar text, readers also considered familiar words or phrases important since they provided readers with a means to begin constructing an understanding of the text. Typically, a familiar word or phrase provided a framework for interpreting the text (see example 2.2). In extreme cases, a familiar word or phrase might serve as a base of operations in otherwise unfamiliar terrain. We call this a foot–in–the–door strategy; a reader might assign importance to any text component that provides a place to start putting together the puzzle (see example 2.3). For example, "carbon-14 readings" was a phrase familiar to a chemistry student reading an otherwise unfamiliar anthropology text.

A related strategy is the reader's construction of an analogy between some part of the text and prior knowledge (see example 2.4). This again helps the reader select key information, or at least eliminate extraneous information. Thus, the part of text to which an analogy could be made was important.

Although most of our readers assigned importance to familiar words or phrases, the effectiveness of this strategy was dependent on their prior knowledge of the particular content domain. At times, keying on a familiar word or phrase in a text from an unfamiliar content domain was an extremely costly strategy. In a sense, readers were putting all their chips behind one card, gambling that the familiar word or phrase indicated which knowledge structure (schema) they should apply. If the schema was inappropriate, the reader sometimes ignored information that might refute the interpretation.

Both familiar and unfamiliar words and phrases were often designated as relatively less important. Expert readers seemed to be quite good at determining how much mental effort they needed to figure out the meaning of an unknown word, and whether the effort would be worth the trouble (see example 2.5). On occasion unfamiliar words were assigned importance, seemingly when readers knew that, while the meaning of a word was unclear, the position of the word in the text signaled importance (see example 2.6).

Readers also used strategies to reduce the amount of text they had to consider, and this required assigning less importance to some text parts than others. Often, a reader would exclude from consideration words that were judged less important (see example 2.7). While deciding what to exclude might require use of memory resources, often the ultimate effect of this strategy was to leave more of these resources available to deal with the parts of text that were considered important. These important words were typically content specific.

Text Structure Cues

While the use of topic relevant knowledge was pervasive, readers did use other cues to aid in assigning importance. These included cues in the text, such as repetition of words or concepts, relational terms, and knowledge of text structure.

The repetition of words or concepts often signaled importance to readers. Readers assumed that a word or concept repeated throughout a paragraph was probably important (see example 2.8). They did not need to be identical, as overlapping of concepts also led to importance assignment (see example 2.9). Apparently, readers' content domain knowledge interacts with text cues. That is, the reader must have appropriate prior knowledge to know that the concepts overlap if they are worded differently.

Readers used relational terms in the text (e.g., *similarly*) in order to organize and assign importance. With unfamiliar text, these cues signal continuity of an argument or relatedness of concepts (see example 2.10). Readers also noted their familiarity with sentence structure, and how they used this knowledge to figure out and assign importance to more difficult portions of text. For example, one reader used context cues to help determine whether a phrase was important (see example 2.11).

Afflerbach and Johnston

With larger segments of text, readers reported using paragraph structure to understand the text. That is, expert readers may determine what is important by considering not only *what* is presented but *how* it is presented. Consequently, readers might use the paragraph structure strategy independently of their general knowledge related to the passage (see example 2.12). Readers also reported using the relationships between paragraphs to impose order on the text or a given segment of text and further determine what was important (see example 2.13).

Readers clearly used their knowledge of the structure and content of scientific text to aid in the assignment of importance. Readers who have much prior experience reading articles in their specific field or specialty know that texts will typically state a problem, describe the way in which the problem is investigated, and then discuss results and implications of the investigation of the problem. Many of our readers did this (see example 2.14).

The Perceived Writer

Readers also determined importance through their perceptions of the author. Sometimes the reader viewed the author as separate from the text and made inferences about his or her intentions (see example 2.15). Such a strategy for determining what is important in text, while dependent both on content domain knowledge and text structure knowledge, seems to warrant separate consideration. The reader might establish perceptions of the author from the style of the writing, or compare what the author is proposing with any relevant knowledge of his or her own (see example 2.16). These strategies can result in the reader being able to understand the writer's style and potential biases. Thus, the reader could react to the text on an evaluative level which influences what is ultimately considered important.

Flexible Importance Assignment

Readers also reported flexibility in determining what was important. That is, criteria for assigning importance might change throughout the reading of a text (see example 2.17). This flexibility has important implications for goal setting which, in turn, may affect what is ultimately considered important. For example, a reader may finish the first paragraph of a relatively difficult text and decide that the amount of unfamiliar material makes constructing a sophisticated main idea statement futile. As a result, the reader's basis for assigning importance may change drastically as might the level of main idea statement originally planned. Related to this are readers' reports of how they approached the main idea construction task, using strategies to limit the amount of information to which they assigned importance (see example 2.18). Here, readers plan in advance their importance assignment strategies, appropriate to the perceived difficulty of the task.

Subjects assigned what might be called conditional importance to certain parts of the text (see example 2.19), which was subject to refinement by subsequent information. Thus, importance assignment may involve hypothesis generation in some instances. Part of a text is hypothesized as being important, and this assignment of importance is subject to verification, refinement, or refutation by subsequent information.

This section has indicated some of the wide variety of strategies readers used to assign importance while reading. Readers used their knowledge of text topic and text structure to determine what to use in constructing a main idea. While importance is relative to a particular text and reader, we would urge, for example, that readers be made aware of how using appropriate prior knowledge may help in accurately assigning importance.

When the procedures for determining importance are combined with having to construct a main idea statement for a paragraph and an entire text, even expert readers may encounter difficulty. This requires the reader to monitor and control the reader's processing with an executive system which we discuss next.

Managing the Reading Process

When the reader's text comprehension system is functioning smoothly, the component main idea construction processes are automated, and verbal report data tend to be sketchy. As mentioned earlier, the texts used in our studies lacked topic sentences, contained unfamiliar content domain material, and sometimes were constructed in a convoluted style. Consequently, main idea construction and other processes which might be automated when reading less challenging texts required conscious attention.

Britton, Glynn, and Smith (1985) note that the reader's working memory is of limited size; thus, it requires careful monitoring of information and execution of processes. This is what we found in many of our protocols. To construct main idea statements successfully, our readers managed their cognitive resources by monitoring their progress and taking appropriate actions when necessary. They monitored many aspects of processing and their consequent actions were similarly diverse. Table 3 contains protocol excerpts that illustrate some strategies for managing reading processes.

Afflerbach and Johnston

Table 3
MANAGING THE READING PROCESS

(3.1)

"...the two sentences are very...I think...too compact...in terms of they're trying to get too much information out at one time...and it's kind of overloading the old...senses right now...."

(3.2)

"...now these two words...'living organisms'...make me think that maybe I'm losing something from the previous chapters...uh—previous sentences...so I'm gonna go back to see if I lost something...important...."

(3.3)

"...I stopped at the comma and went back and skimmed it...to put it together...."

(3.4)

(Reads last sentence of paragraph)

"...OK...first thing...I went over it...and skimmed through the article again...and...uh...I remember basically...where I saw...like important things...."

(3.5)

(Reads sentence)

"...at that particular point I didn't have enough information to make anything out of it...so I wanted to continue reading...to see if I could make a little more sense out of that particular statement...."

(3.6)

"...OK...right now...too many unfamiliar words are...phrases have forced me to not comprehend that sentence...and I have to reread it...."

(3.7)

"...I'm misreading this sentence actually...that's after going back and reading through it again...I'm getting words...that make more sense...."

(3.8)

(Rereads sentence)

"...OK...now that...the second time...that seemed to be more...easy to...it seems that...the recall...or the establishment of what that sentence's saying is better the second time...."

(3.9)

"...I'm just trying to pack all the stuff in...going slow wasn't helping me...figure out what's going on...so I figured I'd just get it all there and then ponder it for a second...."

The task of constructing a main idea statement for difficult text often requires working memory to run at, or near, capacity. Consequently, an important strategy for readers is to monitor memory space availability (see example 3.1). This allows readers to decide if they have room enough to continue adding information and perform further comprehension processes, or if they need to stop for a moment and assess the situation.

In addition to keeping close tabs on how full working memory is, readers also monitored the quality of what they were holding in working memory. That is, they checked to see that information they wanted to hang onto was being maintained (see example 3.2). If needed information was fading, they took appropriate action.

While readers monitored their working memory, they also needed to monitor incoming information. They did this several places, including at the end of a meaning unit, or when they did not comprehend the text. Readers reported using the breaks in text (e.g., commas, semicolons, periods) as points to check to see that things were going smoothly (see examples 3.3, 3.4, 3.5). In other instances, they noted failure to understand incoming information (see examples 3.6, 3.7). In this sense, we can make a distinction between types of comprehension monitoring. One type occurs regularly, at the end of meaning units, and seems to be a sort of doublecheck to make sure things are running smoothly. Another type seems more reactive in nature, prompted by a detected problem with comprehension.

Readers also monitored the effectiveness of strategies in trying to understand (see examples 3.8, 3.9). Thus, they were able to refine, maintain, or switch strategies depending on their success.

Difficult texts require efficient monitoring to keep the main idea construction processes working smoothly. To coordinate these processes within the limited capacity of working memory, readers performed varied managment procedures. We suggest that explicit modeling of these strategies may increase developing readers' ability to keep things under control when difficult tasks, such as main idea construction, are required. For example, we noted earlier that our readers monitored the success of the listing strategy and often stopped reading to avoid overloading their memory system. Thus, students need to learn that they shouldn't bite off more than they can chew. Instruction that equips students with procedures to monitor and manage their memory systems will be beneficial not only for main idea construction tasks, but also in other tasks that have high working memory demands.

Affect and Main Idea Construction

A benefit of think aloud data is that they provide insight into how affect can influence comprehension processes. In the following section, we discuss readers' feelings about what they were reading and the attributions readers made for success or failure during the main idea construction task. We feel this is an important aspect of comprehension that deserves further attention.

Our verbal report data offered many instances where readers' prior knowledge in the form of attitudes, opinions, and beliefs influenced what they took from the text (and added to it) to construct main idea statements. van Dijk and Kintsch (1983) propose that the reader builds a situational model of the text. The model consists of information in the text and knowledge that the reader brings to the text, with which the reader creates the situation in the text. As readers' knowledge varies, we might expect varying degrees of reader interaction with the text. This interaction will depend not only on the reader's familiarity with a text topic but also on the feelings a reader has concerning the text that are a consequence of this knowing. Table 4 contains protocol excerpts that illustrate how readers' feelings, in the form of attitudes, opinions, and beliefs, influence how a text is read.

Table 4

ATTITUDES, OPINIONS, AND BELIEFS

(4.1)

"...I would be skeptical immediately...uh—to be quite honest...uhm...but—but...that's because of my knowledge of the subject...and perhaps I ought to concentrate more on...exactly how they're saying this...."

(4.2)

"...they're jumping to a conclusion right there...uh...but at any rate they're making that assertion...this is a group of people...instead of a group of projectile points...(laughs)...that happen to be associated with people...so—they're a little confused already...."

(4.3)

"...I kind of feel relieved because I finally understand what's going on with petroleum...and...uh...I'm not trying to relate it to anything...I take it as a statement...I take it as a truity also...I have no—no—no knowledge of anything...to...to test this and say 'No! It's wrong! I think petroleum comes from something else or whatever chemical transformation'...so this would probably be my explanation of petroleum for the next twenty years...so...this is it for me!...now I know where petroleum comes from and this guy has a true...has the truth...."

(4.4)

"...they're trying to explain...migration but that I'm—I'm not buying their argument because in the first...thing...is that they're using somebody else—which is not wrong...I mean it's perfect...but they're using somebody else's arguments...and they're not tying them into their own thing...and then they're not explaining me...they're not giving me anything new...and the—the last thing about explaining...explaining the argument by negative evidence...has completely...lost importance...in—in my opinion...so I'm gonna go on reading this...and trying to find...if—if there's anything positive...in their hypothesis...if—if they can prove it...because they still haven't proven anything to me...so I'm gonna go on until this moment...I'm—I'm thinking that this article is a bad article...and he's not saying anything new...and it's criticizable from every point...."

(4.5)

"...that's a peculiar way of putting it...but that's OK...uhm...I mean you wanna say...broadpoint assemblages...overlie...deposits containing broadpoint assemblages overlie...narrow point...narrow stemmed point levels...if you wanna just say that right...as far as I'm concerned...uhm...at any rate...it's a funny way of saying that...uhm... I'm wondering now...how skilled this writer is...at—uh...at—uh... archeological data...and the skills vary among highly...recognized archeologists...."

(4.6)

"...I assume they've left out...uhm...but that's OK...otherwise it's another undergraduate student who doesn't have a TA who's coming down on him...."

(4.7)

"...this is written to give some scientific suspense...uh...it's not...uh...it doesn't seem to be a highly typical article...even though they're displaying...a technical background here...I think...this is still...kind of a...reporting article...a little bit popular...."

In many instances, the higher the prior knowledge for the content domain of the text, the more involved the reader tends to become with it. Typically, readers would make evaluative or judgmental statements about texts they read if their prior knowledge afforded them the opportunity (see examples 4.1, 4.2). Lack of prior knowledge greatly influenced the way in which some readers dealt with text. For example, one reader noted that, due to lack of appropriate prior knowledge, what the author was saying was truth (see example 4.3). On a more familiar text, the same student reported that she was having trouble accepting the author's point because it conflicted with her own beliefs about the text topic (see example 4.4).

We also noted the influence of reading related activities that readers engaged in before the main idea construction task. Such activities seemed to greatly affect the ways in which they approached and read text. One subject had just completed marking written, final exams from an introductory anthropology course as part of his doctoral student duties. Throughout his protocols, many comments indicated he maintained his judgmental approach to written discourse. He made these evaluative comments on both familiar (see examples 4.5, 4.6) and unfamiliar (see example 4.7) content domain texts, and they influenced the main ideas which he constructed.

In addition to the effect of readers' feelings on how text is read, we noted the presence of many attributional statements in our protocols. The power of readers' attributions has been recently noted (Butkowsky & Willows, 1982; Johnston & Winograd, 1985), and we feel that our data emphasize the need to incorporate reader attributions into any adequate model of text comprehension. Our adult expert readers explained their success or failure on the main idea construction task in a variety of ways. Table 5 presents samples of their attributional statements.

Table 5
READERS ATTRIBUTIONAL STATEMENTS

(5.1)
"...I'm trying to...I'm doing a terrible effort to understand this...."
(5.2)
"...it's ambiguous as far as I'm concerned...and...uh...I—I have a feeling that this is either written for—for a public...that is...uh...familiar with what the problem is...or...it's—it needs to be...the author needs to be...a bit more specific about what they're talking about...."
(5.3)
"...I kind of feel insecure reading these things so I would...I'm gonna try to read it again...."
(5.4)
"...I feel relieved after reading this sentence...because it...it explains...at least...as far as I'm concerned...it explains my questions here...so now I feel OK...."

Some subjects noted the effort they were putting into trying to understand a text or part of a text (see example 5.1). In other instances, the reader attributed inability to construct a main idea to the writer's effort or skill (see example 5.2). Butkowsky and Willows (1982) have examined the attributions made by less able readers, and it is clear that these play a very important part in reading activities. Readers were also quite descriptive in relating their emotions while reading different texts. One subject noted feeling "insecure" with an unfamiliar text (see example 5.3) and "relieved" with a more familiar one (see example 5.4).

We have discussed these two affective areas because we feel they need to be more fully considered and investigated by research on comprehension processes. Data from think-aloud protocols indicate that expert readers not only interact with the text in an informational sense but also in an affective way. Failing to consider these dimensions may prevent us from understanding why some readers who fail to get the point press on anyway, and others simply give up the task.

Summary

When we listen, we generally either get the speaker's point easily and automatically, or we do not. And unless we have the opportunity for dialogue, missing the point is terminal. When we read, the permanence of print affords us the possibility of using a variety of strategies to overcome such a failure. These strategies have been the focus of this chapter. Recent work on comprehension instruction suggests that these might be modeled with great effect for less able readers.

We have described how our expert readers construct main ideas when they are not explicitly stated in the text. The difficulty that even experts can have with constructing main ideas supports Brown and Day's contention (1983) that construction is the most difficult of their summarization rules. Thus, the importance of training construction skills is evident. Through analysis of protocol data, we have proposed specific strategies which readers use to construct main ideas. We have also noted the strategies and cues which readers use in assigning importance to text. In addition, we have considered the ways that expert readers manage their memory resources. The explicitness of the protocol data are encouraging, and they may serve as models for teachers to use in their instruction.

Our protocols also indicated that readers bring to the reading task feelings that can greatly influence their efforts to construct main ideas. These feelings may be a result of prior knowledge and its accompanying attitudes, opinions, and beliefs, or they may be related to broader, more

Afflerbach and Johnston

personal factors, such as recent experiences with reading. Reading is not performed in a vacuum, and readers constantly deal with their feelings and experiences as they read. We think that in order to become mature readers, students need to come to grips with these diverse aspects of reading so that they might effectively cope with difficult reading tasks.

References

Afflerbach, P., and Johnston, P. On the use of verbal reports in reading research. *Journal of Reading Behavior,* 1984, *16,* 307-322.

Baumann, J., and Serra, J. The frequency and placement of main ideas in children's social studies textbooks: A modified replication of Braddock's research on topic sentences. *Journal of Reading Behavior,* 1984, *16,* 1, 27-40.

Britton, B., Glynn, S., and Smith, J. Cognitive demands of processing expository text: A cognitive benchwork model. In B. Britton and J. Black (Eds.), *Understanding expository text.* Hillsdale, NJ: Erlbaum, 1985, 227-248.

Brown, A., and Day, J. Macrorules for summarizing texts: The development of expertise. *Journal of Verbal Learning and Verbal Behavior,* 1985, *22,* 1, 1-15.

Brown, A., and Palincsar, A. Inducing strategic learning from texts by means of informed, self-control training. *Topics in Learning and Learning Disabilities,* 1982, *2,* 1-17.

Brown, A., Palincsar, A., and Armbruster, B. Instructing comprehension fostering activities in interactive learning situations. In H. Mandl, N. Stein, and T. Trabasso (Eds.), *Learning and comprehension of text.* Hillsdale, NJ: Erlbaum, 1984, 255-285.

Butkowsky, I., and Willows, D. Cognitive motivational characteristics of children varying in reading ability: Evidence for learned helplessness in poor readers. *Journal of Educational Psychology,* 1982, *72,* 408-422.

Collins, A., and Smith, E. Teaching the process of reading comprehension. In D. Detterman and R. Sternberg (Eds.), *How and how much can intelligence be increased?* Norwood, NJ: Ablex, 1982, 173-185.

Day, J. *Teaching summarization skills: A comparison of training methods.* Unpublished doctoral dissertation, University of Illinois, 1980.

Edfelt, A. *Silent speech and silent reading.* Chicago: University of Chicago Press, 1960.

Ericsson, K., and Simon, H. *Protocol analysis.* Cambridge, MA: MIT Press, 1984.

Johnston, P., and Winograd, P. Passive failure in reading. *Journal of Reading Behavior,* 1985, *17,* 279-301.

Kintsch, W., and van Dijk, T. Toward a model of text comprehension and production. *Psychological Review,* 1978, *85,* 363-394.

LaBerge, D., and Samuels, S. Toward a theory of automatic information processing in reading. *Cognitive Psychology,* 1974, *6,* 293-323.

Palincsar, A. *Reciprocal teaching: Working within the zone of proximal development.* Paper presented at the annual meeting of the American Educational Research Association, New Orleans, April 1984.

Shiffrin, R., and Schneider, W. Controlled and automatic human information processing: II. Perceptual learning, automated attending, and a general theory. *Psychological Review,* 1977, *84,* 127-190.

van Dijk, T., and Kintsch, W. *Strategies for comprehending discourse.* New York: Academic Press, 1983.

Winograd, P. Strategic difficulties in summarizing texts. *Reading Research Quarterly,* 1984, *19,* 404-425.

Afflerbach and Johnston

4

Research and Instructional
Development on Main Idea Skills

Joanna P. Williams

In this chapter, Joanna Williams describes several studies in which she investigated variables that affect how normally achieving children, learning disabled children, and adults comprehend main ideas in expository prose. She then proposes a categorization model of expository text processing that accounts for her findings on children's and adults' main idea comprehension. The chapter also contains a description of an instructional program for teaching learning disabled students to comprehend main ideas and the results of an experimental study that supports the effectiveness of the program. Williams concludes the chapter with a discussion of the implications for further work in this area.

A curriculum in reading comprehension usually includes a substantial emphasis on the skill of finding the main idea. The fact that lessons on main idea are found across a wide range of grade levels underscores the importance of this skill and also reflects the difficulties that pupils often have with it. Many children cannot find the main idea even of rather simple texts (Baumann, 1983).

Recently, research has provided both theory and empirical support for the design of reading instruction. Not surprisingly, some of this work has focused on the skill of finding main ideas, which is fundamental to so many aspects of comprehension. A reader cannot draw appropriate inferences from a text without first understanding the explicitly stated propositions; nor can that reader compare texts, as for example in terms of two authors' points of views, without understanding each author's main points.

The ability to identify main ideas is, however, no different in any real sense from any other comprehension skill. From the demonstrations of schema theorists (Anderson, 1984; Rumelhart, 1980) we know that a reader always brings prior knowledge to the task of understanding text and that such background information interacts with the text information in the reader's cognitive processing. This implies that, even when a main idea appears explicitly in the text, some kind of inferencing may be involved in the process of identifying it. Research on comprehension, whether based on the current information processing paradigm or on the earlier model involving the factor analysis of performance on comprehension tests, indicates the impossibility of delineating separate and independent comprehension skills.

In this chapter we are interested solely in studying children's ability in the task traditionally described as finding the main idea and in attempts to improve this ability. From an educational point of view, this task is a genuine one, one that is important quite apart from the psychological issue of what cognitive processes are involved in finding the main idea (Afflerbach & Johnston, Chapter 3, this volume) and quite apart from the concerns of literary critics (Fish, 1980) and discourse analysts (Wooton, 1975) who argue that we can never determine the true meaning of any text, let alone its main idea.

This chapter presents the results of a series of studies of adults and children, both normally achieving and learning disabled. It also describes an instructional program for teaching main idea skills to learning disabled children, based on the results of the studies, and presents the findings of a preliminary evaluation of the instructional program.

Theoretical Background

The concept of main idea has not been defined consistently either in instruction or in research (Pearson, 1981). Many instructional tasks qualify as main idea tasks, including writing summary statements, writing titles, and choosing among an array of topic sentences (Rosenshine, 1980). However, a great deal of variation surrounds, and little theoretical justification supports, what is judged to be an appropriate title or summary sentence for a given text (Cunningham & Moore, Chapter 1, this volume). And students often do not get guidance in meeting the different task demands involved in these various instructional activities.

The research literature offers a variety of definitions, but while main idea is most often defined in terms of a sentence (Aulls, 1978; Braddock, 1974), there is usually no precise specification of the text factors (how much information the text contains and of what type, and how it is structured) that determine whether a particular sentence represents an appropriate main idea for a particular text. Perhaps this is inevitable, given the fact that natural—and therefore often loosely structured—text is used extensively in the research.

Winograd and Bridge (Chapter 2, this volume) and Baumann (1982, 1984) have reviewed the recent literature, which is heterogeneous and therefore hard to integrate. According to Baumann, most research indicates that fluent adult readers are quite proficient at comprehending main ideas. But he has also noted that while some studies indicate that children can comprehend main ideas relatively easily (e.g., Meyer, 1977; Waters, 1978), other studies suggest that they have substantial difficulty with this task (e.g., Taylor, 1980; Winograd, 1984). Perhaps such conflicting results are at least partly due to the wide and unspecified variations in texts and tasks that have been used in the studies (see Winograd & Bridge, Chapter 2, this volume).

The models of discourse structure introduced in the 1970s provide the basis for a new approach to the study of main idea. These models typically describe text in terms of a set of propositions that are organized into a hierarchy that reflects their relative importance in the text (e.g., Fredericksen, 1975; Kintsch & van Dijk, 1978; Meyer, 1975). Much empirical evidence supports the usefulness of these discourse models in the study of comprehension. Early studies demonstrated that the higher the level of a proposition in the hierarchical organization, the greater the probability of its being recalled and comprehended (Kintsch & Keenan, 1973; Meyer, 1975) and also that well structured text leads to better recall and comprehension than does a disorganized version of the same content (Kieras, 1978). Children's performance is similarly influenced by the propositional structure of texts (Aulls, 1975; Danner, 1976; Meyer, 1977). None of this early work, however, specifically addressed the notion of main idea.

The Kintsch and van Dijk Model

One aspect of the Kintsch and van Dijk (1978) model of text comprehension is particularly relevant to research on main idea: its theory of macrostructure. According to this model, as readers proceed through a text, and as they convert sentences to propositions, they are also deleting, generalizing, and integrating those propositions. These macroprocesses yield a macrostructure, which can be described as those propositions in the text that represent the information that would appropriately summarize that text. (It should be noted that the reader's schema also influences macroprocessing: propositions are deleted, generalized, and/or integrated not only in terms of what the author intended as important but also in terms of the readers's own goals, knowledge, and interests.)

The expressions of macrostructure in actual language can take several forms. More or less information from the top of the text's propositional hierarchy can be represented in a particular expression of macrostructure. There are, for example, one word titles, topic sentences that express one or two propositions, and in the case of complex text, several sentence summaries. Such expressions of marcrostructure may not appear explicitly in the text, and readers do not necessarily express what they generate as macrostructure.

An Explicit Definition of Main Idea

In order to avoid the problems that arise from the lack of a consistent definition of main idea (Cunningham & Moore, Chapter 1, this volume), we have chosen to work with short, simple paragraphs, structured in a very specific way according to the Kintsch and van Dijk (1978) model, from which clear main ideas can be reliably derived. Consider the following paragraph:

> Cowboys had to protect the herd from cattle robbers. They had to brand cattle to show who owned them. Sometimes cowboys had to separate the cattle that were to be sent to market.

In this paragraph, each sentence instantiates a global topic, and the reader can construct a proposition that at a higher level subsumes the three sentences (van Dijk, 1980, p. 46): "Cowboys had jobs to do." Each sentence in the paragraph semantically implies this macroposition.

While this paragraph is too simple to consider for it a several-sentence-long expression of macrostructure, various titles and topic sentences do represent adequate expressions. For example, the paragraph could be entitled "Cowboys," or it could be entitled "The Jobs of Cowboys." In van Dijk's terminology (1980), the first title contains the *general topic* of the paragraph and the second, the *specific topic of discourse*. Instead of titles, sentences might express either the general topic or the specific topic of discourse: "The paragraph is about cowboys," or "Cowboys had jobs to do."

Research on Main Idea Comprehension

To provide some foundation for our instructional design, we performed several studies on children's main idea skills. We investigated performance on a variety of tasks, some of which were similar to those used in school in main idea instruction and some of which were more sensitive laboratory tasks. We worked solely with short, highly structured paragraphs (and variations on them) that allow analysis and evaluation in terms of the precise definitions of van Dijk (1980). This section of the paper presents a brief summary of our findings.

The Ability to Perform School Like Tasks

How well *can* children identify and construct main ideas for short, simple expository paragraphs? Our research confirms Baumann's conclusion (1983) that these tasks are not necessarily easy ones for children. We asked fourth and sixth graders and adults (Williams, Taylor, & Ganger, 1981, experiments 1 and 3) to read short paragraphs, and to choose either the best title from an array of four titles or to write one sentence that expressed the main idea. The four title choices included 1) the specific topic of discourse (The Jobs of Cowboys); 2) the general topic (Facts about Cowboys); 3) the general topic plus a detail from the paragraph (How Cowboys Brand Cattle); and 4) the general topic plus an intrusion (The Movies that Cowboys Like).

Table 1 shows the proportion of correct responses, scored two ways: First, we called an answer correct if it represented either the specific topic of discourse (STD) or at least the general topic. In this case, even fourth graders were reasonably proficient at the task (84 percent correct title choices). When the scoring was more stringent, however, requiring "The Jobs of Cowboys," performance was considerably lower: Only 58 percent of the fourth graders chose the correct title, and fewer than half could write an adequate sentence. We replicated the study with adults; their scores were considerably higher—though, surprisingly for such simple paragraphs, far from perfect. Another comparison is not shown in the table: The adults scored higher on paragraphs that had topic sentences than on those that did not, but the children showed no such differences.

We then replicated the study with fifth graders (Williams, Taylor, & Ganger, 1981, experiment 5) with one modification: We drew lines around

Table 1

PROPORTION OF CORRECT RESPONSES, LENIENT CRITERION
(Specific Topic of Discourse or General Topic)

	Fourth Grade	Sixth Grade	Adult
Title Task	.84	.93	.99
Production Task	.74	.88	.97

PROPORTION OF CORRECT RESPONSES, STRINGENT CRITERION
(Specific Topic of Discourse Only)

	Fourth Grade	Sixth Grade	Adult
Title Task	.58	.78	.87
Production Task	.43	.57	.80

the first sentences of all the paragraphs, half of which were topic sentences. Under these conditions, children performed better on the topic sentence paragraphs, indicating that children can use the information in topic sentences effectively when they have extra support.

We replicated these findings with learning disabled children (Taylor & Williams, 1983). In this study, we matched learning disabled children with normally achieving children on IQ and on the word knowledge subtest of the SRA Achievement series (Level E). All children were reading at the fourth or fifth grade level. Thus, the learning disabled children were older. Table 2 presents descriptive data on the two groups of children and also the results of the study, which indicated that the performance of the learning disabled children was not different from that of the nondisabled children, $F (1,44) = .72$.

Thus, learning disabled readers' problems do not appear to be due specifically to a particular inability to develop macrostructure. This finding suggests that instruction that focuses on the development of main idea skills should not necessarily be different for learning disabled children than for other children—a conclusion that is consonant with the general point of view that instructional development for the learning disabled should focus on whatever strategies and techniques are effective for the general category of slow learners (Williams, 1980).

Table 2
DESCRIPTIVE INFORMATION ON THE SUBJECTS

	Nondisabled Children	Learning Disabled Children
Age (mean)	10.9	12.9
IQ (mean)	97.1	93.5
Word Knowledge (mean)	5-1	4-4
N	24	24

PROPORTION OF CORRECT RESPONSES (STD)

	Nondisabled Children	Learning Disabled Children
Title Task	.61	.59
Production Task	.45	.34

The Detection of Anomalous Content

Certainly, not all expository prose consists of well structured paragraphs. Natural text often contains content anomalous both in terms of intuitive analysis of the passage content and in terms of a text structure analysis. What we call parenthetical information, for example, might often be unrelated to (or only tangentially related to) the hierarchy of propositions that underlie the text. How does the inclusion of such information influence comprehension?

We constructed anomalous paragraphs from the same well structured paragraphs used in the earlier studies. One sentence in each paragraph was replaced by one of two kinds of anomalous sentences. In one type, the sentence was completely *unrelated* to the paragraph macrostructure (e.g., "Birds sit on their eggs to keep them warm," in reference to the cowboy paragraph), that is, it contained neither the general topic nor the specific topic of discourse. In the other type, called *related* (e.g., "Cowboys sing and dance every evening), the sentence contained the general topic but not the specific topic of discourse. Although we used two versions of related and two versions of unrelated anomalous sentences, I will not discuss them here. (See Williams, Taylor, & Ganger, 1981, experiments 2 and 4 for details.)

In this experiment, we asked the reader to identify the inappropriate sentence in each paragraph. As predicted, both children and adults turned out to be quite sensitive to these anomalous sentences. Moreover, the detection of completely unrelated sentences was superior to detection of sentences that contained the general topic (the related sentences), $F (1,102) = 397.30$, $p < .001$ for the children, and $F (1,59) = 79.34$, $p < .01$ for the adults. Other aspects of this work indicated that several additional text variations at the level of the individual sentence also affected children's ability to process information in these paragraphs. (See Williams, Taylor, & Ganger, 1981, experiment 2.)

Finding the Main Idea in Less Well Structured Paragraphs

Our next question was whether the presence of anomalous sentences in text affected the development of the macrostructure of the text, that is, the ability to find the main idea. We designed a study for third, fifth, and seventh graders and adults (Williams, Taylor, & deCani, 1984).

We used the same two tasks, choosing titles and writing summary statements, and we also added one more task: Subjects had to add an appropriate next sentence to some paragraphs. This task required the generation of macrostructure *plus* the selection of an additional detail about the specific topic of discourse. To do this required adequate prior knowledge of the topic and also the ability to assess that knowledge and to evaluate its appropriateness in terms of the specific topic of discourse.

The pattern of findings for the adults was complex. The adults did show sensitivity to the presence of the anomalous content. On the Title task, the number of specific-topic-of-discourse choices on paragraphs containing a related anomalous sentence was lower than on paragraphs containing either an unrelated anomaly or no anomaly at all. This indicated that adults did modify their judgments as to what the main idea of the paragraph was in light of the anomalous sentence. What they did on the related paragraphs was to choose more often the title that reflected the general topic ("Facts about Cowboys"), thereby incorporating the anomalous sentence into their representation. (Since none of the four title options reflected the information contained in the unrelated anomalous sentence, most subjects chose the specific-topic-of-discourse title for the Unrelated paragraphs.)[1]

The results on the other tasks were different. The anomalous material had no effect on the Summary task. On the Next Sentence task, the effect was different from that on the Title task. In this case, the number of specific-topic-of-discourse responses decreased as a function of the degree of the anomaly. A common response was for adults to generate a Next Sentence on the basis of whatever information was contained in the fourth and final sentence of the paragraph; they did not consider the paragraph as a whole.

In general, then, adults did take account of anomalous information in their formation of macrostructure, and the way that they did depended on the particular task they were asked to perform. The children's pattern however, was quite different. For these readers, performance never changed as a function of the presence of anomalous information. Thus while children could detect these sentences as anomalies (as the previous study showed), they evidently did not tap this ability when they undertook tasks that involved identifying or formulating a main idea.

Overall, across tasks and across paragraph types, adults tended to provide broad, general main ideas. That is, they attempted to encompass all of the information presented and even some that was not presented. Young children, on the other hand, tended to pick out a narrow detail that represented a single sentence in the paragraph.

We replicated this study with learning disabled children, who showed patterns of performance similar to those of nondisabled children matched on IQ and word knowledge (Williams, Taylor, & deCani, 1983).

A Categorization Model of Expository Text Processing

Description of the Model

After completing the studies summarized above, we looked again at our experimental paragraphs. Could we be more specific about what readers are doing when they read this particular type of text?

The macroprocesses described by Kintsch and van Dijk (1978, 1983) are basic cognitive processes and, as such, are not restricted to comprehension of written text or, indeed, of language in general. These cognitive processes form the basis of all of our categorization and classification skills.

Our cowboy paragraph illustrates the similarity of text processing on one hand, and simple classification on the other; each sentence entails, that is, semantically implies, the topical macroproposition "Cowboys had jobs to do." A proficient reader can generate the macroproposition that underlies the paragraph by reading the three detail sentences.

An understanding of the above paragraph implies the knowledge that branding, separating, and protecting cattle are exemplars of the category *jobs,* that is, that readers understand the category *job* and certain exemplars of that category. We are talking here about simple comprehension and not the more complex situation that occurs when readers are learning from text, as when they understand the category *jobs,* but have never known, before reading a paragraph, that branding cattle is one of a cowboy's jobs.

We are also talking about a model of concept identification rather than of concept formation. The reader who is reading a series of detail sentences of the type shown above presumably understands that the activities specified in those sentences are indeed jobs. (Of course, this may not always be true: It may be that a reader has never learned that an individual might get paid for performing a particular activity. But we are not here dealing with the formation—or expansion—of categories.)

In concept identification, as in other domains, expectations about the nature of one's task play a large role in determining one's performance. Readers usually assume that the text will contain only relevant information (cf. Grice's "cooperative principle," 1975). Thus, in terms of our simple paragraphs, the reader would, under ordinary conditions, expect that all the detail sentences are intended as positive exemplars of the main idea. Consider a reader who, having read enough of that paragraph (with or without a topic sentence) to have formed, however hazily, the mental representation "This is about cowboys' jobs," comes upon a sentence that he does not identify as an exemplar of the general category "jobs." The reader reidentifies that proposition to include it in the set of exemplars, i.e., relabels it "a job." (This would be a case of learning from the text.) Or the reader might reject the proposition as an exemplar and enlarge the representation of what the paragraph is about; this is in fact what proficient readers do with simple paragraphs.

For example, a young reader encountering "Cowboys sing and dance every evening" within the above paragraph might infer that singing and dancing are jobs that cowboys do. A more proficient reader might offer as a topic sentence, "Cowboys do many different things at work and at play." Note that in each case the reader is assuming that the text is well organized and that all information is relevant. Only in extreme cases will a reader reject anomalous portions of text instead of trying to make sense of them and incorporate them into their representations (Markman, 1981).

Obviously, natural text is much more complex and varied than a simple classification model, strictly applied, can handle. The ability to deal with such complexities—and, at more advanced levels, the ability to make the adjustments in the basic model that are necessary to process sophisticated text—derive from gradual refinements in macroprocessing ability as children develop and gain further experience.

Empirical Support for the Model

Does this basic categorization model really underlie text processing? It is an inductive model, such that the addition of more and more exemplars should lead to a greater probability of identifying the category. This is comparable to the macroprocessing of a series of detail sentences and the development of macrostructure. Presumably, then, if this model is valid, several detail sentences should lead to better macrostructure development than only one or two. Of course, paragraphs often have explicit topic sentences. In this case, the category is provided explicitly, and so a greater number of exemplars (or detail sentences) should offer no advantages.

To test this hypothesis, we asked fourth and sixth graders from a middle class parochial school in New York City to read a series of paragraphs that were either one or three sentences long, with or without topic sentences (Williams, 1984). At the end of each paragraph a target sentence appeared, and the task was to say whether that sentence belonged in the paragraph. The ones that did belong were detail sentences like the ones that appear in the paragraph about cowboys. The ones that did not belong contained the general topic but did not exemplify the specific topic of discourse. For example, the inappropriate target sentence for the cowboy paragraph read, "Cowboys wear fancy boots that are handsomely decorated."

Table 3 presents the findings. For the sixth graders, performance was better after three sentences than after one, $F (1,46) = 10.41$ p < .01;

Table 3

MEAN NUMBER OF CORRECT RESPONSES

Number of Sentences	Fourth Grade		Sixth Grade	
	With Topic Sentence	No Topic Sentence	With Topic Sentence	No Topic Sentence
1	5.46	4.17	6.62	4.42
3	5.83	4.33	6.50	6.13

Maximum score per cell = 8.00

performance was better if there was a topic sentence, F (1,46) = 40.28, p < .01; and the predicted interaction was also significant, F (1,46) = 14.66, p < .01. That is, when no topic sentence appeared, increasing the number of examples via a sequence of detail sentences did lead to better identification of the main idea of paragraph (i.e., the category). This finding indicated that a simple categorization model can indeed describe the processing of at least one simple type of expository text.

Fourth graders, however, did not show the same pattern of results. Only the topic sentence variable was significant at this grade level, F (1,46) = 39.93, p < .01. This relative lack of sensitivity to variations in the text was not expected in the younger children, but it is consistent with other results, which will be reported below.

Instructional Development

An Instructional Program for the Learning Disabled Student

Durkin (1978-1979, 1981) has pointed out that most of what is commonly called instruction in reading comprehension is in actuality not much more than assessment and practice. Our project (Williams, et al., 1983) was an attempt to provide genuine instruction on finding the main idea designed on the basis of 1) certain fundamental and classic principles of instruction and 2) implications for instruction drawn from recent advances in theories of text processing. The text materials used in the instructional sequence came from our own experiments discussed above, which also provided some of the basis for the instructional design.

The decision to develop instruction in main idea identification was based on our judgment that the ability to extract the most essential information from text is not only important in itself but is also an important component of the ability to use text based knowledge in reasoning and problem solving. The instruction is based on the idea, discussed in an earlier section of this chapter, that comprehension of main idea rests strongly on basic categorization and classification skills. We also spelled out a clear and explicit definition of main idea (van Dijk's specific topic of discourse, 1980)—something that has not been done in most instruction.

In addition, we incorporated general principles of instruction into the design: 1) the use of well structured examples of the prototypic task, 2) consistent modeling of the strategies being taught, 3) a sequence of tasks,

4) a sequence of response demands that reflected a progression from easier to more difficult material, and 5) provision for extensive practice. We also chose to externalize some of the steps in the comprehension process that are, in actuality, implicit. We did this by having the students highlight some of the textual cues, that is, circle or underline them or cross them out.

The paragraphs used in the instruction were simple. Like the paragraphs we used in our experiments, they contained 1) a topic sentence which reflected the specific topic of discourse and 2) several detail sentences, each of which independently supported the topic sentence. An example follows:

> Bike riders should follow certain rules. They ought to ride in the same way that the traffic is moving. Bike riders must watch out for people in parked cars who may suddenly open a door. Bike riders should give signals before making turns.

The ten lessons of the instructional sequence were divided into two parts. The first part, consisting of five lessons, emphasized the application of categorization skills to the tasks of identifying the specific topic of discourse and of writing summary sentences. We used only well structured paragraphs. In the second part, we introduced paragraphs containing anomalous sentences to help sharpen the students' skills.

The sequence began with activities in which objects and pictures of objects were classified. For example, the teacher showed the students an eraser, a pencil, a pen, and some crayons and elicited the general concept of "things to write with." Then the students provided superordinate labels for lists of words, of phrases, and of sentences. For example, the phrases *a wooden ball, a red wagon,* and *some paper kites,* were presented and classified as *toys.*

We were not attempting to teach prerequisite classification skills. Rather, we were demonstrating the relationship between these skills, in which we assumed the students were already proficient, and the task of identifying and stating the general and specific topics of discourse. We quickly moved to applying these classification skills in identifying the general and specific topics in short paragraphs. We avoided the use of the term *main idea* in our work because of the notorious lack of precision (and of consensus) about this term (see Cunningham & Moore, Chapter 1, this volume). The terms *general topic* and *specific topic* were defined and demonstrated in terms of our paragraphs. To help the students identify the specific topic, we developed a sequence of questions along with activities in which the students circled and underlined the important aspects of the text. We hoped in this way to help them develop a strategy to use in determining the specific topic.

Having found in our research that when asked what a paragraph is about, a good proportion of young children and learning disabled children could not even provide the general topic of the paragraph, our series of questions began with a focus on that skill. We started by asking, "What is this paragraph about?" (This question was later replaced by "What is the general topic?") Having identified the general topic, the students then circled the reference to the general topic in each sentence in the paragraph.

Next, we went through a question and answer sequence to direct attention to the specific topic, starting with, "Does this paragraph tell us everything about bicycles?" *No, it doesn't.* "What is the specific topic?" We often asked questions in order to get the students started: "Does the paragraph tell us about how bikes are made?" *No.* "Well, what does the paragraph tell us about bikes? What is the specific topic?" At this point, responses usually tended to be one of two types. Sometimes a student would answer with a detail, in which case we would identify (and underline) all the details in the paragraph and then determine what they had in common (e.g., "All the details are about the rules that bike riders should follow.") Sometimes a student would give the correct response. In this case we would agree, and then review, by enumerating and underlining the examples in the supporting detail sentences.

Paragraphs were presented in an easy-to-difficult sequence. The instruction started with paragraphs that contained topic sentences. Paragraphs without topic sentences were introduced later. Response demands were also carefully sequenced; we started with title choice activities and then moved to writing summary sentences.

During the second half of the instruction, we introduced anomalous sentences into some of the paragraphs. Students had to determine whether an anomalous sentence was present and, if it was, they had to cross it out (another example of making explicit and overt some of the steps of the comprehension process). The crossing out was designed to help the students disregard the anomalous sentence when they wrote their summary sentence for the paragraph.

We introduced these paragraphs containing anomalous sentences because research has demonstrated that negative instances are valuable for concept attainment (Klausmeier, 1977). Moreover, as pointed out above, natural text is not always well structured; thus, children must learn to read less than optimally structured prose. Well written text sometime contains parenthetical information, for example, which the reader must process without allowing it to be a source of confusion.

The anomalous sentences were of two types. Some contained neither the general nor the specific topic of the paragraph; they did, however, contain material relevant to the general topic, that is, material that had, in Halliday and Hasan's terms (1976), collocational ties to the general topic. For example, the sentence "Skateboarding has become a very popular sport in the past few years" served as the anomalous sentence in the paragraph about bike riders. This type of anomalous sentence (unrelated) was introduced first, because its detection required only that the student recognize that the general topic was not mentioned.

The second, more difficult type of anomalous sentence was then introduced. The general topic was represented in those related sentences, but the rest of the sentence information was not consonant with the specific topic of the paragraph, e.g., "Some bike riders can learn to do special tricks." When paragraphs containing anomalous sentences were introduced, we continued with our basic sequence of questions on each paragraph, but we added a question pertinent to the detection of the anomalous sentence: "Is there a sentence that doesn't tell us about the rules that bike riders should follow?"

An Evaluation of the Instructional Program

In order to determine whether our instructional program was, in fact, effective in helping learning disabled children learn to identify and produce the main idea of short, expository paragraphs, we conducted a small evaluation study (Williams et al., 1983). We also wanted to determine whether any improvement in performance was due simply to exposure to and practice on the specific materials covered in the instruction or whether, in fact, the results of the training generalized to content not specifically addressed in training.

Description of the study. Subjects were eighteen middle school level learning disabled children who were participating in after school tutoring programs. Nine of the children were given the instruction, and nine were not. The instructed (M = 11.33 years) and the comparison (M = 11.27 years) groups were equated on age, t(16) = .11, and on their standard scores on the reading subtest of the Wide Range Achievement Test (instructed group: M = 91.1; comparison group: M = 96.1; t(16) = 1.04). In oral reading performance, they were judged informally to be about two grade levels below average for their age.

Subjects were given two tests as both pretests and posttests. (See Table 4 for examples of the test items.) In the first, main test, children wrote a summary sentence after reading each of twelve paragraphs. The paragraph was removed from view during the writing. Six of the paragraphs contained a topic sentence, and six did not. Half of the paragraphs of each type were randomly selected to be used as examples in the instructional sequence, and the other half appeared only in the tests.

A secondary test was given after the main one. This test consisted of twelve paragraphs developed from the paragraph bases of the first test. Four of the twelve paragraphs contained a normal structure. In each of the other eight paragraphs, an anomalous detail sentence was substituted for one of the normal detail sentences; half of these were related details and half, unrelated details. In addition, half the paragraphs of each type contained a topic sentence and half did not. The children's task was to determine which, if any, of the sentences did not belong to each paragraph.

In the test booklets, each paragraph was written in ordinary format, and directly below it, the same sentences appeared in list form (as response choices), with the additional choice of "all sentences belong." Instructions were to "mark the sentence that does not belong in the paragraph you just read."

The justification for the main test is obvious. Writing a sentence that summarizes the main idea of the paragraph is the goal of the instructional sequence; its importance is reflected in the fact that almost all school curricula—at several levels—include it.

We included the deviant sentence detection test for three reasons. First, it provided another measure of main idea comprehension, one in which the child must use the specific topic in the evaluation of the appropriateness of detail sentences. Second, it required no writing. Since writing is such a difficult task for learning disabled students, instruction might have had an effect that would show up only on a test that incorporated an easy response mode. Third, the deviant sentence detection task corresponded to an important part of our instructional sequence, as explained above.

The procedure was as follows. Fifteen sessions were spread over ten weeks. On Day 1, we gave the main pretest; on Day 2, the second pretest. Then followed five instructional sessions devoted to the first part of the instructional program. These sessions focused on identifying and stating general and specific topics in normal paragraphs. After each lesson, the children worked independently on a worksheet that provided further practice. At the end of these five sessions, the students were again given the main summary sentence test. Then followed another five lessons in which they focused on the detection of anomalous sentences and learned to disregard such sentences when writing summary sentences. Following

Table 4
EXAMPLES OF TEST ITEMS

A. Main Test (Write Summary Sentence)
1. *Normal with topic sentence.*
   The catcher is a very important person on a baseball team. The catcher has to know the hitting weaknesses of every player on the other teams. He can tell whether the players on his team are in the right spot. The catcher gives the signal that starts every play.
2. *Related anomalous with no topic sentence.*
   The wolf often breaks into beavers' lodges and ruins them. The wolf was once common throughout the colder parts of North America. It raids trappers' camps and takes things that it has no use for. The wolf steals food that other animals have hidden away.
   Note. Students are instructed to write one sentence that summarizes the paragraph they just read. A separate sheet of paper is provided in each booklet for answers, so that the paragraph is not in front of the students when they write their answers.

B. Secondary Test (Identify Anomalous Sentences)
1. *Normal with no topic sentence.*
   Newspapers need reporters to track down the stories that get printed. They have editors who read the stories and decide which one should be printed. Artists sometimes draw cartoons for newspapers. Newspapers have delivery people to take the papers to newsstands and stores.

   Mark the sentence that does not belong in the paragraph which you just read.
   ☐ Newspapers need reporters to track down the stories that get printed.
   ☐ They have editors who read the stories and decide which ones should be printed.
   ☐ Artists sometimes draw cartoons for newspapers.
   ☐ Newspapers have delivery people to take the papers to newstands and stores.
   ☐ All sentences belong.
2. *Unrelated anomalous with topic sentence.*
   Bike riders should follow certain rules. Bike riders ought to ride in the same way the traffic is moving. Skateboarding has become a very popular sport in the past few years. Bike riders should give signals before making turns.

   Mark the sentence that does not belong in the paragraph which you just read.
   ☐ Bike riders should follow certain rules.
   ☐ Bike riders ought to ride in the same way the traffic is moving.
   ☐ Skateboarding has become a very popular sport in the past few years.
   ☐ Bike riders should give signals before making turns.
   ☐ All sentences belong.

the instruction were two sessions of posttesting; first the main test was given, and then the secondary one. Each of the ten lessons lasted about 25 minutes and took place when the children were regularly scheduled for remediation. The children were instructed in small groups of two to four.

Approximately the same number of days elapsed between pretesting and posttesting for the comparison group, which did not receive instruction. This group also took the main summary sentence test midway through the interval between pretest and posttest. (This administration of the test has not been evaluated.)

Results of the study. Table 5 represents the mean scores on the main (summary sentence) test as a function of group and type of item. An analysis of covariance, with pretest score as the covariate, was performed on the posttest scores. The instructed group performed significantly better than did the comparison group, F $(1,15)$ = 17.76, p < .01. This indicated that our instructional sequence had in fact been effective in helping the children to learn to identify and construct main ideas. In addition, there was no significant difference between instructed and noninstructed items, F $(1,15)$ = 2.12; this indicated that the results of our training were not restricted to the specific paragraphs used in the instruction but, rather, that the effects of the training generalized to other content. The two variables did not interact.

Table 5

EVALUATION OF THE INSTRUCTIONAL PROGRAM

Mean Number Correct
(Main Test: Writing Summary Sentences)

| | Pretest | |
	Instructed Items	Noninstructed Items
Instructed Group	1.89	1.89
Comparison Group	1.33	1.44

| | Posttest | |
	Instructed Items	Noninstructed Items
Instructed Group	3.56	4.00
Comparison Group	1.78	2.33

Maximum score per cell = 6.00

Table 6 presents the data on the secondary test, the identification of anomalous sentences. This test reflected the same pattern of findings as did the main test. That is, the instructed group performed significantly better than the comparison group, $F (1,15) = 40.06$, $p < .01$, and there was no difference between the instructed and the noninstructed items, $F (1,15) = 3.35$. There was no interaction between the two variables.

The results of this evaluation study indicated that systematic focused training can improve performance on main idea comprehension. Children were able to apply known classification skills to the task of recognizing and formulating the main idea statements. Although the texts used in this study were structurally simple, we are convinced that work with materials such as these is an appropriate beginning step in the development of a sophisticated understanding of main idea and in using this comprehension skill in a variety of more complex materials.

Main ideas are directly stated in expository prose rather infrequently, it turns out (Baumann & Serra, 1984; Braddock, 1974). This is an important argument for focusing instructional attention on texts that do not have topic sentences, and the simple texts used in this program appear to be appropriate as introductory examples of paragraphs in which the main idea is not stated explicitly.

Table 6

EVALUATION OF THE INSTRUCTIONAL PROGRAM

Mean Number Correct
(Secondary Test: Identifying Anomalous Sentences)

	Pretest	
	Instructed Items	Noninstructed Items
Instructed Group	3.22	3.56
Comparison Group	2.67	3.44

	Posttest	
	Instructed Items	Noninstructed Items
Instructed Group	5.78	5.11
Comparison Group	3.22	2.89

Maximum score per cell = 6.00

Implications for further work. This work has implications for further instructional design. First, the tasks that are used in school to assess the ability to understand main idea vary considerably in difficulty. If task demands are too stringent, or too complex, performance will not accurately reflect actual ability to generate macrostructure. Both instructional tasks and assessment materials must be carefully selected.

Second, in our research, third graders did not perform well on the simplest task (title choice) even with very easy texts. The ability to understand the main idea of these paragraphs depends on knowledge of specific content, including classification of that content into categories and exemplars. Basic instruction is often neccessary at this early level, involving the teaching of content or categorization skills. The fact that the younger children in our studies tended to offer narrow main ideas suggests that they need help in developing their generalization processes.

At the fourth grade level and beyond, instruction should focus on the application of existing abilities in the performance of more complex or novel tasks. One specific focus should be on teaching students how to use effectively the information presented in topic sentences. The issue of how to deal with anomalous material appropriately should also be addressed at this time. The first step here is to get students to attend to anomalous information, and then to evaluate such information with a view toward either rejecting *or* incorporating it into their mental representation of the paragraph, i.e., the macrostructure.

At more advanced levels, other instructional emphases are warranted. At times even proficient readers have difficulty focusing on the global coherence of the text without being diverted by specific detail information. Special attention should be devoted to this matter in instruction at higher levels.

We are working further on materials and procedures that address these issues at different stages of instruction.

Note

[1] To confirm our hypothesis that these subjects were in fact incorporating the anomalous sentence into their representation, we later asked another sample of adults to do a Title task that offered broadened options. Three of the four title choices were, as before, 1) the specific topic of discourse; 2) the general topic; and 3) the general topic plus a detail from the paragraph. However, the fourth choice, instead of containing the general topic plus an intrusion, contained the general topic plus the unrelated information represented in the anomalous

sentence (e.g., "About Cowboys and Birds"). In this situation, we would expect, on the related paragraphs, a substantial number of choices of the title that reflected the general topic and, on the unrelated paragraphs, a substantial number of choices of the title that reflected the general topic plus unrelated information. This is just what happened.

All of these results derive from four sentence paragraphs. With longer paragraphs, it would be expected that adults would not attempt to incorporate the information contained in a single anomalous sentence into their representation. We have collected some preliminary evidence on this point. The unrelated cowboy paragraph was written in both a four-sentence and an eight-sentence version, and each version was given to 22 subjects. On the short paragraph, 13 subjects chose the general–plus–unrelated information title and 8, the specific topic of discourse title, whereas on the long paragraph, only two subjects chose the general–plus–unrelated information and 17 chose the specific topic of discourse ($\chi^2(1) = 11.24$, p < .001).

References

Anderson, R.C. Role of the reader's schema in comprehension, learning, and memory. In R.C. Anderson, J. Osborn, and R.J. Tierney (Eds.), *Learning to read in American schools*. Hillsdale, NJ: Erlbaum, 1984, 243-257.

Aulls, M.W. *Developmental and remedial reading in the middle grades*. Boston: Allyn & Bacon, 1978.

Aulls, M.W. Expository paragraph properties that influence literal recall. *Journal of Reading Behavior*, 1975, *7*, 391-400.

Baumann, J.F. Research on children's main idea comprehension: A problem of ecological validity. *Reading Psychology*, 1982, *3*, 167-177.

Baumann, J.F. Children's ability to comprehend main ideas in content textbooks. *Reading World*, 1983, *22*, 322-331.

Baumann, J.F. The effectiveness of a direct instruction paradigm for teaching main idea comprehension. *Reading Research Quarterly*, 1984, *20*, 93-115.

Baumann, J.F., and Serra, J.K. The frequency and placement of main ideas in children's social studies textbooks: A modified replication of Braddock's research on topic sentences. *Journal of Reading Behavior*, 1984, *16*, 27-40.

Braddock, R. The frequency and placement of topic sentences in expository prose. *Research in the Teaching of English*, 1974, *8*, 287-302.

Danner, F.W. Children's understanding of intersentence organization in the recall of short descriptive passages. *Journal of Educational Psychology*, 1976, *68*, 174-183.

Durkin, D. What classroom observations reveal about reading comprehension instruction. *Reading Research Quarterly*, 1978-1979, *14*, 481-533.

Durkin, D. Reading comprehension instruction in five basal reader series. *Reading Research Quarterly*, 1981, *16*, 515-544.

Fish, S. *Is there a text in this class?* Cambridge, MA: Harvard University Press, 1980.

Fredericksen, C.H. Representing logical and semantic structure of knowledge acquired from discourse. *Cognitive Psychology*, 1975, *7*, 371-458.

Grice, H.P. Logic and conversation. In P. Cole and J.L. Morgan (Eds.), *Syntax and semantics, volume 3: Speech acts*. New York: Seminar Press, 1975, 41-58.

Halliday, M.A.K., and Hasan, R. *Cohesion in English*. London: Longman, 1976.

Kieras, D.E. Good and bad structure in simple paragraphs: Effects on apparent theme, reading time, and recall. *Journal of Verbal Learning and Verbal Behavior*, 1978, *17*, 13-28.

Kintsch, W., and Keenan, J.M. Reading rate as a function of the number of propositions in the base structure of sentences. *Cognitive Psychology*, 1973, *5*, 257-274.

Kintsch, W., and van Dijk, T.A. Toward a model of text comprehension and production. *Psychological Review*, 1978, *85*, 363-394.

Klausmeier, H.J. Instructional design and the teaching of concepts. In J.R. Levin, and V.L. Allen (Eds.), *Cognitive learning in children: Theories and strategies*. New York: Academic Press, 1976, 191-217.

Markman, E.M. Comprehension monitoring. In W.P. Dickson (Ed.), *Children's oral communication skills*. New York: Academic Press, 1981, 61-84.

Meyer, B. *The organization of prose and its effect on memory*. Amsterdam, The Netherlands: North Holland, 1975.

Meyer, B.F. What is remembered from prose: A function of passage structure. In R.O. Freedle (Ed.), *Discourse, production and comprehension*. Norwood, NJ: Ablex, 1977, 41-58.

Pearson, P.D. A retrospective reaction to prose comprehension. In C.M. Santa and B.L. Hayes (Eds.), *Children's prose comprehension: Research and practice*. Newark, DE: International Reading Association, 1981, 117-132.

Rosenshine, B.V. Skill hierarchies in reading comprehension. In R.J. Spiro, B.C. Bruce, and W.F. Brewer (Eds.), *Theoretical issues in reading comprehension*. Hillsdale, NJ: Erlbaum, 1980, 535-554.

Rumelhart, D.E. Schemata: The building blocks of cognition. In R.J. Spiro, B.C. Bruce, and W.F. Brewer (Eds.), *Theoretical issues in reading comprehension*. Hillsdale, NJ: Erlbaum, 1980, 33-58.

Taylor, B.M. Children's memory for expository text after reading. *Reading Research Quarterly*, 1980, *15*, 399-411.

Taylor, M.B., and Williams, J.P. Comprehension of learning disabled readers: Task and text variations. *Journal of Educational Psychology*, 1983, *75*, 743-751.

van Dijk, T.A. *Macrostructures*. Hillsdale, NJ: Erlbaum, 1980.

van Dijk, T.A., and Kintsch, W. *Strategies of discourse comprehension*. New York: Academic Press, 1983.

Waters, H.S. Superordinate-subordinate structure in semantic memory: The roles of comprehension and retrieval processes. *Journal of Verbal Learning and Verbal Behavior*, 1978, *17*, 587-597.

Williams, J.P. Teaching decoding with an emphasis on phoneme analysis and phoneme blending. *Journal of Educational Psychology*, 1980, *72*, 1-15.

Williams, J.P. Categorization, macrostructure, and finding the main idea. *Journal of Educational Psychology*, 1984, *76*, 874-879.

Williams, J.P., Taylor, M.B., and deCani, J.S. *How learning disabled and nondisabled readers construct macrostructure (find the main idea) for expository text*. Technical Report No. 22. Research Institute for the Study of Learning Disabilities, Teachers College, Columbia University, 1983.

Williams, J.P., Taylor, M.B., and deCani, J.S. Constructing macrostructure for expository text. *Journal of Educational Psychology*, 1984, *76*, 1065-1075.

Williams, J.P., Taylor, M.B., and Ganger, S. Text variations at the level of the individual sentence and the comprehension of simple expository paragraphs. *Journal of Educational Psychology*, 1981, *73*, 851-865.

Williams, J.P., Taylor, M.B., Jarin, D.C., and Milligan, E.S. *Determining the main idea of expository paragraphs: An instructional program for the learning-disabled and its evaluation*. Technical Report No. 25. Research Institute for the Study of Learning Disabilities, Teachers College, Columbia University, 1983.

Winograd, P.N. Strategic difficulties in summarizing texts. *Reading Research Quarterly,* 1984, *19,* 404-425.

Wooton, A.J. *Dilemmas of discourse: Controversies about the sociological interpretation of language*. London: Allen and Unwin, 1975.

5

Actively Teaching Main Idea Skills

Mark W. Aulls

This chapter focuses on instructional issues related to main idea comprehension. Aulls begins by defining topic *and* main idea, *offering guidelines for their instruction, and specifying the types of declarative knowledge (knowing what) and procedural knowledge (knowing how to) required for main idea instruction. He then discusses four basic responsibilities and the learning goals in main idea instruction, making the distinction between context bound and context free learning outcomes. Aulls then describes the general components of active teaching—verbal explanation, verbal modeling, practice and feedback, and independent practice—and then specifies what is involved in the active teaching of main ideas in a systematic instructional cycle. He concludes the chapter with several guidelines for the preparation of instructional materials that will facilitate the active teaching of main idea skills.*

Defining Main Idea Skills

In *Developmental and Remedial Reading in the Middle Grades* (Aulls, 1978), I devoted a chapter to teaching main idea skills. Even though other reading texts typically only gave two to three pages to teaching main ideas, I felt that greater instructional emphasis was justifiable given its pervasive occurrence in published programs, its relevance to carrying out a variety of study reading skills, and its relevance to composing exposition (see Flood & Lapp, Chapter 10, this volume). In addition, I assumed that a reader needs two complex and different sorts of knowledge to establish the importance of text information and to interpret the author's signals as to what is important. These two forms of knowledge are 1) declarative knowledge, knowing *what* a skill or strategy entails and 2) procedural knowledge, knowing *how* to perform a skill or strategy.

Declarative Knowledge

Main idea skills entail acquiring two primary forms of declarative knowledge: 1) knowledge of what a topic is and 2) knowledge of what the explicit or implicit main idea statement is. I defined topic and main idea in the following way:

Topic. The topic of a paragraph signals to the reader the subject of the discourse. Topics usually are signified by single words but they can be phrase units. The subject that dominates one or more paragraphs is the superordinate word (or phrase) to which all other subjects (subordinate words) refer. The referential relationships between the subtopics and superordinate topic coordinate the between sentence relationships in a paragraph. When you ask, "What is this chapter, article, or paragraph about?", you are asking for the major subject that is being explained.

Main Idea. The main idea of a paragraph signals to the reader the most important statement the writer has presented to explain the topic. This statement characterizes the major idea to which the majority of *sentences* refer. This statement is usually developed in a single sentence. However, it sometimes is developed by two coordinate sentences. The main idea presents more information than a word or phrase representing the topic of the discourse. As a single sentence it may occur at any point in a paragraph. It may be implied rather than explicitly stated. An implied main idea may be inferred from postulating the *dominant* relationship between the superordinate topics of a paragraph. When you ask, "What is the most important idea the writer is trying to explain with regards to the subject?", you are asking for the one main idea statement presented by the writer to explain the major subject. (Aulls, 1978, pp. 92-93)

While other forms of declarative knowledge may be involved in teaching main idea skills, topic and main idea are central concepts to define. Furthermore, how these concepts are applied to designing instructional procedures, developing materials, and sequencing what to teach varies considerably. Therefore, it seems worthwhile to raise and discuss questions regarding how these concepts apply to planning instruction.

Should students be taught that a topic is different from a main idea? In my view, the answer is definitely *yes*. These two concepts help signal importance in text in different ways. The prior definitions spell out how they provide different signals to the reader. Students who do not distinguish between them are deprived of conscious access to both when they need to distinguish the general topic from the specific topic. Furthermore, an inability to distinguish between the topic of a text and the main idea creates considerable cognitive confusion when the same terms are used interchangeably.

Should students be taught what a topic is before being taught what a main idea is? In my opinion, the answer to this question is *yes*, based on one primary consideration. Cognitive developmental studies (Applebee, 1978; Baker & Stein, 1978; Nelson, 1977a; Stein & Glenn, 1979) demonstrate that children acquire the cognitive knowledge necessary to organize semantic concepts such as objects, events, and actions as they read a text before they acquire a sense of the function of explicit text structure signals to important information like main idea statements.

Should students be taught how to identify the topic before being taught to identify the main idea? Again the answer is *yes*. Children are better equipped cognitively to learn how to identify a topic than to identify main ideas. In both narrative and expository material, the central topic is introduced early in the text (as the story problem in a narrative story or the central concept of an exposition). In contrast, the main ideas can be introduced at any point in the text (Baumann & Serra, 1984; Braddock, 1974). This strong topical order signal probably makes the central topic more salient to the reader than the main idea. In addition, in exposition the main ideas may be implied rather than stated, but the central topic is almost always stated in even poorly written exposition. In short, we should first teach students how to identify topics and later how to identify main ideas. This assertion applies to both narration and exposition.

Should we define topic and main idea for narrative stories and expository texts differently? This is a difficult question for two reasons. First, clear explicit research regarding how experts and novices derive these two concepts and apply them to both kinds of texts is yet to be done. Second, teachers usually use narrative material to teach topic and main idea in the primary grade reading programs but rely heavily on exposition in the middle grades.

Regardless of these overwhelming pragmatic considerations, my view is that main idea and topic should be defined differently and taught differently for narration and exposition. In fact, I recommend teaching only the concept of topic in the primary grades by first using narratives and later simple expositions. I would suggest teaching main idea only using exposition. If main idea is taught with narrative stories, then it should not be done until high school where serious literary analysis occurs in literature classes.

Evidence has slowly begun to emerge that exposition is much more difficult to comprehend than narrative stories from grades one (Dixson, 1981) through grades three, four, five, six, and eight (Baker & Stein, 1978; Berkowitz & Taylor, 1981; Freedle & Hale, 1979; Guzzetti, 1982; Marshall, 1982; Mosenthal, 1979; Olson, Mack, & Duffy, 1981). In the reported studies a variety of comprehension measures were used. This provides some indirect evidence that distinguishing between narration and exposition when teaching main idea skills is a potentially sound notion. However, the greater difficulty that students have with exposition may be due to the fact that formal schooling does little to teach students how to read exposition (Calfee & Curley, 1984). In the elementary school, reading programs are primarily based on narrative stories, even in the intermediate grades. But students are required to read increasingly more exposition from elementary school through college, as a function of reading assignments in subject areas. By the time they enter the work force, 93 percent of their reading time involves various forms of expository material (Guthrie & Seifert, 1982).

Thus, within the present educational context, it seems reasonable to teach topic in the primary grades as all the literal events of a story which tell what it is about. For exposition, the definition given earlier applies. In the intermediate grades, the definitions of topic and of main idea given earlier apply to exposition. In high school, the central meaning of a narrative story seems readily derivable from the relationship between the story problem and its resolution or from criteria for evaluating the social, psychological, and moral factors which enable us to understand characters' actions (Andresen, 1965; McConaughy, Fitzhenry-Coor, & Howell, 1981). Some literary theorists and psychologists would argue against the notion of assuming a story has one central meaning or main idea (Bruce, 1980; Iser, 1974).

Procedural Knowledge

In *Developmntal and Remedial Reading in the Middle Grades* (Aulls, 1978), I also stressed that teaching main idea skills required teaching students two forms of procedural knowledge. Remember that procedural knowledge refers to any form of knowing *how* to do something. For main idea skills it is how to identify, infer, and generate main ideas or topics. The first type of procedural knowledge needed is classification and categorization (cf., Williams, Chapter 4, this volume). Each cognitive procedure is relevant to how to identify the topic. The second type of procedural knowledge is how to use rules or strategies to identify, infer, or generate a main idea. These forms of knowledge are acquired through discovery or taught by explanation *and* verbally modeling how to use classification, categorization, and rules.

Categorization and Classification. Categorization is a slightly different thinking process than classification. Suppose you had a wood pencil, paper, a wooden ruler, and a clay coffee cup in front of you. Now, suppose I asked you to put together the objects which were alike in some way. This is a classification thinking task. You have to think of a context or a physical dimension in which to relate these objects. You might, for example, say they are all objects used when studying. In a categorization task, on the other hand, I would give you a criterion (or category) for relating information. If I said, "Put together all the objects that are made of wood," you would group the wood pencil, paper, and wood ruler.

These procedural distinctions are important to make when teaching students how to identify the central topic because the student must distinguish the superordinate topic category from the subordinate ones. For example, a paragraph about objects used while studying may have as its subordinate topics, pencils, paper, rulers, and books. Class inclusion reasoning is needed to draw these relationships, that is, to relate the superordinate to subordinate categories. Well written exposition and all narratives first signal the superordinate topic and then the subordinate. To relate expository paragraphs together, the reader must classify the superordinate topics. When there is no superordinate topic, the reader must infer it from the subordinate topics by classification. To do this requires the reader to transform the topic of each paragraph to a subordinate status in order to generate the superordinate topic of the entire selection.

To help students control the procedures they use to identify the central topic, first teach them to classify and categorize words, phrases, and then the topics of a paragraph. Later, they can be taught to classify the topic from the paragraph topics in the entire selection. Learning how to categorize story events into problem and resolution categories may also be useful to teach students how to infer the central theme (Armbruster, Echols, & Brown, 1983).

My own research suggests that both average and poor readers in the middle grades can become competent in identifying the central topic of an expository paragraph or selection through direct instruction which includes training in categorizing and classifying words, phrases, sentences, and topics of paragraphs (Aulls, 1980).

Rules and Strategies. The second form of procedural knowledge involves rules for how to identify main ideas. These rules help the reader to use signals in the text structure to formulate strategies for how to arrive at the main idea. Evidence of the usefulness of explicitly explaining and verbally modeling rules is offered by the research carried out by Day (1981) and reported by Brown and Day (1983).

Day taught junior college students who were good or poor readers and good readers but poor writers to write summaries. Writing a summary entails both a reading comprehension step and a composing step. This study is a marvelous example of an instructional procedure for teaching study skills.

What is instructionally important here is that Day had four levels of instruction using rules. The instruction varied in how explicit the rules were for identifying the important parts of a text (in writing and verbally by the teacher) and whether the teacher trained the students to monitor how effectively they used the rules to extract the most important information while reading and while composing an eighty word summary.

The least explicit instruction provided vague directions to be concise and efficient without any mention of how to accomplish this. Furthermore, the readers recieved no directions for what to do during reading except to read the text three times. They were told to keep the text in front of them if they wanted to in preparing the summary, make sure they understood the important points, and check their summary against the original text to be sure no important information was left out. The teacher verbally modeled these steps with a text and explained what she was doing. Students then were given a different text and asked to read it and write an eighty word summary. On the next day, written feedback was given on the students' written product as opposed to the process used. Then a new text was given, and the teacher and students repeated the same process.

The second group received a handout listing five rules for summarization, but they were not explained or verbally modeled. The rules were:
1. Delete trivia, circle any lists, and write a one word superordinate (e.g., replace lists like *daisies, tulips, sweet peas* with *flowers)*.
2. Underline the topic sentences—sentences that include the superordinate topic and state the main idea of a paragraph.
3. If there is no topic sentence, make up one.
4. Delete redundant and unimportant information.

The third group received a handout which listed the rules for summarization and three general steps for writing a summary: 1) state the theme, 2) reread the text, 3) check and doublecheck the summary against the original text.

The fourth group received the same handout as group two, but specific methods were explained and verbally modeled. In other words, the processes needed to read and extract the summary information and then to write the summary were explicitly stated and modeled.

The results showed that the rules groups produced the best summaries. Furthermore, the group given the most explicit explanation of how to use the rules was most successful in using most of them. The only exception was the rule to generate the unstated main idea. Poorer readers did not significantly improve in the two days, but the good readers who were poor writers did significantly improve their summaries. The authors concluded that the poor readers needed more instructional time to get better at inventing implicit main ideas. Whether or not this is the case, explaining rules and showing students how to use them and how to write the summary did significantly improve the quality of the students' summaries. That is a very powerful short term instructional effect, and it has been replicated by McNeil and Donant (1982) with fifth graders.

Will explaining and modeling rules that teach students how to identify, infer, and generate main ideas, lead to their internalization and spontaneous use? Existing research does not show this, but the possibilities for future research are many.

Why should there be so much potential in explicitly explaining and verbally modeling rules for how to identify main ideas, followed by the same training in how to infer main ideas, and still later how to use both processes to carry out study skills such as summarizing, outlining, or notetaking? Answers to this question are, of course, preliminary and will be varied.

Max Black gives educators some strong arguments for teaching rules in his essay "Rules and Routines" (Black, 1967). From that essay, several arguments support teaching rules for how to identify or infer main deas. First, rules enable deliberate mental activity which leads to an end result or product. In the context of executing reading study skills (like summarizing, internalizing the important information in text in preparation for an essay test, and preparing for a discussion of the main ideas in an exposition), the reader must deliberately activate any prior knowledge that will help in identifying or generating main ideas. Without deliberately accessing rules for how to organize the knowledge required to get the main ideas, students will not be very successful at the task. And deliberate access to rules implies the learner already possesses the declarative knowledge needed to understand the concepts (Brown, Day, & Jones, 1983).

In a six week study, Ritchie (1983) taught sixth graders rules for how to identify the main idea and verbally modeled how to generate main idea questions that adhered to the rules. The students most successful in generating better quality main idea questions had been taught main idea skills, knowledge, and rules for using it before the teacher verbally modeled the process of generating main idea questions. For those who only participated in the question asking, verbal modeling instructional sessions were not as successful. Both groups were significantly more successful on a variety of measures for using and getting the main idea than those not given either form of instruction. Thus, teaching the knowledge of what topic and main idea is, in conjunction with rules for how to identify topics and main ideas, seems to lead to more powerful question asking strategies.

Rules offer a recipe for how to arrive at a defined goal or achievement. After defining the term *main idea,* students need a plan for how to arrive at it whether explictly stated or merely implied. But learning how to respond to a rule requires students to learn from experience that they cannot use the rules unthinkingly (Armbruster, Echols, & Brown, 1983). The student must understand the concepts in each rule and how to transform them into a procedure or plan to arrive at the goal. This understanding is developed instructionally through explaining each rule, repeated verbal modeling of how to use the rules mentally, and repeated student practice and teacher feedback. The latter should especially emphasize procedural processes that lead to the outcome of rule use. Thus a teacher cannot just hand out a list of rules and expect students to benefit from them.

From a recent year long study (Aulls & Holt, 1984) of how to teach junior high school students how to write expository paragraphs, preliminary evidence suggests that junior high students will write longer and better quality paragraphs if they are taught what a topic is, what a stated main idea is, and how to identify and infer both from expository paragraphs. Their performance also improves if they are given extensive opportunity to practice and get feedback on strategies for using their knowledge of text structure during the process of planning and revising their paragraphs. What was particularly encouraging in this study was evidence of transfer, over a three month period, to the geography essays students wrote. This suggests that if the rules taught about text structure and the procedures taught for planning and drafting specify good ways to approach a meaningful writing task, students use them. These results are further strengthened by the fact that the students were unaware that their performance on geography writing assignments would be evaluated on the basis of what they had been taught in English class.

For rules to be more than unthinking routine, they also must be tested by the students throughout instruction. Only in an instructional climate which supports testing rules will students use the rules as their own and recognize how to alter them or adapt their content for different contexts. Whether the rules are good ones is ultimately a cognitive issue tested by common sense and against the facts regarding how often they work, in what contexts they work, and for whom they are workable.

In short, teaching students rules for how to identify stated main ideas serves as a starting place, but learners must be able to use the rules with what they already know. Giving out a list of rules will not teach students how to do tasks like identifying or inferring main ideas or writing summaries. At first, the teacher must explain and model. As the learner and teacher use them in many practice contexts, the student should discover that even rather workable rules have exceptions and will have to be challenged, discussed, and revised or allocated to use in specific situations. This process is a metacognitive one of monitoring, testing, and self correcting the use of rules for how to identify, infer, or generate main ideas with a variety of texts (Brown, Campione, & Day, 1981). The gradual internalization of rules enables the learner to take control over getting main ideas, establishing what is important in a text, and composing texts that clearly signal what is important for a reader to understand.

In summary, the preceding research seems to indicate that active teachers will be as explicit as possible in their explanation of rules and their key concepts. They will also provide verbal models of how to use the rules, as strategies, to arrive at the learning goal. Lastly, active teachers will be collaborators who guide student practice and give feedback focused on the process of using rules as well as the product.

Basic Responsibilities in Main Idea Instruction

In my opinion, teachers in elementary school, high school, and in college methods courses all have essentially the same responsibilities to face and fulfill with regard to teaching main idea skills. I believe there are four basic instructional responsibilities.

The first responsibility is for the teacher to know what a main idea is, be able to explain what it is, to explain why it is important to learn, and to explain how to go about identifying, inferring, or generating main ideas. Furthermore, a teacher must be able to reason whether students must use the same types of knowledge to get the main idea as they do to get the topic for narrative stories and explanation.

The second responsibility is to recognize that testing will not substitute for direct instruction in improving students' main idea skills. Asking main idea questions as an instructional activity does not teach the knowledge students need to answer them. Asking "What is the main idea of this selection?" for both narrative stories and expository texts may confuse students because the types of text structure cues underlying these two kinds of text are inherently different. Treating the questions "What is this about?" and "What is the main idea?" as interchangeable may also confuse students or lead them to believe both questions require the same knowledge. Moreover, how to interpret the criteria for acceptable responses to main idea questions should not be a mystery to the students. Students should not perceive the tasks given by teachers to be mysterious or solved by magical means, or they will consider such tasks too ambiguous and risky (Doyle, 1982). Finally, just as testing is not a reasonable way to teach new knowledge, neither is telling students to identify, infer, or generate main ideas on practice exercises from published materials that again only test (rather than explain or show how to do) these tasks (Beck, 1984; Durkin, 1981).

Third, a teacher must present an understandable and usable definition of *main idea*. A definition, with good examples, makes explicit what knowledge the teacher expects the students to learn and rely upon when identifying, inferring, or generating main ideas.

The fourth teaching responsibility is to explain what cues in the text signal main ideas and then to model verbally the thinking procedures for how to identify or infer main ideas and answer main idea questions (see Afflerbach & Johnston, Chapter 3, this volume). The knowledge needed for identifying stated main ideas may not be the same as the knowledge needed to infer implied main ideas. Stated main ideas are identified in an author's text because the reader knows how a main idea sentence differs from the other explicitly stated sentences in the text. Implied main ideas must be recognized as being implied. The reader must know what other text information or signals in the text to use in order to infer and generate a main idea sentence that satisfies the same functions as any stated main idea.

Verbally modeling the mental procedures necessary to use knowledge about text to identify and especially infer main ideas makes explicit to the novice what to do. For example, knowing what parts are needed to put a model airplane together is different from knowing how to put the parts together so that you end up with a plane that will fly. Verbally modeling strategies for using rules provides the learner with rules or a plan for how to identify a stated main idea and infer an implied main idea. It gives learners a place to start when looking for stated main ideas or when they must infer implied main ideas. However, the teacher should be aware that the rules or plans used by an adult may not work for younger, less expert readers who have not yet obtained an adult's knowledge of text structure. This knowledge precedes knowledge of procedures for how to use it (Brown, et al., in press). The teacher simply needs to remain flexible and sensitive to this relationship between knowledge *about* and knowledge *how to*. The teacher must also resist putting students in situations where the text is more complex than the knowledge they have or the procedures they can use to identify, infer, or generate main ideas.

The Learning Goals in Main Idea Instruction

The teacher and the student should be comfortable with the learning goals entailed in acquiring main idea skills. This is not easy because they are demanding and conceptual in nature rather than simple and concrete. Equally important, it is not easy to establish the criteria for judging the extent to which main idea skills have been learned. Closely related to this issue is the determination of what function these skills can be expected to play in the process of reading or writing per se as well as reading or writing for specific purposes. In short, teachers must clarify these issues in order to become comfortable with why main idea skills are important and why an active instructional role is necessary.

Among the many comprehension skills which are relevant to reading study skills, main idea skills are probably among the most basic. The extent to which these skills are developed appears to play a powerful role in how effectively a student can carry out the more global strategies of outlining, underlining, note taking, skimming and scanning, summary writing, and question asking. All of these more global strategies emphasize establishing what is most important to understand or remember from all the information provided by an author. Each strategy assumes the reader already possesses the knowledge to identify the central topic and stated main ideas, to recognize when main ideas are not explicitly stated, and when to infer and generate an implied main idea.

Anytime a reader wades through a long text, or a writer composes a long text, it is essential to establish what is important in order to prevent information overload and a loss of the overall meaning of the text (see Afflerbach & Johnston, Chapter 3, this volume). For students to sort out the levels of importance of information in a text, they must, of course, first distinguish the irrelevant from the important information. But they must also distinguish levels of importance within the relevant information in order to organize and relate it. In this task, knowledge is required to discern superordinate and subordinate relationships among semantically related topics. This situation also requires an understanding of what a main idea is and how main ideas function to cue what the author deems as the most important relationships among the topics in exposition or events in narrative stories. Thus, one way of defining the learning goal for main idea skill is the extent to which the learner can use the skills successfully to carry out study reading strategies.

Research studies show that students who have limited skills in establishing what is important in a text are not as successful in rereading and memorizing (Brown, Campione, & Day, 1981), in underlining (Brown & Smiley, 1977a, 1977b), or in writing sound summaries (Brown & Day, 1983; Day, 1981; Winograd, 1984). Reviews of research also show that these reading study skills are late in developing (Brown, et al., in press). Hence, it may be assumptive and ineffective instruction to teach students global reading study skills without first teaching the knowledge and strategies required to identify, infer, or generate main ideas. Research suggests this seems especially likely in the middle grades and high school for all but the very brightest students, but it also applies to junior college and college students when the material read is long and complex.

The knowledge of text structure required to learn main idea skills may also play an important role in learning to plan and revise expository compositions. While less research directly supports this contention, some studies do point in this direction (Aulls & Holt, 1984; Berieter & Scardamalia, 1982; McGee, 1981; Taylor & Beach, 1984). Therefore, one reasonable learning goal is to expect main idea skills to aid the writer in composing. This seems especially likely for planning and revising expository writing such as paragraphs, reports, and summaries. These writing tasks are frequent in schools and also in professional job settings where brief, topic driven writing is valued as a basic communication tool (*Time*, 1980).

A formal but general goal for learning main idea skills might be stated in this way: The learning goal for main idea skills is for the student to acquire sufficient knowledge and strategies so that she/he can feel comfortable in how to establish the levels of importance implicit in a body of information during a reading or writing task, and in order to achieve deliberately a broader academic or communication goal.

The declarative and procedural knowledge entailed in learning main idea skills must be more *context free* than *context bound*. Knowledge which is context bound cannot be used (Brown et al., in press; Brown, Collins,

& Harris, 1978; Newell, 1979; Tuma & Reif, 1979) outside the specific context in which it is learned. For example, students who learn to infer implied main ideas with exercises that provide multiple choice answers may perform the skill rather well. But when asked to read texts without such cues and write out the main idea, they may perform poorly. Why? The skill is cognitively bound to the context of the original learning tasks. In fact, what such students may have actually learned is how to use multiple choice responses to cue them to what to look for in the text, thereby bypassing the use of knowledge and procedures required to infer and generate an implied main idea. Of course, to some extent all knowledge is context bound. In the case of main idea skills, students will always find it easier to identify or infer main ideas when they are knowledgeable about the central topic of a selection. Being knowledgeable about the central topic already guarantees knowing what information may be important or relevant. Therefore, readers comprehend more and writers write more when knowledgeable about the topic (Chi, 1978; Hare, 1982; Langer, 1984; Pearson, Hansen, & Gordon, 1979).

A *context free* main idea skill refers to the ability to determine the main idea across many texts: some where the topics are very familiar and others where they are less familiar. It also refers to being able to determine the stated main idea in a paragraph whether it is presented first as the topic sentence, as a concluding sentence, or midway in the paragraph. In addition, the reader who possesses context free skills will possess a strategy, a plan, or rules for how to determine the central topic and the main idea time after time. Also, the more skilled readers will be able to explain how they do it. Most skilled readers will be able to monitor the process of main idea comprehension by using the plan or rules as a guide. They will also be able to use the plan or rules to check their success in determining the main idea. Finally, main idea skills are context free when they are spontaneously or deliberately used to carry out a global study reading strategy or writing strategy. This is not only an indication that the skills are transferable to a variety of topics and texts but that the learner has been able to transfer them to an entirely different learning context.

Active Teaching

Even if teachers do not hold the same definition of what to teach as the main idea or order what to teach in the same instructional sequence, the responsibility for teaching this skill entails active verbal teaching.

Active teaching involves four interlocking types of teacher instructional behaviors. First, the teacher must explain what a main idea is and rules for how to identify, infer, or generate main ideas. Next, in order to make visible the mental process entailed in how to use these rules, the teacher must verbally model (i.e., think out loud) the application of the rules for understanding main ideas. Following this, the teacher must begin to release the responsibility (Baumann, 1983, 1984; Pearson, 1982; Pearson & Gallagher, 1983) for identifying, inferring, or generating main ideas to the students. To do this, the teacher walks students through practice sessions in which teacher and students take turns performing the mental act (identification, inference, or generation) of getting the main ideas. During this time, the teacher guides students in using the rules to support their results. In this activity, student and teacher discussions and further teacher verbal modeling of how to apply the rules should be done so that feedback focuses on the nature of the mental process rather than only on whether students correctly obtain the main ideas. Finally, students need plenty of practice at applying their skill on texts which represent a continuum from short texts in which organizational structure explicitly cues what the important information is to long texts which represent a variation in the explicitness of the structural cues (number of cues, type of cues, and order of the cues) which signal importance.

In short, active teaching entails the teacher instructional behaviors of explaining, verbal modeling, collaborative feedback, and student independent practice sessions (see Figure 1) which emphasize particular learning

Learning Goals

Awareness	Declarative	Procedural	Metaknowledge	Transfer
↑	↑	↑	↑	↑
Verbal Explanation		Verbal Modeling	Collaborative Practice and Feedback	Independent Practice

Teacher Instructional Behaviors

Sequence of Instruction

Figure 1. Relationships between learning goals and phases of instruction.

outcomes. In addition, the texts used for practice should be designed to provide initial success, support the intended correspondence between teacher instructional behaviors and student learning goals and progressively increase in complexity and length over the sequence of instruction in order to engender the student expertise needed to establish importance in day-to-day school reading materials.

A considerable body of research has been devoted to discerning what effective teachers do to teach reading comprehension (Berliner, 1981; Duffy, 1982; Duffy, Roehler, & Mason, 1984; Pearson, 1982; Stallings, 1979) as well as a variety of other subjects (Anderson & Smith, 1984; Brophy, 1983; Gage, 1978; Rosenshine, 1983). The need for active teaching embodies principles of direct instruction (Berliner, 1981; Duffy & Roehler, 1982). As Baumann (1983) states, the heart of any direct instruction approach is the teacher who "in a face to face, reasonably formal manner tells, shows, models, demonstrates, teaches the skill to be learned" (p. 287).

Notice that Baumann's definition excludes questioning. While asking questions can be a useful tool, Duffy, Book, and Roehler (1982) emphasize that active teaching places a premium on the teacher's role in making statements which aid the learner in gradually internalizing what to do, how to do it, why do it, and when to do it. In contrast, in answering questions the learner merely demonstrates the result of cognitive processes. If questions are used in main idea instruction, then they should serve the function of invoking students to access what they have already been taught (about what to do, how to do it, and when to do it) as they verbally think aloud how to identify or generate main ideas with a specific text.

Finally, instructional research reported by Aulls (1980), Baumann (1984), Day (1982), Duffy, Book, and Roehler (1982), and Taylor and Beach (1984) suggests that explanatory teacher talk has a significant effect on learning comprehension skills. Research by Brown and Palinscar (1982) and Ritchie (1983) demonstrates the positive effects of verbal modeling on the process of identifying, inferring, or generating ideas. Both also support the value of collaborative feedback and practice which emphasizes metcognitive acts such as self checking results using rules. Baumann's (1984) and Aulls' (1980) research on teaching main idea demonstrates the significant influence of a properly designed continuum of independent practice activities for students in order to establish the transfer of knowledge acquired through direct instruction and to compensate for differences in the amount of practice needed by low and high ability students.

Four Teacher Instructional Behaviors in Active Teaching

The interlocking instructional components which make up active teaching (see Figure 1) seem very important to understand in order to consider direct ways of teaching main idea skills. Therefore, each form of instruction will be described further. In addition, the special function of teaching rules for how to identify or infer main ideas will be further elaborated.

Verbal Explanation

Explanations are intended to teach declarative knowledge (how to do something) rather than to direct or simply inform. In other words, concepts, information, or behaviors and their relationships are taught in order to make explicit how to acquire a skill or learn how to perform a strategy.

First, explaining declarative knowledge entails introducing what will be learned (what a main idea is) by using metaphors, definitions, and examples. Second, explaining entails describing or illustrating why this knowledge is useful so that the students will have a sense of purpose for learning it and a desire to learn it.

Following these two activities, explaining often entails specifying rules for how to achieve the learning outcome (identify stated main ideas, infer implied main ideas, or generate main ideas). A rule in this sense refers to a strategy stated verbally as a series of guidelines for thinking out what is to be done to obtain the learning outcome. It is like a recipe for identifying the main idea of a paragraph, an article, or a story. Rules specify a good way, not the only way, to approach the stated or assumed learning outcome. Good rules work in a broad array of contexts and can be adapted to work in contexts which do not seem to apply. Rules must first be practiced as they are stated, tested, and eventually criticized and transformed by the learner into a simpler personalized form.

Explaining is done to help the student learn when and how to employ the skill or criteria for monitoring its successful use. This is done to enable students to make progress toward using the skill independently in appropriate circumstances. In the case of the main idea, when to identify, infer, or generate main ideas is often a critical part of successfully carrying out many study skills. It is also useful in resolving breakdowns in comprehension during reading situations where the text is long or complex, or the topic is not familiar.

Verbal Modeling

Verbal modeling refers to showing students how to carry out the use of rules to achieve a goal, how to enact a strategy, how to solve a comprehension problem, or to help them envision the otherwise covert mental processes used to make sense out of a word, sentence, paragraph, or complete text. Unlike explaining, verbally modeling how to do mental activities entailed in identifying or generating topics or main ideas is done to make salient how to use concepts, rules, or relevant text information in the context of a specific text.

The teacher first uses verbal modeling to introduce students to the complete pattern of mentally working toward a learning outcome and to allow them to acquire a sense of how they should go about it. Usually the teacher will talk aloud and show what he or she does to identify, infer, or generate a main idea and then invite students to try to do just what she or he did. Second, the teacher attempts to clarify what she or he did by giving feedback on how well what the student did resembled the thinking process verbally modeled by the teacher. Rather than trying to explain what to do differently, the teacher simply describes what he or she does using the same text the student was using and asks the student to try again.

One primary benefit of modeling the use of knowledge, the use of rules to achieve a specific learning outcome, or the steps of a strategy to solve a problem is in making otherwise covert processes observable for the student. Verbal modeling is also a concrete means of getting the student to learn how to achieve goals which would otherwise be impossible to learn through telling or explaining what to do. You cannot get some students to internalize a process by simply telling or even explaining what the steps are. One must practice and test rules for them to become internalized and to be meaningful. Strategies must be actively engaged in to become a personal plan for taking action.

Verbal modeling provides the opportunity to show how to do something. Since most comprehension skills like identifying or inferring main ideas entail a complex series of mental activities, they cannot be learned by just memorizing the steps. The rules and steps *only* become useful and understandable by doing them and reflecting upon what is done to put them to use. Doing this also fosters metacognitive skills. These skills allow students to check and self correct themselves.

Finally, having students talk about what they are doing mentally when they attempt to identify, infer, or generate a main idea gives the teacher deeper insights into a student's procedural problems in using knowledge to achieve a learning outcome.

Practice and Feedback

Collaborative teaching occurs when the teacher helps students learn how to work through a text by giving a variety of forms of assistance. Students then carry out the processes of identifying, inferring, or generating main ideas while completing the more general task of making sense out of the entire text. The students should be overtly aware that the teacher will act as a partner in constructing the text meaning as well as figuring out how to identify, infer, or generate main ideas as one major means of constructing the entire text meaning. An important aspect of collaboration for the teacher is knowing when to shift the burden of processing to the child or back to the teacher. A teacher needs considerable skill to pace a group of students so they maintain active attention and to ensure that individuals are successful enough to remain positive about new strategies. Maintaining student attention is, of course, a basic of effective instruction.

Feedback, in the context of collaborative teaching events, refers to providing relevant information about what one does to identify, infer, or generate main ideas and to the success of the outcome achieved. The primary goal of feedback is to get students to continue to use a definition, a rule, or a strategy for getting or producing main ideas. Feedback makes explicit for students what they did that worked. Feedback can also cue the reader to when to use a skill and how to self correct the inappropriate use of knowledge, rules, or strategies.

In the context of lessons devoted to collaborative practice of the use of rules to identify, infer, or generate main ideas, the success of teacher feedback depends on when and how it is given. Three guidelines seem especially important.

1. Do not provide feedback on every mistake a student makes. Instead, wait to see whether the readers can correct themselves. Try to preserve a reasonable flow in the student's execution of the process of identifying, inferring, or generating main ideas.

2. Observe whether a group of students' mistakes have a pattern. Focus feedback on just one type of mistake over the course of several collaborative practice lessons. Select the most common mistake and shift to a new mistake when the first appears to be reduced markedly.

3. Feedback and practice which does not result in a change in students' accuracy in identifying, inferring, or generating main ideas during reading should be discontinued and replaced with reteaching using verbal explanation or modeling.

Independent Practice

The traditional view of practice has been to define it as something the student does to become more accurate and automatic in performing a skill. This concept of practice appears to apply to many reading skills (Stanovich, 1980), but not necessarily to complex comprehension skills. For main idea skills, practice may serve a distinctly different function. The function of practice may be to enable the reader to gain conscious and deliberate control over how to use procedures to identify, infer, or generate main ideas. Through this achievement, the student slowly becomes able to transfer the use of main idea skills to a wide variety of text situations and reading study skills. Some students may never become automatic at using these skills, although they may become much more accurate in using them when cued to do so by teacher directions or comprehension problems. In fact, getting the main idea (in contrast to establishing the topic) may only be of value to conscious, deliberate, and goal directed reading acts like studying.

Practice as a means of instruction assumes the student already possesses the knowledge needed (declarative and procedural) to perform the skill. In the context of the interlocking phases of active instruction, practice is only initiated when the appropriate knowledge has been successfully taught. For practice to benefit students, it must enable them to begin to coordinate their declarative and procedural knowledge independently as well as to monitor the outcome of this activity. By doing these things, students will progress from sporadic control over a skill to consistently greater control in a variety of text situations. Consistent control is evidenced by being able to use a skill with better than chance success, by having a feeling of knowing what you are doing, and by having some ability to say what and how you do it.

To facilitate successful practice, the teacher must choose texts that progress from less to more complex. For example, identifying main ideas stated in the first sentence of a paragraph is easier for adults (Kieras, 1978) and intermediate grade students (Aulls, 1975; Williams & Stevens, 1972), and identifying a main idea stated in the last sentence of a paragraph is easier than one between the first and last sentence (Aulls, 1975). It is easier to identify a stated main idea in a paragraph than to infer one (or invent one) that is implied even for college students (Brown & Day, 1983), and it is easier to identify or infer main ideas from short, well structured paragraphs than the main idea of a selection made up of a series of paragraphs (Baumann, 1984).

To facilitate practice which leads to subsequent transfer and success in easy and difficult text situations, the directions provided for practice must invoke students to use their knowledge actively through emphasizing generative responses. For example, requiring students to underline the main idea is a generative activity and more representative of real study reading than providing multiple choice answers from which students select the main idea. Having students write down a main idea which must be inferred is much more representative of real reading than answering a multiple choice question that cues an acceptable inferred main idea. Furthermore, a rather substantial body of research suggests that, in general, generative responses promote high levels of comprehension (Linden & Wittrock, 1981; Taylor & Berkowitz, 1980; Wittrock, 1981).

Thus, to lead to independence and effectiveness in using a skill, practice reading tasks should be representative of the range of text complexity the reader will encounter during real day to day reading in school and at home. Furthermore, the practice tasks should demand student responses like those required in natural school and home study reading contexts.

The practice teaching sessions should be followed frequently by review of what students did to establish importance and discussion of the problems they encountered. The discussion should emphasize student–to– student as well as student–to–teacher verbal modeling of relevant rules or strategies which demonstrate how to solve the specific problem of getting or generating main ideas.

Answers are not nearly as important as learning how to arrive consistently at those answers. The hallmark of independence in using main idea skills is knowing how to get sensible answers and how to solve comprehension problems when they arise. Students who achieve this criterion for independent use of main idea skills will be able to use them to bridge the gap between what they already know and new knowledge conveyed by the text.

Actively Teaching Main Idea Skills

The distinction between context bound and context free learning goals provides a different educational context for envisioning the purposes of instruction. Context free learning goals require more powerful instructional procedures, and the teacher's role changes when trying to implement more powerful forms of instructions (Aulls & Graves, in press; Duffy, Roehler, & Mason, 1984; Pearson, 1982; Pearson & Gallagher, 1983). The teacher and the student must be more active during instructional events. The teacher must also learn to transfer the responsibility for learning to the student during the course of teaching.

One potentially powerful instructional procedure for teaching main idea skills based on the principles of active teaching is the following series of interlocking instructional routines. *Routines* is used here to refer to crisp bits of teaching which, once learned, can be used repeatedly to teach a single main idea skill or a sequence of main idea skills. For example, to teach students how to identify the central topic in a paragraph, all six of the following routines would be used before moving on to the next skill in the sequence such as identifying stated main ideas. The reader can use this interlocking instructional procedure with any sequence of skills.

1. Make students *aware* of a need to know about the target knowledge. For example, ask students to tell other students how to get the topic or main idea of a paragraph rather than what it is.

2. Define, and clarify by example, what knowledge is to be learned. For example, define what a topic or main idea is and give examples (words or phrases) of the stated topics (statements) or main ideas in texts.

3. Explain rules for how to use the knowledge. For example, provide "text signaling" rules such as where to find a stated main idea placed in a paragraph.

4. Verbally model the thinking steps (procedures) used to apply the rules that were previously explained, and discuss how you did it. For example, talk aloud about what text signals to look for and how to use them in order to identify a stated main idea. Do this as you read a text aloud while the students follow along. Allow students to ask questions and try to copy the thinking steps you model by using a handout specifying the "text signaling" rules for what text cues to look for.

5. Provide guided practice, and later independent practice, in using rules to solve reading tasks that require the knowledge taught earlier through explanation and verbal modeling. For example, provide multiple paragraphs of varied lengths with the placement of the stated main idea in the first sentence, the last sentence, and the middle of the paragraph. Have students underline the stated main idea and list the rules used to make their decision for each paragrph.

6. Provide appropriate practice texts and the opportunity for students to practice the main idea skill independently. Initially, students must be as successful as possible. Later, they can be challenged. A good rule of thumb

is to present students initially with practice texts slightly longer than those used during direct instruction but entailing the same structural cues emphasized in those texts. To increase the need for deliberate use of the skill, provide a mixture of short, medium, and lengthy text examples. To increase the need to monitor and check the use of a skill, provide texts of mixed lengths but vary the structural organization patterns of the text.

The roles of the teacher and learner change as they progress through the six interlocking phases of this instructional procedure, and there are a number of issues to be understood regarding these changes.

Figure 2 represents the learning goals for teaching main idea skills, the type of instruction which corresponds to each goal, and how the responsibility for learning shifts from the teacher to the students as they pass from one phase of instruction to the next.

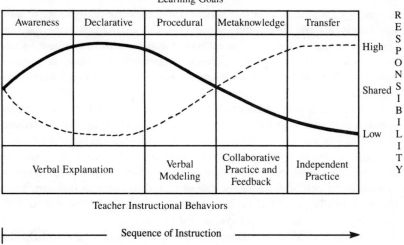

Figure 2. Relationships among learning goals, phases of instruction, and responsibility for learning.

The cognitive learning goals progress from being context bound to context free. However, the extent to which main idea skills become context free for the learner depends upon a slow compilation of each type of knowledge for each skill in the entire domain. For example, students who can transfer the skill of identifying the central topic of a text only possess one of the several skills needed in the entire domain of main idea skills. A student who can transfer identifying the central topic, identifying stated main ideas, and inferring main ideas has considerably more awareness, declarative, procedural, and metacognitive knowledge than one who only possesses one of the skills. Skilled readers use a variety of skills to establish what is important during study reading or composing, and therefore, their main idea skills are more context free than context bound.

One additional point about the series of cognitive learning goals must be made: They are ordered in a sequence which seems to represent the range of knowledge frequently reported when novices and experts are contrasted who perform the same task. Experts tend to possess the entire range of knowledge shown in Figure 2. Novices usually possess none of these knowledge bases. The progression from novice to expert status seems to entail at least the acquisition of declarative knowledge (knowledge that a topic is such and such) before procedural knowledge (knowledge of how to identify a topic in different kinds of texts). Metaknowledge may be acquired before evidence of context bound transfer is available, and awareness of the need for a skill may precede, accompany, or follow the acquisition of declarative or procedural knowledge. Awareness is represented in Figure 2 as an initial learning goal to strive for early in the course of instruction. This is based on results from developmental training studies which report increased learning when learners are informed about why and how what they are to be taught is useful to learn (Brown, et al., in press).

All in all, the progression from awareness of a need for a skill to metacognitive knowledge of how to monitor and check its use prepares the learner to be able to transfer the use of a skill to contexts different from those originally presented during instruction. Transfer learning should be the primary outcome of effective, active instruction.

The five interlocking phases of instruction are designed to help the student progress through the five phases of knowledge acquisition and organization entailed in acquiring context free main idea skills. Since each of these kinds of instruction were discussed in detail earlier in the chapter, they need not be discussed here. These instructional routines are not difficult, although they may place some new responsibilities on the teacher.

Creating awareness requires putting students in situations where they will be aware that although they lack the target skill they can learn it. Coupling this experience with an explanation of how a skill will help students accomplish other goals, such as studying or composing, gives them a sense of why they will be asked to participate in subsequent instructional routines.

Explanations require simple definitions and good examples or analogies to support them. Explaining entails more than simply telling. It requires introducing concepts, procedures, or rules.

Verbally thinking aloud how to use concepts, procedures, or rules will be a different experience for many teachers as well as for students. Often teachers initially fall into the trap of using a series of questions to lead students into using the declarative or procedural knowledge they explained rather than simply showing how to use it by thinking out loud what they do to identify, infer, or generate main ideas. Sometimes teachers panic and think they do not know what to do. Teachers are by virtue of experience more expert than their students. They simply need to relax and do what comes naturally using example materials that the students can read silently as they talk aloud how to identify or infer a central topic or main idea.

Finally, the collaborative practice and feedback routine should be done at a relaxed pace and focus primarily on how to do the skill rather than on the correct answer. The teacher sets the pace by calling on students to use their skill and models skill use when several students cannot identify or infer a main idea on a sample paragraph. The teacher also guides better students to model a skill which is difficult for another student. And the teacher encourages students to verbalize their procedural knowledge of their rules in order to monitor or check their success in identifying or inferring main ideas. Maximum student participation is encouraged by the teacher, and feedback is selectively used. Students should look forward to participating in this routine. The teacher should welcome the opportunity to observe the extent to which students are able to use new knowledge. A teacher cannot know what a student has learned without observing the thinking processes that lead to a student's answer.

The role of the teacher is most active in the explanation, modeling, and collaborative phases of instruction. The responsibility for learning is slowly transferred from the teacher to the student. At the awareness and explanation phase, the student is responsible for learning the what and the why. In the verbal modeling phase, students take turns trying to think out loud like the teacher does on a few sample texts. But in the collaborative phase, most of the doing, discussing, and giving aid to other students is primarily up to the student. During the independent practice phase, the responsibility for using a skill is almost solely the student's. Teacher feedback is delayed until after students have used a skill on their own. This is quite different from being cued to use a skill during the collaborative phase.

The amount of time spent on each form of instruction will depend on the range of students' ability and the complexity of each skill. However, normally there would be one twenty minute lesson devoted to awareness or one thirty minute lesson that combines awareness and defining the skill by explanation. At least one to two lessons will be needed to further explain rules for text cues, and one or two lessons to model verbally how to use the rules while reading. The collaborative feedback and practice instruction will require as many lessons as needed for the teacher to observe substantial progress by most students. Independent practice also allows the teacher to assess students' performance. This can inform the teacher about who may benefit from more collaborative feedback and practice and who should continue with independent practice. Independent practice should continue until students can consistently demonstrate that they can apply the skill to both short and lengthy materials having the structural features of those used during instruction.

It may seem that this interlocking series of instructional procedures is too excessive to be practical. While they can be used independently or in combinations, it may not be as productive to do so. What is practical is whatever is needed to produce lasting and transferable skills for a large proportion of the students in a class. With reading skills as complex as main idea skills, a great deal of active teaching is necessary. This is especially true when transfer is desired for the skill of inferring implied main ideas across a variety of texts whose structures will differ (Heibert, Englert, & Brennan, 1983).

Preparing Materials Which Facilitate Actively Teaching Main Idea Skills

At the present time, only a few instructional reading programs include materials explicitly designed to facilitate actively teaching comprehension skills (Aulls & Graves, in press). Materials which support active teaching should provide explicit directions to teachers for how to teach comprehension skills verbally. Student materials should emphasize generative responses to texts (Doctorow, Wittrock, & Marks, 1978; Van Blaricom & White, 1976). Recent evaluations of teachers' manuals (Durkin, 1981a and 1981b) and student materials (Osborn, 1981; Winograd & Brennan, 1983) clearly suggest that neither provision is common.

Many teachers will find ways to apply active teaching procedures to available published materials, but to help curriculum personnel and teachers to imagine how student materials can be designed to support active teaching procedures, several guidelines will be discussed. Specific examples of such student materials for teaching main idea skills can be found in other sources (Aulls, 1978; Aulls & Holt, 1984).

Guideline One

Design student materials to follow a deliberately reasoned sequence for teaching main idea skills. The sequence should specify and link the declarative and procedural knowledge entailed in each skill. What is unique in such a sequence is the specific recognition that teaching any main idea skill requires teaching both the text structures and how to determine or use them.

For expository materials, the following four step sequence is recommended: 1) Teach what a topic is and how to categorize and classify topics in a text on the basis of synonymity, general to specific, and superordinate relationships; 2) teach what a stated main idea is and how to identify it from signals in the text such as inclusion of the central topic as its subject or sentence placement in a paragraph; 3) teach what an implied main idea is and how to infer it from a paragraph as well as how to check that the main idea invented makes sense for a paragraph; 4) teach what a superordinate main idea of a complete text is and how to use main idea skills to carry out specific study reading strategies like summary writing.

For narrative stories, the sequence for teaching main idea skills would include at least two steps: 1) Teach the basic structures of tne narrative story and how to determine the central problem, and 2) teach what the relationship is between the problem and its resolution and how to infer relationships between a story problem and its resolution. This sequence could be extended by teaching criteria (social, psychological, or moral) for inferring story themes and how to use these criteria to generate possible themes.

Guideline Two

Design student materials and teacher guides so that teachers will use the student materials to explain, model, and collaboratively guide students to practice a skill. Most existing published programs almost solely emphasize that students use materials alone without accompanying teacher explanations, verbal modeling, and collaborative practices. Feedback procedures provide little or no emphasis on the knowledge and strategies which must be used to get the answers (Durkin, 1978-1979).

Materials designed to teach each skill should be used jointly by the teacher and students to explore what students need to know about text structures and how to use this knowledge to identify and infer topics and main ideas. For example, in introductory lessons where the emphasis is on explaining the concept of topic and main idea, student materials should provide clear, consistent definitions followed by examples that obviously fit the definitions. These would be read and discussed by the teacher and students together. Follow up student materials for introductory lessons should provide the text examples which the teacher uses in modeling the concepts entailed in the definition. These lessons should be followed by exercises which allow the teacher to guide students in how to use rules and test their sensibility. The exercises should be done collaboratively, with the teacher taking turns with the students; the teacher should also verbally model a strategy and thereby show how to identify or infer a topic or main idea. The teacher's manual accompanying the student materials should provide a brief think aloud script to help teachers imagine how to go about modeling. The scripts are not to be used verbatim. This would be impractical and unnecessary, but teachers do need a mechanism to envision how to verbalize to students a covert strategy they themselves use unconsciously.

Guideline Three

Student materials prepared for the awareness and explanatory phases of instruction should only provide cued responses. Cued responses refer to additional information provided to the student that would not be found in the natural reading situation where the reader interacts with only a test. For example, multiple choice answers following a paragraph provide cues to find the topic or main ideas. Thus, cued responses can help students to perceive more rapidly the concepts defined or explained. They can also facilitate the initial use of specific thinking procedures.

Guideline Four

Generative responses predominantly should be included in student materials prepared for the teacher to use during verbal modeling and the collaborative feedback and practice phase of instruction. Only generative responses should be used for the independent student practice phase of instruction. For example, students might write out topics and main ideas, with no cues other than those found in natural text. This of course, represents how people normally respond in a written form to a text. Students who have to infer implied main ideas would write out a main idea sentence. Students who classify which topics are related in a text would make an outline or draw a diagram. Generative responses require deliberate, reasoned thinking and encourage the use of rules rather than guesses. Moreover, they force the learner to construct relationships between parts of a text or between the text information and their own prior knowledge

(Linden & Wittrock, 1981). When a student does not possess the proper knowledge, it is immediately obvious to the teacher and to the student. It is probably as important that the student is aware she or he does not know how to respond as it is for the teacher. This cognitive state helps make apparent to the student why further instruction is useful.

Guideline Five

Design student materials so that examples isolate the salient, cognitive procedures or text structure signals to be learned. Suppose you wanted to teach the cognitive procedures for categorizing and classifying topics in a text. The purpose is to help students establish the levels of importance of text information and semantic relationships among topics. To do this, it is much easier for students to start by learning to categorize a subordinate word meaning such as *cat* to a superordinate one like *animal*. Then, phrases, such as *Persian cat* and *domestic animals* could be introduced and categorized. Next, sets of words and phrases can be introduced in which one word or phrase in the set is superordinate and the others are subordinate to it. This requires students to classify information using the criteria previously taught. Last of all, simple paragraphs could be introduced where the subjects in each sentence can be extracted and put into the categories of superordinate topic and subordinate topics. The result makes explicit the hierarchical network of topics underlying a paragraph. This progression slowly simulates the use of cognitive procedures entailed in identifying the superordinate or central topics in a text. Each step would entail a different set of materials, and within each set, the initial materials would be designed for teachers to define, explain, model, and guide students in practicing the cognitive procedures. After simple paragraphs have been worked through, another graded series of materials could be introduced in order to work through more complex paragraphs entailing several levels of topical organization.

One salient text signal for stated main ideas is where they are typically placed in a paragraph. The main idea may be placed in the first sentence, the last sentence, or between these two sentences. Student materials would provide separate exercises which emphasize each placement and conclude by presenting paragraphs with the main idea occurring in all of the possible positions.

Guideline Six

Recognize that the paragraph is a basic processing unit within exposition (Calfee & Curley, 1984; Koen, Becker, & Young, 1969). For the sole purpose of simplifying learning, exercises designed to teach how to identify and infer topics or main ideas should be based at first on these conventional text units. After students show confidence and control in the use of main idea skills in paragraphs, they should be exposed to longer texts. When faced with complete expositions, students will inevitably face the reality that paragraphs do not always have an explicit or implicit main idea. In this case, their importance must be derived from their function within the entire exposition. Teaching reading study skills is appropriate at this point and gives additional meaning to the use of main idea skills when reading longer expository text.

Closing Comments

Evidence has been cited throughout this chapter that teaching main idea skills will lead not only to determining the central topic and main ideas from texts but will also lead to the development of other forms of reading comprehension and perhaps lead to more expertise in composing exposition. Nevertheless, there are limitations to these claims. Suppose a reader is not already knowledgeable about the semantic content of the text being read. Does establishing the central topic, main ideas, or other text structures which signal what information is important help comprehension? The answer seems to be yes and no. Yes, it does help college age readers to remember the gist of the text. It also helps younger readers remember more when they have a good deal of prior knowledge of the text content. However, only college students with high prior knowledge of the text content will acquire new information from reading. Those with low knowledge do not (Schmalhofer, 1983); they only remember the gist of the text itself. Thus, main idea skills may only promote certain kinds of comprehension.

College students who have low prior knowledge of the text topic can derive main ideas surprisingly well, even with poorly written text (Kieras, 1980; 1982). When college students are compared to intermediate grade students on the ability to determine main ideas from text with familiar content, the older readers do markedly better (Williams, Taylor, & Ganger, 1981). Also, older readers do better than younger ones in using main ideas to help them detect irrelevant paragraph information. Therefore, low prior knowledge of a text topic may depress the use of main idea skills in younger readers but not college students.

Research has shown that insufficient prior knowledge of the text content may prevent college students from spontaneously generating many questions about its content (Miyaki & Norman, 1982). Without considerable training in main idea skills, middle grade students may not benefit much from being asked to generate questions about main ideas (Ritchie, 1983). With training, however, the benefits of asking questions about the main ideas, in conjunction with other strategies for organizing text information, appear to be considerable by grade seven (Brown & Palinscar, 1982). By grade eleven, even short periods of training in asking main idea questions enable poor students to increase their literal comprehension (André & Anderson, 1978-1979).

In short, the prior knowledge the student brings to the text, the extent of main idea skills previously acquired, and the extent of training in a strategy for when and how to ask main idea questions will affect the potential for students' main idea questions to influence text comprehension.

Four instructional studies have reported success in teaching students to establish what text information is important (Brown & Day, 1983; McNeil & Donant, 1982; Taylor, 1982; Taylor & Beach, 1984). Three studies have successively asked students to ask questions about main ideas (André & Anderson, 1978-1979; Brown & Palincsar, 1982; Ritchie, 1983). Other studies have reported success in teaching students to identify and infer main idea (Aulls, 1980; Baumann, 1984; Peterson, 1975). One study demonstrates improvement in composing exposition through direct instruction in main idea skills combined with teaching composing processes (Aulls & Holt, 1984). In all eleven studies, students have been taught main idea skills in a concentrated time period. Instruction lasted from between two and eight weeks. All studies used some form of direct instruction in which the teacher played an active verbal role in teaching the students. None of these studies has been carried out with students below grade five. Long term transfer effects have not been demonstrated with students below grade seven.

In contrast to the successful instructional studies, major published reading programs tend to spread out rather than concentrate main idea instruction at each grade level. Concentrated direct instruction of main idea skills may be much more productive. Further, we have no justification yet for teaching main idea skills before grade four. This widespread practice seems especially curious since primary grade reading is almost solely focused on narrative stories. Last, few of the major basal reader programs provide guidelines in the teacher's manuals for how to teach main ideas actively.

It does appear to be important and challenging to teach main idea skills not only to improve reading comprehension but to also improve composing and subject matter learning. It is important because both school academic training and many professional occupations require being able to wade through pages of information, sorting the important from the unimportant, and then relating and reacting to its meaning. It is challenging because active, direct instruction seems to be warranted for even average students to acquire and use main idea skills successfully. Active, direct instruction is necessary because the use of main idea skills entails standing back from one's own composition or someone else's text and examining the explicit and implicit signals to what is important in an abstract, rational, and generalized way. As Brown (1977), Goody (1977), Olson, (1977), and Scribner and Cole (1978) have all stated in different ways, the acquisition of skills of this nature transforms the nature of cognitive processes. Both teachers' roles and publishers' materials will have to change in order to meet this challenge. Can this happen? The answer is yes. Will it happen during the 1980s and 1990s? If it does not, it ought to happen. We know enough. But publishers and teacher trainers will have to take the first step because main idea instruction entails facing an even larger educational problem. As Calfee and Freedman (1983) put it: "Schools spend too much time teaching students the surface forms of reading and writing . . . and fail to lead students to the deeper levels that are basic to the education of the modern man" (p. 5).

References

Anderson, C.W., and Smith, E. L. Children's preconceptions and content area textbooks. In G.G. Duffy, L.E. Roehler, and J.E. Mason (Eds.), *Comprehension instruction*. New York: Longman, 1984, 187-201.

André, M.E., and Anderson, T.H. The development and evaluation of a self-questioning study technique. *Reading Research Quarterly*, 1978-1979, *14*, 605-625.

Andresen, O.S. Evaluating profundity in literature. *Journal of Reading*, 1965, *6*, 387-390.

Applebee, A.N. *A child's concept of story*. Chicago: University of Chicago Press, 1978.

Armbruster, B.B., Echols, C.H., and Brown, A.L. *The role of metacognition in reading to learn: A developmental perspective*. Reading Education Report No. 40. Urbana-Champaign: University of Illinois, Center for the Study of Reading, 1983.

Aulls, M.W. *Developmental and remedial reading in the middle grades*. Boston: Allyn and Bacon, 1978.

Aulls, M.W. Expository paragraph properties that influence literal recall. *Journal of Reading Behavior*, 1975, *7*, 391-400.

Aulls, M.W. *The influence of types of learners and methods of instruction on understanding expository text*. Unpublished paper, McGill University, Montreal, 1980.

Aulls, M.W., and Graves, M.F. *Quest*. New York: Scholastic, in press.

Aulls, M.W., and Holt, W. *Helping seventh graders learn how to write expository paragraphs: The role of procedural facilitation as a means of instruction*. Paper presented at the thirty-third National Reading Conference, Austin, December 1984.

Baker, L., and Stein, N. *The development of prose comprehension skills*. Technical Report No. 102. Urbana-Champaign: University of Illinois, Center for the Study of Reading, 1978.

Baumann, J.F. A generic comprehension instructional strategy. *Reading World*, 1983, *22*, 284-294.

Baumann, J.F. The effectiveness of a direct instruction paradigm for teaching main idea comprehension. *Reading Research Quarterly*, 1984, *20*, 93-115.

Baumann, J.F., and Serra, J.K. The frequency and placement of main ideas in children's social studies textbooks: A modified replication of Braddock's research on topic sentences. *Journal of Reading Behavior*, 1984, *16*, 27-40.

Beck, I.L. Developing comprehension: The impact of the directed reading lesson. In R.C. Anderson, J. Osborn and R. J. Tierney (Eds.), *Learning to read in American schools*. Hillsdale, NJ: Erlbaum, 1984, 56-79.

Bereiter, C., and Scardamalia, M. From conversation to composition: The role of instruction in a developmental process. In R. Glasser (Ed.), *Advances in instructional psychology*, vol. 2. Hillsdale, NJ: Erlbaum, 1982, 1-64.

Berkowitz, S., and Taylor, B. The effects of text type and familiarity on the nature of information recalled by readers. In M.L. Kamil (Ed.), *Directions in reading: Research and instruction*. Washington, DC: National Reading Conference, 1981, 159-171.

Berliner, D.C. Academic learning time and reading achievement. In J.T. Guthrie (Ed.), *Comprehension and teaching: Research review*. Newark, DE: International Reading Association, 1981, 203-226.

Black, M. Rules and routines. In R.S. Peters (Ed.), *The concept of education*. London: Routledge and Kegan Paul, 1967, 92-104.

Blake, K. Review summaries, review questions, and retarded and normal pupils finding the main idea in connected discourse. *Journal of Research and Development in Education*, 1973, *10*, 65-70.

Braddock, R. The frequency and placement of topic sentences in expository prose. *Research in the Teaching of English*, 1974, *8*, 287-302.

Bridge, C., Thomas, S., and Evers, L. The effects of textual cohesion on cloze comprehension scores. In M. L. Kamil (Ed.), *Directions in reading: Research and instruction*. Washington, DC: National Reading Conference, 1981, 187-192.

Brophy, J.E. Classroom organization and management. *Elementary School Journal*, 1983, *83*, 265-285.

Brown, A.L. *Knowing when, where and how to remember: A problem of metacognition*. Technical Report No. 47. Urbana-Champaign: University of Illinois, Center for the Study of Reading, 1977.

Brown, A.L., Bransford, J.D., Ferrara, R.A., and Campione, J.C. Learning, remembering and understanding. In J.H. Flavell and E.M. Markman (Eds.), *Carmichael's manual of child psychology*, vol. 2. New York: Wiley, in press.

Brown, A.L., Campione, J.C., and Day, J.D. Learning to learn: On training students to learn from texts. *Educational Researcher*, 1981, *10*, 14-21.

Brown, A.L., and Day, J.D. *Strategies and knowledge for summarizing text: The development and facilitation of expertise*. Technical Report No. 270. Urbana-Champaign: University of Illinois. Center for the Study of Reading, 1983.

Brown, A.L., Day, J.D., and Jones, R.S. *The development of plans for summarizing texts*. Technical Report No. 268. Urbana-Champaign: University of Illinois, Center for the Study of Reading, 1983.

Brown, A.L., and Palincsar, A.S. *Inducing strategic learning from texts by means of informed, self-control training*. Technical Report No. 262. Urbana-Champaign: University of Illinois, Center for the Study of Reading, 1972.

Brown, A.L., and Smiley, S.S. *The development of strategies for studying prose passages.* Technical Report No. 66. Urbana-Champaign: University of Illinois, Center for the Study of Reading, 1977a.

Brown, A.L., and Smiley, S.S. Rating the importance of structural units of prose passages: A problem of metacognitive development. *Child Development,* 1977b, *48,* 1-8.

Brown, A.L., Smiley, S.S., and Lawton, S.C. The effects of experience on the selection of suitable retrieval cues for studying texts. *Child Development,* 1978, *49,* 829-935.

Brown, J.S., Collins, A., and Harris, G. Artificial intelligence and learning strategies. In H.F. O'Neil (Ed.), *Learning strategies.* New York: Academic Press, 1978, 12-89.

Bruce, B.C. Analysis of interacting plans as a guide to the understanding of story structure. *Poetics,* 1980, *9,* 295-311.

Bruner, J.S. *Toward a theory of instruction.* Cambridge, MA: Belknap Press of Harvard University, 1966.

Calfee, R.C., and Curley, R.G. Structures of prose in the content area. In J. Flood (Ed.), *Understanding reading comprehension.* Newark, DE: International Reading Association, 1984, 161-181.

Calfee, R.C., and Freedman, S. *Understanding and comprehension.* Paper presented at the International Reading Association Convention, Anaheim, May 1983.

Chi, M.T.H. Knowledge structures and memory development. In R.S. Siegler (Ed.), *Children's thinking: What develops?* Hillsdale, NJ: Erlbaum, 1978, 73-96.

Christie, D.J., and Schumacher, A.M. Developmental trends in the abstraction and recall of relevant versus irrelevant thematic information from connected verbal materials. *Child Development,* 1975, *46,* 598-602.

Danner, F.W. Children's understanding of intersentence organization in the recall of short descriptive passages. *Journal of Educational Psychology,* 1976, *68,* 174-183.

Day, J.D. *Training summarization skills: A comparison of teaching methods.* Doctoral dissertation, University of Illinois, 1980. *Dissertation Abstracts International,* 1981, *41,* 4282B.

Denhiere, G., and LeNy, J. Relative importance of meaningful units in comprehension and recall of narratives by children and adults. *Poetics,* 1980, *9,* 147-161.

Denny, N.W. Evidence for some developmental changes in categorization criteria. *Human Development,* 1974, *17,* 41-53.

Dixson, C.N. Text type and children's recall. In M.L. Kamil (Ed.), *Directions in reading: Research and instruction.* Thirtieth yearbook of the National Reading Conference. Washington, DC: National Reading Conference, 1981, 82-86

Doctorow, M.J., Wittrock, M.C., and Marks, C.B. Generative processes in reading comprehension. *Journal of Educational Psychology,* 1978, *70.*

Doyle, W. *Academic work.* Technical Report No. 6179. Austin: University of Texas, Research and Development Center for Teaching, 1982.

Duffy, G.G. Fighting off the alligators: What researach in real classrooms has to say about reading instruction. *Journal of Reading Behavior,* 1982, *14,* 357-373.

Duffy, G.G., Book, C., and Roehler, L.R. *A study of direct teacher explanation during reading instruction.* Paper presented at the National Reading Conference, Clearwater, Florida, December 1982.

Duffy, G.G., and Roehler, L.F. Direct instruction of comprehension: What does it really mean? *Reading Horizons,* 1982, *23*(1), 35-40.

Duffy, G.G., Roehler, L.R., and Mason, J. (Eds.) *Comprehension instruction: Perspectives and suggestions.* New York: Longman, 1984.

Durkin, D. What classroom observations reveal about reading comprehension instruction. *Reading Research Quarterly,* 1978-1979, *14,* 481-533.

Durkin, D. Reading comprehension instruction in five basal reader series. *Reading Research Quarterly*, 1981a, *16*, 515-544.

Durkin, D. *Do basal reader materials provide for reading comprehension instruction?* Paper presented at the Center for the Study of Reading Publisher's Conference, Tarrytown, New York, October 1981b.

Freedle, R., and Hale, G. Acquisition of new comprehension schemata for expository prose by transfer from narrative schema. In R.O. Freedle (Ed.), *Advances in discourse processes, Vol. 2: New directions in discourse processing*. Norwood, NJ: Ablex, 1979, 121-127.

Gadway, C.J. *Main idea and organization: Theme 6, reading*. Denver: National Assessment of Educational Process, 1973. (ED 079 668)

Gage, N.L. *The scientific basis of the art of teaching*. New York: Teachers College Press, 1978.

Gagne, R. M., and Wiegand, V.K. Effects of superordinate context on learning and retention of facts. *Journal of Educational Psychology*, 1970, *61*, 406-409.

Goody, J. *The domestication of the savage mind*. London: Cambridge University Press, 1977.

Guthrie, J. and Seifert, M. *Reading competencies and practices*. Technical Report No. 4. Newark, DE: International Reading Association, 1982.

Guzzetti, B.J. *A psycholinguistic analysis of the reading strategies of high, average, and low ability readers across selected content areas*. Doctoral dissertation, University of Colorado, 1982. *Dissertation Abstracts International*, 1982, *43*, 1026A.

Hare, V.C. Preassessment of topical knowledge: A validation and extension. *Journal of Reading Behavior*, 1982, *14*, 77-86.

Hiebert, E.H., Englert, C.S., and Brennan, S. Awareness of text structure in recognition and production of expository discourse. *Journal of Reading Behavior*, 1983, *15*, 63-80.

Iser, W. *The implied reader*. Baltimore: Johns Hopkins University Press, 1974.

Johnson, N. What do you do if you can't tell the whole story? The development of summarization skills. In K.E. Nelson (Ed.), *Children's language*, vol. 4. New York: Gardner Press, 1981, 93-111.

Kieras, D.E. Good and bad structures in simple paragraphs: Effects on apparent theme, reading time, and recall. *Journal of Verbal Learning and Verbal Behavior*, 1978, *17*, 13-28.

Kieras, D.E. Initial mention as a signal to thematic content in technical passages. *Memory and Cognition*, 1980, *8*, 345-353.

Kieras, D.E. *Thematic processes in the comprehension of technical prose: Final report*. Technical Report No. UARZ/DP/TR-82 ONR-10. University of Arizona, 1982.

Koen, F., Becker, A., and Young, R. The psychological reality of the paragraph. *Journal of Verbal Learning and Verbal Behavior*, 1969, *8*, 49-53.

Koenke, K.R. *The effects of a constant relevant picture on the comprehension of the main idea of a paragraph*. Doctoral dissertation, University of Wisconsin, 1973. *Dissertation Abstracts International*, 1973, *29*, 149A. (University Microfilms No. 68-7109)

Langer, J.A. Examining background knowledge and text comprehension. *Reading Research Quarterly*, 1984, *19*, 468-481.

Linden, M., and Wittrock, M.C. The teaching of reading comprehension according to the model of generative learning. *Reading Research Quarterly*, 1981, *17*, 44-57.

Marshall, N. *The effects of discourse type upon comprehension*. Paper presented at the American Educational Research Association, Montreal, May 1982.

McConaughy, S.H. *Cognitive structures for reading comprehension: Judging the relative importance of ideas in short stories*, doctoral dissertation, University of Vermont, 1980. *Dissertation Abstracts International*, 1980, *40*, 5843B.

McConaughy, S.H., Fitzhenry-Coor, I., and Howell, D. Developmental differences in story schemata. In K.E. Nelson (Ed.), *Children's language*, vol. 4. Hillsdale, NJ: Erlbaum, 1981, 385-421.

Actively Teaching Main Idea Skills

McGee, L.M. Good and poor readers' ability to distinguish among recall ideas on different levels of importance. In M.L. Kamil (Ed.), *Directions in reading: Research and instruction*. Thirtieth yearbook of the National Reading Conference. Washington, DC: National Reading Conference, 1981, 162-168.

McNeil, J., and Donant, L. Summarization strategy for improving reading comprehension. In J.A. Niles and L.A. Harris (Eds.), *New inquiries in reading research and instruction*. Thirty-first yearbook of the National Reading Conference. Rochester, NY: National Reading Conference, 1982, 215-219.

Miyaki, N., and Norman, D. To ask a question, one must know enough to know what is not known. *Journal of Verbal Learning and Verbal Behavior*, 1982, *18*, 357-364.

Mohr, P., Glover, J.A., and Ronning, R.R. The effect of related and unrelated details on the recall of major ideas in prose. *Journal of Reading Behavior*, 1984, *26*, 97-108.

Mosenthal, P. Three types of schemata in children's recall of cohesive and noncohesive text. *Journal of Experimental Child Psychology*, 1979, *27*, 129-142.

Nelson, K. The syntagmatic-paradigmatic shift revisited: A review of research and theory. *Psychological Bulletin*, 1977a, *84*, 93-116.

Nelson, K. Cognitive development and the acquisition of concepts. In R.C. Anderson, R.J. Spiro and W. Montague (Eds.), *Schooling and the acquisition of knowledge*. Hillsdale, NJ: Erlbaum, 1977b, 215-239.

Newell, A. One final word. In D.T. Tuma and F. Reif (Eds.), *Problem solving and education: Issues in teaching and research*. Hillsdale, NJ: Erlbaum, 1979, 175-189.

Olson, D.R. From utterance to text: The bias of language in speech and writing. *Harvard Educational Review*, 1977, *47*, 257-281.

Olson, D.R. On the language and authority of textbooks. *Journal of Communication*, 1980, *30*, 186, 196.

Olson, A.M., Mack, R.L., and Duffy, S.A. Cognitive aspects of genre. *Poetics*, 1981, *10*, 283-315.

Osborn, J. *The purposes, uses, and contents of workbooks and some guidelines for teachers and publishers*. Technical Report No. 27. Urbana-Champaign: University of Illinois, Center for the Study of Reading, 1981.

Otto, W., Barrett, T.C., and Koenke, K. Assessment of children's statements of the main idea in reading. In J.A. Figurel (Ed.), *Reading and realism*. Newark, DE: International Reading Association, 1969, 692-697.

Palincsar, A.S. The quest for meaning from expository text: A teacher guided journey. In G. Duffy, L. Roehler, and J. Mason (Eds.), *Comprehension instruction: Perspectives and suggestions*. New York: Longman, 1984, 251-264.

Pearson, P.D. *A context for instructional research on reading comprehension*. Technical Report No. 230. Urbana-Champaign: University of Illinois, Center for the Study of Reading, 1982.

Pearson, P.D., and Gallagher, M.C. The instruction of reading comprehension. *Contemporary Educational Psychology*, 1983, *8*, 317-349.

Pearson, P.D., Hansen, J., and Gordon C. The effect of background knowledge of young children's comprehension of explicit and implicit information. *Journal of Reading Behavior*, 1979, *11*, 201-209.

Perry, W.G. Students' use and misuse of reading skills: A report to faculty. *Harvard Educational Review*, 1959, *29*, 193-200.

Peterson, V.R. *A comparison between two instructional approaches teaching topic and main idea*. Unpublished master's thesis, University of Minnesota at Minneapolis, 1975.

Pichert, J.W. *Sensitivity to importance as a predictor of reading comprehension.* Paper presented at the annual meeting of the National Reading Conference Convention, San Antonio, Texas, November 1979.

Rennie, B.J., Neilsen, A.R., and Braun, C. The effects of typographical cuing on memory for superordinate structures in connected discourse. In M.L. Kamil (Ed.), *Directions in reading: Research and instruction.* Thirtieth yearbook of the National Reading Conference, 1981, 169-173.

Ritchie, P. *Effects of instruction on the reading comprehension of grade six students.* Unpublished master's thesis, McGill University, 1983.

Rosch, E., Merris, C.B., Gray, W.D., Johnson, D.M., and Boyes-Braen, P. Basic objects in natural categories. *Cognitive Psychology,* 1976, *8,* 382-439.

Rosenshine, B.V. Skill hierarchies in reading comprehension. In R.J. Spiro, B.C. Bruce and W.F. Brewer (Eds.), *Theoretical issues in reading comprehension.* Hillsdale, NJ: Erlbaum, 1980, 112-130.

Rosenshine, B. Teaching functions in instructional programs. *Elementary School Journal,* 1983, *4,* 335-351.

Ross, E. *The development and evaluation of exercises to teach main idea and outlining in grade eight.* Unpublished doctoral dissertation, Boston University, 1970.

Schmalhofer, F. *Text processing with and without prior knowledge: Knowledge versus heuristic-dependent representations.* Discussion paper No. 32, University of Heidelberg, 1983.

Scribner, S., and Cole, M. Literacy without schooling: Testing for intellectual effects. *Harvard Educational Review,* 1978, *48,* 448-461.

Smiley, S.S., Oakley, D.D., Worthen, D., Campione, J.C., and Brown, A.L. Recall of thematically relevant material by adolescent good and poor readers as a function of written versus oral presentation. *Journal of Educational Psychology,* 1977, *69,* 381-387.

Smiley, S.S., and Brown, A.L. Conceptual preference for thematic taxonomic relations: A non-monotomic age trend from preschool to old age. *Journal of Experimental Child Psychology,* 1979, *28,* 249-257.

Spilich, A.J., Vesonder, A.T., Chiesi, H.L., and Voss, J.F. Text processing of domain related information for individuals with high and low domain knowledge. *Journal of Verbal Learning and Verbal Behavior,* 1979, *18,* 275-290.

Stallings, J.A. *Effective instructional practices for teaching basic reading in secondary schools.* Paper presented at the preconference institute of the National Reading Conference, Austin, Texas, November 1979.

Stanovich, K.D. Toward an interactive compensatory model of individual differences in the development of reading fluency. *Reading Research Quarterly,* 1980, *16,* 32-71.

Stein, N.L., and Glenn, C.G. An analysis of story comprehension in elementary school children. In R.O. Freedle (Ed.), *Advances in discourse processes, vol. 2: New directions in discourse processing.* Norwood, NJ: Ablex, 1979, 123-220.

Taylor, B.M. Text structure and children's comprehension and memory for expository material. *Journal of Educational Psychology,* 1982, *74,* 323-340.

Taylor, B., and Beach, R. The effects of text instruction on middle grade students' comprehension and production of expository text. *Reading Research Quarterly,* 1984, *29,* 134-145.

Taylor, B.M., and Berkowitz, S. Facilitating children's comprehension of content material. In M.L. Kamil and A.J. Moe (Eds.), *Perspectives in reading research and instruction,* Twenty-ninth yearbook of the National Reading Conference. Clemson, SC: National Reading Conference, 1980, 64-68.

Tenny, Y.J. The child's conception of organization and recall. *Journal of Experimental Child Psychology*, 1975, *19*, 100-114.

Time. The righting of writing. *Education*, May 19, 1980, 55-58.

Tuma, D.T., and Reif, F. (Eds.). *Problem solving and education: Issues in teaching and research*. Hillsdale, NJ: Erlbaum, 1979.

Van Blaricom, G., and White, S. Testing comprehension of the central thought: Selecting versus generating main idea. In W. D. Miller and G. H. McNinch (Eds.), *Reflections and investigations on reading*. Twenty-fifth yearbook of the National Reading Conference. Clemson, SC: National Reading Conference, 1976, 317-323.

van Dijk, T.A. Relevance assignment in discourse comprehension. *Discourse Processes*, 1979, *2*, 113-126.

Weaver, P.A. Comprehension, recall, and dyslexia: A proposal for application of schema theory. *Bulletin of the Orton Society*, 1978, *28*, 92-113.

Weaver, P.A., and Dickinson, D. Scratching below the surface structure: Exploring the usefulness of story grammars. *Discourse Processes*, 1982, *5*, 225-243.

Williams, M., and Stevens, V. Understanding paragraph structure. *Journal of Reading*, 1972, *6*, 313-316.

Williams, J.P., Taylor, M.B., and Ganger, S. Text variations at the level of the individual sentence and the comprehension of simple expository paragraphs. *Journal of Educational Psychology*, 1981, *73*, 851-865.

Winograd, P.N. Strategic difficulties in summarizing texts. *Reading Research Quarterly*, 1984, *19*, 404-425.

Winograd, P.N. *Strategic difficulties in summarizing texts*, Technical Report No. 274. University of Illinois, Center for the Study of Reading, April 1983.

Winograd, P., and Brennan, S. Main idea instruction in the basal readers. In J. Niles and L.A. Harris (Eds.), *Searches for meaning in reading/language processing and instruction*. Thirty-second yearbook of the National Reading Conference. Rochester, NY: National Reading Conference, 1983, 80-86.

Wittrock, M.C. Reading comprehension. In F. J. Pirozzolo and M.C. Wittrock (Eds.), *Neuropsychological and cognitive process in reading*. New York: Academic Press, 1981, 229-259.

Yussen, S.R., Mathews, S.R., Buss, R.R., and Kane, P.T. Development change in judging important and critical elements in stories. *Development Psychology*, 1980, *16*, 213-219.

6

The Direct Instruction of Main Idea Comprehension Ability

James F. Baumann

Direct instruction has several different definitions and interpretations. In this chapter, James Baumann defines direct instruction in terms of teacher behaviors that have been consistently associated with student gains in reading. Based upon this literature, he presents a five-step direct instruction strategy for teaching main idea comprehension: introduction, example, direct instruction, teacher-directed application, and independent practice. Next, three model lessons for teaching several different main idea skills at various grade levels are presented which exemplify the direct instruction model. Suggestions and an example that depict how teachers might adapt or modify existing instructional materials to include more direct instruction of main idea skills conclude the chapter.

Across a large number of studies, investigators have found that 1) students who receive much of their instruction from the teacher do better than those expected to learn on their own or from each other and 2) students learn to read most effectively when teachers use systematic instruction, monitor student responses, and give students feedback about their performance. (Rosenshine & Stevens, 1984, p. 746)

Millions of federal and private dollars and years of effort by educational researchers have resulted in research findings that demonstrate the seemingly simple-minded notion that students learn what they are taught. That is, what teachers directly teach to students, students learn; what students are not taught, they do not learn. This is true for teaching students science, mathematics, language, spelling, and a variety of reading abilities. You might ask yourself why so much time, money, and effort have been expended in proving the obvious, the common sense. Indeed, that is a reasonable question, but unfortunately, observations of teachers in classrooms (e.g., Durkin, 1978-1979) indicate that much of what occurs in schools is not directly instructional; that is, oftentimes, students are not taught directly. Instead, students are engaged in extended assessment and practice activities. As Berliner (1981) stated, "The research community has validated some commonsense notions about education [i.e., students learn what they are taught]. But *common sense is not common practice,* as a visit to the schools will reveal" (p. 224).

In this chapter I will present a direct instruction strategy for teaching students to comprehend main ideas. The strategy is based upon what is known about effective classroom instruction. After defining direct instruction, research that discriminates effective teachers from less effective teachers is presented. Then the five-step, direct instruction strategy, which is based upon this teacher effectiveness research, is presented along with validating research. A scope and sequence of main idea tasks and relations and several model lessons that employ the direct instruction strategy are presented next. The chapter concludes with suggestions about how existing reading curricula (e.g., basal readers) can be adapted, when necessary, to incorporate elements of direct instruction.

Direct Instruction in Reading: What Is It?

The term *direct instruction* has several definitions and interpretations. Direct instruction was first popularized by way of the University of Oregon Direct Instruction Model as an effective way to teach disadvantaged children (Becker, 1977; Becker & Carnine, 1980). This original direct instruction model "emphasizes small-group, face-to-face instruction by a teacher using carefully sequenced, daily lessons in reading, arithmetic, and language" (Becker, 1977, p. 428). This direct instruction approach was subsequently marketed by Science Research Associates as the familiar DISTAR programs (Engelmann & Bruner, 1969). What is most distinctive about the original direct instruction model is the highly structured, scripted lessons from which the teacher must not deviate.

> The scripts permit the selection and testing of sequences of examples that produce efficient learning if followed. Most teachers simply do not have time to find appropriate words and examples or to sequence skill hierarchies in the most efficient possible manner. When teachers phrase their own questions, they may choose terms unknown to lower

performing children or may include unnecessary verbiage. In choosing examples, moreover, they may teach incorrect rules. (Becker, 1977, p. 430)

In this conception of direct instruction (see Kameenui, Chapter 11, this volume), the teacher's role is rather limited. Altering the scripted lessons or any other modifications of the direct instruction methods and materials are not allowed. In effect, the teacher simply delivers the lesson and engages in little, if any, instructional decision making.

Other researchers and theorists, however, began to use the term direct instruction in a somewhat different manner, emphasizing the child and teacher more, rather than the design of instruction or the method of delivery, as was the case with the University of Oregon model. Rosenshine (1979) typified direct instruction in a manner similar to that of Becker (1977) and Becker and Carnine (1980), although he deemphasized the regimented, scripted lessons and looked more toward teacher behaviors associated with student achievement. Berliner (1981) defines direct instruction as consisting of a conflux of conditions and teacher behaviors that have been associated with effective classroom instruction, such as content coverage, opportunity to learn, academic engaged time, allocated time, success rate, and the like. Similarly, Duffy and Roehler (1982) emphasize teacher variables, not task variables: "Direct instruction means an academic focus, precise sequencing of content, high pupil engagement, careful teacher monitoring and specific corrective feedback to students" (p. 35). Baumann (1983) reinforced the notion that at the real heart of direct instruction lies the teacher:

> In direct instruction, the teacher, in a face-to-face, reasonably formal manner, tells, shows, models, demonstrates, *teaches* the skill to be learned. The key word here is *teacher,* for it is the teacher who is in command of the learning situation and leads the lesson, as opposed to having instruction "directed" by a worksheet, kit, learning center, or workbook. (p. 287)

Therefore, it is the teacher behavior aspect of classroom instruction that underpins the instructional strategy for teaching main ideas that is presented in this chapter. The following section discusses the research findings on teacher effectiveness (i.e., teacher behaviors) that support this direct instruction strategy.

Teacher Effectiveness and Direct Instruction*

Much has been learned about teacher behaviors that discriminate successful teachers from less successful teachers. Many of the teacher effect studies have been correlational (e.g., Fisher et al., 1978) in which certain teacher behaviors and conditions of the instructional environment have been linked to high student achievement. Other studies have been experimental (e.g., Anderson, Evertson, & Brophy, 1979) in which students of teachers trained to adopt effective teacher behaviors (as identified by correlational studies) have made gains greater than students of teachers not so trained. A comprehensive review of this large body of teacher effectiveness research is beyond the scope of this chapter; interested readers are referred to one of several excellent reviews of this literature (Baumann, 1984a; Berliner, 1981; Brophy & Good, 1985; Duffy 1981, 1982; Good, 1979, 1983; Rosenshine, 1976; Rosenshine & Stevens, 1984). What follows, however, is a selective review of aspects of teacher effectiveness that are germane to the subsequent discussion of the direct instruction model for teaching main idea comprehension.

Underlying Assumptions

Effective teachers consistently make two assumptions about teaching and learning. First, they assume that the school (faculty and administrators) is primarily responsible for student achievement (Brophy & Evertson, 1974, 1976; Hoffman & Rutherford, 1984; Samuels, 1981; Venezky & Winfield, 1979). In other words, teachers and principals do not engage in academic "buck passing." Rather, they accept the social, economic, and political realities of their situation and work within the constraints present. They do not use limited resources or family difficulties as excuses for failure to learn. Second, effective teachers *expect* that their students will learn (Brookover & Lezotte, 1979; Brophy & Evertson, 1974, 1976; McDonald & Elias, 1976; Rutter et al., 1979). As Duffy (1982) stated, "When teachers believe that students can learn, they *do* learn" (p. 365). In effect, these two assumptions reflect teacher confidence—confidence in their ability to teach and in students' ability to learn (Brophy, 1979).

Goals and Objectives

When teachers have clearly formulated instructional objectives, and when they are able to communicate them effectively to children, learning

*Portions of this section are taken from J.F. Baumann, "Implications for reading instruction from the research on teacher and school effectiveness," *Journal of Reading*, 1984, 28, 109-115.

is enhanced (Anderson, Evertson, & Brophy, 1979; Emmer, Evertson, & Anderson, 1980; Tikunoff, Berliner, & Rist, 1975). In turn, effective instruction is typified by children who also know what they are about to learn and why it is important; teachers and students in effective classrooms are rarely confused about what the academic goals are.

Allocated Time

In effective reading programs, enough time is allocated for instruction; that is, there is a direct relationship between the length of the reading period and reading achievement (Fisher et al., 1978; Berliner, 1981). It would be safe to predict that if Teacher A had a 40 minute reading period daily and Teacher B had a 75 minute period, Teacher B's students would outperform those of Teacher A. Obviously, other factors affect reading achievement beyond simple time allocation (see the following items), but by setting aside a reasonable amount of time for reading instruction, students are afforded a sufficient opportunity to learn.

Academic Engaged Time

A factor with a stronger relationship to student achievement than time allocation alone is academic engaged time (Berliner, 1981; Fisher et al., 1978; Rosenshine & Berliner, 1978). Academic engaged time is the amount of allocated time that students are attending to (i.e., engaged in) reading instruction, or more simply stated, "time on task." When students are academically engaged, they pay attention to and participate in the instructional task at hand (e.g., skill instruction by the teacher, oral or silent reading, doing a workbook page, working in a reading kit, reading independently), as opposed to nonacademic engagement which would be transition times, talking, disciplining, and the like.

Academic Emphasis

Teachers who ran their classrooms in a task oriented or businesslike manner were more effective than teachers who were less formal and student oriented (Solomon & Kendall, 1979; Stallings et al., 1977; Stallings & Kaskowitz, 1974; Stallings, Needles, & Stayrook, 1979). An environment with an academic emphasis was typified by teachers who lead lessons themselves (as opposed to self teaching), used time efficiently, did not digress from the lesson at hand, held students accountable for classroom work and homework, had instructional materials ready, provided substantive feedback to students about their performance, and encouraged students to employ good work habits. Conversely, in classes with less of an academic emphasis, teachers allowed much more unstructured group sharing time and employed many activities that involved arts, crafts, games, puzzles, and toys.

Teacher Directed Instruction

Teachers with the highest achievement gains select and direct classroom activities themselves (Soar, 1973; Solomon & Kendall, 1979; Stallings et al., 1977; Stallings & Kaskowitz, 1974). Teachers who placed the student as the center of attention, organized learning around student generated problems, and joined in and participated in student activities has been negatively related to achievement. As Rosenshine and Stevens (1984) note:

> Classrooms in which students chose their own activities, followed their own interests, were responsible for class planning, and were not teacher dependent were also the classrooms which were characterized by rowdiness, shouting, noise, and disorderliness. In addition, these factors of permissiveness, spontaneity, and lack of control were *negatively* related, not only to achievement gain, but also to growth in creativity, inquiry, writing ability, and self-esteem for the students in those classrooms. (pp. 746-747)

High Success Rates

Effective teachers enable their students to be regularly successful (Anderson, Evertson, & Brophy, 1979; Brophy & Evertson, 1976; Fisher et al., 1978). Berliner (1981) defines high success as "the student understands the task and makes only occasional careless errors" (p. 209). For example, high success would mean that students respond to most questions correctly, read aloud with minimal miscues, and get a high proportion of items correct on written assignments. In other words, the psychologically intuitive notion that "success breeds success" has empirical support. The importance of high success rates, however, does not mean that students should not be challenged or that students do not learn from errors ("Common sense suggests that too high a rate of 'high success' work would be deleterious," Berliner, 1981, p. 211); instead, it merely means that regular failure (i.e., low success rates) discourages or interferes with learning.

Baumann

Effective Managers

Not surprisingly, teachers who are effective managers are effective in teaching children reading skills (Anderson, Evertson, & Brophy, 1979; Brophy & Good, 1985; Emmer, Evertson, & Anderson, 1980; Duffy, 1981, 1982). Management behaviors linked to effective reading instruction include thorough, advanced preparation by the teacher, a brisk pace of instruction, minimal transition time, the installation of unambiguous rules and procedures, and an ability to *prevent* misbehavior (Anderson, Evertson, & Brophy, 1982).

Teacher Monitoring

Teacher monitoring also has been shown to be directly related to student achievement (Anderson, Evertson, & Brophy, 1979; Brophy & Good, 1985; Emmer, Evertson, & Anderson, 1980). Monitoring involves teachers' ability to check students' understanding, to provide corrective feedback, to reteach when necessary, and to insure the completion of assigned work. Monitoring is obviously closely tied to engagement and management, for these are the teachers who create more opportunities for students to learn by organizing themselves and their classrooms to enhance efficiency and minimize wasted time (Anderson, Evertson, & Brophy, 1982).

Large or Small Group Instruction

Although one-to-one instruction is the most effective organizational pattern (Smith & Glass, 1980), given the impracticality of much one-to-one instruction in classrooms of 20-30 students, the research indicates that traditional, large or small group instruction is more effective than highly "individualized" instruction in which students are expected to learn by themselves (Fisher et al., 1978; Kean et al., 1979; Stallings & Kaskowitz, 1974). When reviewing this literature, Rosenshine and Stevens (1984) noted, "when students worked in groups under adult supervision, correlations with achievement were positive and often significant, but when small groups met without an adult, correlations between this pattern and achievement were negative and often significant" (p. 748). Although the research provides no definitive answer to the question of the relative merits of large versus small group instruction (Brophy & Good, 1985), small group instruction is probably necessary for teaching reading, especially in highly heterogeneous classes (Anderson, Evertson, & Brophy, 1982; Brophy & Good, 1985). In other words, when students work in homogeneous groups (usually achievement level groups), achievement is greater than when students are working independently on learning packets or centers (Brophy & Good, 1985). This does not mean that individual differences should not be taken into consideration. Whole class or large group instruction in which each student, regardless of instructional level, must use the same materials is unwise. But when teachers group on the basis of achievement level and assign appropriate instructional materials, students increase their reading ability (Anderson, Evertson, & Brophy, 1982).

Classroom Atmosphere

Given all the emphasis on academic focus, teacher directed instruction, effective management, strict monitoring, and the like, one might be left with the impression that effective teachers run classrooms like Marine drill sergeants, in which the climate is authoritarian, discipline is harsh, rules are unbending, and punishment is administered arbitrarily. Quite to the contrary, effective classrooms have been found to be warm, cooperative, "convivial" environments (Anderson, Evertson, & Brophy, 1979; Berliner & Rosenshine, 1977; Brophy & Evertson, 1974; Emmer, Evertson, & Anderson, 1980). Teachers were in charge in effective classrooms, no doubt, and there was little tolerance for nonacademic activities, but these teachers also had a sense of humor, administered praise, and communicated to children a sincere feeling of caring. In effect, these classrooms were happy places where students felt secure and comfortable.

A Direct Instruction Strategy for Teaching Reading Comprehension Skills

Most of the teacher behaviors just described have been clustered under the rubric "direct instruction" (Baumann, 1983; Berliner, 1981; Berliner & Rosenshine, 1977; Duffy, 1981, 1982; Rosenshine, 1976). In this global sense, when direct instruction occurs, enough time is allocated to reading instruction, teachers accept responsibility for student achievement, and they expect that their students will learn. Teachers understand the objectives for their lessons and are able to communicate them effectively to their students. The academic atmosphere is businesslike and serious but, at the same time, is nonthreatening, warm, and convivial. The teacher selects the instructional activities and directs the lessons; instruction is not administered by a workbook, learning center, textbook, or another student. Instruction usually occurs in small or large groups, students succeed more often than not, and students are on task a high proportion of the time. The teacher is well prepared, is able to prevent misbehavior, checks students' understanding, provides corrective feedback, and reteaches when necessary. But most important, the teacher is in command of the learning situation by showing, telling, demonstrating, modeling, *teaching* the skill to be learned.

Ample evidence supports the effectiveness of a direct instruction approach to teaching reading comprehension skills. For example, Hansen (1981) and Hansen and Pearson (1983) were effective in teaching children to increase markedly their inferential comprehension skill; Raphael and Pearson (1982) and Raphael and McKinney (1983) reported positive effects of metacognitive training on children's question/answering strategies; Reis and Spekman (1983) were successful in training upper grade poor comprehenders in the use of comprehension monitoring strategies; Fitzgerald and Spiegel (1983) enhanced children's comprehension of stories by direct instruction on narrative structure; Tharp (1982) reported consistently higher levels of reading comprehension achievement in a longitudinal study involving educationally high risk, Polynesian-Hawaiian primary grade children who received massed, active comprehension instruction when compared to children who experienced a more traditional decoding focused program; and Patching, et al. (1983) trained fifth grade students in critical reading comprehension skills (faulty generalization, false causality, and invalid testimonial) and found that students who received a systematic, direct instruction approach outperformed comparable students who received a workbook-with-corrective-feedback approach and controls.

The five step direct instruction strategy for teaching main idea comprehension that follows is taken from an earlier work of mine (Baumann, 1983). The effectiveness of this approach for teaching reading comprehension skills has been documented in two studies. In one study (Baumann, 1984b) I randomly assigned sixth grade students to one of three treatments: a direct instruction group which employed the five-step procedure, a basal group which was administered main idea lessons from basal readers for teaching main ideas, or a control group which received vocabulary development instruction. Results revealed that the direct instruction group significantly outperformed both the basal group and controls on a series of measures that assessed varying aspects of main idea comprehension. In a similar study (Baumann, 1986), I found again that the direct instruction strategy was superior to a basal group and a control group in teaching third grade students to comprehend anaphoric relationships (word referents). A description of each of the five steps in this direct instruction comprehension strategy follows. The strategy is then exemplified by the model main idea lessons in this chapter.

Introduction

In this step, the students are provided a purpose for the ensuing lesson, and they are told why the acquisition of the skill will help them become better readers. In effect, the introduction is simply a structured overview, so the students have a clear understanding of the content and purpose of the lesson that follows. The introduction is built upon the teacher effectiveness findings related to Underlying Assumptions and Goals and Objectives (see previous review).

Example

The example is an extension of the introduction. In this step, a section of text that contains an example of the skill to be taught is shown to the students. This helps the students understand more fully what they will learn about. The example demonstrates how this relationship or convention exists in written text and how the ability to understand the relationship or convention will help students comprehend better what they read. Like the introduction, the example builds upon what is known about Underlying Assumptions, Goals and Objectives, and Academic Emphasis.

Direct Instruction

In direct instruction, the teacher is actively engaged in showing, telling, modeling, and demonstrating the target skill. As in the introduction and example, the teacher is leading the lesson. The students are actively involved by responding to questions and working out the comprehension of text, but the teacher is in charge. That is, the primary responsibility for learning rests with the teacher; shared pupil–teacher responsibility and full pupil responsibility for learning come in later steps (Pearson, 1985; Pearson & Gallagher, 1983). Heuristics are an important part of direct instruction;

they provide students with some structure or method to use when they apply the skill in the future independently. In addition the teacher requires students to compose answers whenever possible in direct instruction (and in following steps), for when students must generate responses, learning is greater than when they are simply required to recognize or identify answers (Bridge et al., 1984; Doctorow, Wittrock, & Marks, 1978; Taylor & Berkowitz, 1980). Direct instruction is founded upon the teacher effectiveness findings related to Academic Emphasis, Academic Engaged Time, Teacher Directed Instruction, High Success Rates, Effective Management, and Small Group Instruction.

Teacher Directed Application

In this step, the responsiblity for skill acquisition begins to shift to the student (Pearson, 1985; Pearson & Gallagher, 1983). In teacher directed application, the teacher still initiates the activities, but the students "puzzle out" texts which contain the target skill under the supervision of the teacher. In other words, the teacher is present for guidance and feedback, but the students are forced to apply the skill taught previously. This enables the teacher to monitor students' success in skill acquisition so that reteaching can occur if necessary. Research related to Academic Emphasis, Teacher Directed Instruction, Effective Management, and Teacher Monitoring underpin this step.

Independent Practice

In the final step, the transition from full teacher responsibility for learning, to shared pupil/teacher responsibility, to full student responsibility is complete (Pearson, 1985; Pearson & Gallagher, 1983). In independent practice, students are provided exercises that consist of materials not used in instruction or application and which require them to exercise the skill independently. The use of passage length texts and generative responses are also desirable characteristics of this step. Teacher effectiveness research provides considerable evidence of the need for substantial amounts of independent practice after instruction has occured (e.g., Brophy & Evertson, 1976; Fisher et al., 1978; Stallings et al., 1977; Stallings & Kaskowitz, 1974). In addition, research related to Underlying Assumptions, Allocated Time, Academic Engaged Time, and Teacher Monitoring relate to this step.

Scope and Sequence of Main Idea Instruction

Many authors have suggested instructional strategies for teaching main ideas (e.g., Alexander, 1976; Aulls, 1978; Axelrod, 1975; Baumann, 1984b; Dishner & Readence, 1977; Donlan, 1980; Jolly, 1967; Pearson & Johnson, 1978). The scope and sequence of main idea instruction presented in Table 1 is founded upon work by several of these authors but draws most heavily from a sequence of main idea instruction that I have recommended (Baumann, 1984b).

When using the Scope and Sequence for instructional purposes, note that although considerable research has focused on young and developing readers' ability to comprehend main ideas (Winograd & Bridge, Chapter 2, this volume), the research has not identified a definitive developmental hierarchy of main idea tasks and relations. Therefore, the order of tasks as presented in Table 1 and the recommended grade levels for initiating instruction on each task are based upon the best estimates from the research literature and from intuition and feedback from experienced classroom teachers. Therefore, use Table 1 only as a guide for developing and sequencing instruction in main idea comprehension, not as a definitive developmental hierarchy.

The grade column in Table 1 represents the lowest grade level at which instruction in that task is deemed appropriate. For example, tasks 5 and 6 (main ideas and details in passages—explicit and implicit) are not considered to be appropriate for students below grade five. Keep in mind, however, that these grade level designations represent only the *lower* limit of instruction, not the *upper* limit. In other words, tasks 5 and 6 are not appropriate for students below grade five; students in higher grades, however, would benefit from such instruction. Therefore, a fifth grade teacher who wished to initiate instruction in main idea could teach students tasks 1 through 6; similarly, a sixth grade teacher could use tasks 1 through 8. In fact, the tasks on Table 1 are sequenced in a developmental order, that is, mastery of lower order skills is assumed before proceeding to more sophisticated main idea tasks. Thus, when using the sequence, teachers should have students begin at task 1 and proceed to the highest appropriate level.

Model Main Idea Lessons

In addition to using the five-step, direct instruction approach, several other features incorporated into the model lessons are worthy of note. First,

Table 1

SCOPE AND SEQUENCE OF MAIN IDEA TASKS AND RELATIONS

Main Idea Task	Description	Grades
1. Main ideas in lists of words	Students are taught the basic concept of main idea by learning how to analyze a list of related words to determine the superordinate category or class (e.g., *shirt, pants, dress, hat, shoes = clothing*). When using such lists, students should be taught to liken the words within the list to details and the word list title to the main idea. Classification activities similar to those in Johnson and Pearson (1984) are effective in teaching students this introductory skill.	1 and up
2. Main ideas in sentences	Students are taught to generalize the main idea concept to a larger unit of text: the sentence. For sentences, the main idea is defined as the topic (one or several words that tell what the sentence is about) and what is said about the topic (i.e., *sentence main idea = topic + what is said about the topic*). Students are taught to apply this definition for single sentences by identifying the main idea and discriminating it from other information in the sentence (analogous to details). For example, in the sentence, *Susan, the girl who lives down the street in the blue house, goes to Girl Scouts every Wednesday afternoon,* the topic is *Susan;* what is said about the topic is *goes to Girl Scouts;* and the main idea of the sentence is *Susan goes to Girl Scouts.*	2 and up
3. Main ideas and details in paragraphs — explicit	Students are taught to generalize the main idea/detail concept to paragraphs. For paragraphs, main idea is defined as the topic of the paragraph (one or several words that tell what the paragraph is about) and what is said about the topic (i.e., *paragraph main idea = paragraph topic + what is said about the topic*). *Details* consist of other information in the paragraph that supports, or goes along with, the main idea of the paragraph (although students should ultimately be taught that authors frequently include extraneous information that is neither the main idea nor details). Students are directly taught to identify explicit main ideas in paragraphs and to associate supporting details with them. Instruction also includes a discussion of the location of explicit paragraph main idea statements, indicating that when main ideas are explicit, they are most likely to be found at the beginning of the paragraph (Baumann & Serra, 1984). The teacher may use the term	3 and up

Main Idea Comprehension Ability   145 *topic sentence* if deemed appropriate, informing students that this term is synonymous with *main idea sentence* or with *explicit paragraph main idea.*

4. Main ideas and details in paragraphs — implicit	After achieving mastery in identifying explicit paragraph main ideas, students should be informed that many paragraphs do not have a main idea stated directly (i.e, they have no topic sentence, Baumann & Serra, 1984). During instruction in identifying implicit paragraph main ideas, students should identify the topic of the paragraph, determine what is said about the topic, and then compose a main idea statement that captures the gist of the paragraph. Students need to be shown how to use details in the paragraph to infer what the main idea is, and to test main idea statements by asking, "Does this main idea statement tell me about all the details in this paragraph?"	3 and up
5. Main ideas and details in short passages — explicit	After mastery of explicit and implicit paragraph main ideas, students are taught to generalize the main idea/detail concept to short passages (text sections of three or more paragraphs; similar to subsections in a content textbook). Students are taught that a passage main idea statement consists of the topic of the passage (one or several words that tell what the passage is about) and what is said about the topic (i.e., *passage main idea = passage topic + what is said about the topic*). Instruction leads students to inspect passages for the presence of an explicit main idea statement, which, if present, will most likely be located at the beginning of the passage (Baumann & Serra, 1984). Students are taught to look for passage details (which might be paragraph main ideas) that support the main idea statement and to verify their selection by asking, "Does this main idea statement tell me about all the information in the passage?"	5 and up
6. Main ideas and details in short passages — implicit	Students are taught to compose a main idea statement for a short passage that does not have an explicit passage main idea. Instruction for this task parallels instruction for task 4, implicit paragraph main ideas. Students are led to inspect paragraphs to determine what information is being said about the topic in order to compose a passage main idea statement. Passage details are used to support a hypothesized main idea statement, having students ask, "Does this main idea statement tell me about the details in this passage?"	5 and up

7. Main idea outlines for short passages – explicit	As an extension of task 5, students are taught to construct main idea outlines for short passages with explicit main idea statements. Individual paragraph main ideas are likened to details, and students are taught to compose a two-level outline in which the explicit passage main idea is at the upper level and individual paragraph main ideas (either explicit or implicit) are at the subordinate level.	6 and up
8. Main idea outlines for short passages – implicit	Instruction in this task is identical to task 7, except students must infer the short passage main idea. Again, main ideas within the passage are likened to details and reside at a level subordinate to the inferred passage main idea.	6 and up
9. Main ideas in long passages	Students are taught to inspect long texts (major subsections in content textbooks or entire chapters) and generalize the main idea skills developed in preceding lessons. Students are taught to inspect long passages for the macro-structure, that is, to identify the overall passage main idea (i.e., the theme statement, either explicit or implicit), a second subordinate level (analogous to short passage main ideas either explicit or implicit), and a third subordinate level (analogous to paragraph main ideas either explicit or implicit). To conceptualize the hierarchical nature of such texts, students are taught to construct three-level outlines similar to those taught in tasks 7 and 8.	7 and up

instruction in supporting details is integrated into all main idea instruction. Too frequently, instructional materials ignore the relationship between main ideas and supporting details, making mastery of main idea incomplete and instruction difficult.

Second, many heuristics are used in instruction. These enable the learner to use some visual or conceptual structure first to acquire the main idea skill and later to apply the skill when reading independently.

Third, research indicates that having students *generate* answers results in better comprehension than having them simply recognize correct answers (Bridge et al., 1984; Doctorow, Wittrock, & Marks, 1978; Taylor & Berkowitz, 1980). Therefore, the instructional tasks involve the students in composing (i.e., writing) main idea statements and supporting details whenever appropriate, as opposed to tasks in which students must simply identify main ideas.

Fourth, the instructional sequence includes activities that require students to summarize text, that is, to convey the main point concisely (tasks 4-9 in Table 1). These activities are included because many readers, especially less capable readers, have difficulty summarizing text (Brown & Day, 1983; Tierney & Bridge, 1979; Winograd, 1984) and mastery of summarization is essential for proficiency at higher level main idea comprehension.

Three model lessons follow. Lesson 1 involves instruction in task 1 from the Scope and Sequence (main ideas in lists of words; see Table 1). Lesson 2 provides instruction in task 4 (main ideas and details in paragraphs—implicit), and Lesson 3 teaches task 7 (main idea outlines for passages—explicit). Each lesson specifies certain background information: the main idea task, the grade level of student for which the lesson is intended, and assumptions about the students' capabilities and prior instruction. To facilitate the presentation of the model lessons, several typographical conventions are used: 1) direct statements by the teacher are presented in upper case type; 2) annotations or other comments are printed in lower case type; 3) linguistic examples are printed in lower case italics; and 4) boxed text denotes materials that the teacher would have reproduced on wall charts or transparencies for the direct instruction parts of the lessons, and on class handouts for the teacher directed application and independent practice steps of the lessons.

One final comment is necessary before proceeding with the model lessons. The following lessons represent possible transcripts of actual direct instruction administered by a classroom teacher; they do not represent scripts for such lessons. Scripts are prepared texts to be read or dictated verbatim by teachers to students, much like the scripts Becker (1977) and Kameenui (Chapter 11, this volume) recommend. The direct instruction approach presented in this chapter involves careful teacher planning and preparation to be sure, but it in no way implies that the teacher teach from a prepared script. Rather, this conception of direct instruction requires the teacher to be spontaneous and able to respond to the ebb and flow of instruction, modifying examples and procedures on the basis of feedback from the students as the lesson proceeds. Therefore, each of the following model lessons should be viewed as *one* possible course each lesson took with a particular group of students, not as the *only* possible manner or way in which a lesson could unfold.

Model Lesson 1
Background information.

Main idea task: Main ideas in lists of words.
Grade level: Second semester first grade students.
Assumptions: No prior knowledge or instruction in main ideas
                    is assumed. All students are developmental read-
                    ers capable of handling primer or first grade
                    level materials, so that decoding does not inter-
                    fere with their ability to grasp the concept of
                    main ideas in lists of words.

Introduction. WHEN YOU LISTEN TO OR READ STORIES, THERE ARE BIG IDEAS
AND LITTLE IDEAS. FOR EXAMPLE, THINK OF THE STORY I READ TO YOU YESTERDAY
CALLED *ALEXANDER AND THE TERRIBLE, HORRIBLE, NO GOOD, VERY BAD DAY*. DO
YOU REMEMBER THAT STORY? WELL, THE BIG IDEA OF THAT STORY WAS THAT
POOR ALEXANDER HAD A VERY BAD DAY. THE LITTLE IDEAS IN THAT STORY WERE
ALL THE TERRIBLE AND HORRIBLE THINGS THAT HAPPENED TO ALEXANDER THAT
MADE HIS DAY HORRIBLE, LIKE HIS SWEATER FALLING IN THE SINK WHEN HE
BRUSHED HIS TEETH, HAVING TO EAT LIMA BEANS WHEN HE HATED THEM, BEING
THE ONLY ONE IN HIS FAMILY TO HAVE A CAVITY WHEN THEY WENT TO THE DENTIST,
NOT BEING ABLE TO BUY THE SNEAKERS HE WANTED AT THE SHOE STORE, HAVING
TO WEAR HIS RAILROAD PAJAMAS THAT HE HATED, AND BITING HIS TONGUE WHEN
HE WENT TO BED. LITTLE IDEAS ARE INTERESTING AND IMPORTANT, BUT IT IS
ALSO VERY IMPORTANT TO GET THE BIG IDEA FROM A STORY. IF YOU DON'T GET
THE BIG IDEA, YOU WILL NOT UNDERSTAND WHAT SOMEONE HAS WRITTEN. FOR
EXAMPLE, IF YOU DIDN'T GET THE BIG IDEA IN THE STORY ABOUT ALEXANDER,
YOU WOULD HAVE MISSED THE WHOLE IDEA OF THE STORY—THAT HE HAD A VERY
BAD DAY.

ANOTHER NAME FOR THE BIG IDEA IS THE MAIN IDEA. TODAY WE WILL BEGIN
TO LEARN ABOUT MAIN IDEAS, BUT NOT MAIN IDEAS IN A STORY. TODAY WE WILL
LEARN HOW TO FIGURE OUT THE MAIN IDEA IN A LIST OF WORDS. WHEN YOU
LEARN HOW TO FIGURE OUT THE MAIN IDEA IN A LIST OF WORDS, IT WILL MAKE
IT EASIER WHEN YOU LEARN LATER HOW TO FIND THE MAIN IDEA IN STORIES.

Example. HERE IS AN EXAMPLE OF WHAT WE WILL LEARN ABOUT TODAY:
MAIN IDEAS IN LISTS OF WORDS. Teacher points to the chart (Box 1). ON THE
TOP YOU SEE THE WORD *clothes*. UNDERNEATH, YOU SEE THE WORDS *shirt*, *shoe*,
socks, *pants*, *hat*, and *skirt*. *Clothes* IS THE MAIN IDEA FOR THIS LIST OF WORDS
BECAUSE ALL THE WORDS IN THE LIST ARE DIFFERENT KINDS OF CLOTHES. *Shirt*,
shoes, *socks*, *pants*, and *skirt* ARE ALL WORDS THAT NAME DIFFERENT CLOTHES.

```
        Clothes
        shirt
        shoe
        sock
        pants
        hat
        skirt
```

Box 1

Direct instruction. LOOK AT THIS NEXT CHART. Teacher points to another chart (Box 2). HERE I HAVE WRITTEN ANOTHER LIST OF WORDS, BUT THERE IS A BLANK ABOVE THE LIST. LET'S LOOK AT THE LIST AND SEE IF WE CAN FIGURE OUT WHAT THE MAIN IDEA OF THE LIST IS. REMEMBER, THE MAIN IDEA WILL BE A WORD THAT TELLS US ABOUT THE WHOLE LIST; THAT IS, EACH WORD MUST GO WITH OR FIT UNDER THE MAIN IDEA.

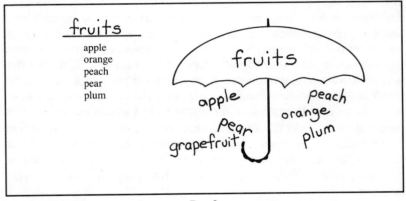

Box 2

LOOK AT THE LIST: *apple, orange, peach, pear, plum.* NOW THE MAIN IDEA FOR THESE WORDS WILL BE A WORD THAT TELLS US ABOUT ALL OF THE WORDS. DOES ANYONE HAVE AN IDEA WHAT THE MAIN IDEA MIGHT BE? Student response. YES, THE MAIN IDEA IS *fruit* BECAUSE ALL THESE WORDS ARE DIFFERENT KINDS OF FRUITS. LET'S CHECK TO MAKE SURE. IS AN APPLE A FRUIT? Student response. YES, AN APPLE IS A FRUIT. HOW ABOUT AN ORANGE? Student response. YES, AN ORANGE IS A FRUIT, TOO. HOW ABOUT A PEACH, A PEAR, AND A PLUM? Student response. YES, THEY ARE ALL FRUITS TOO, SO *fruit* MUST BE THE MAIN IDEA FOR THIS LIST OF WORDS.

Baumann

NOTICE THAT NEXT TO THIS LIST OF WORDS I HAVE DRAWN AN UMBRELLA. I BET YOU ARE WONDERING WHAT AN UMBRELLA HAS TO DO WITH THE MAIN IDEA FOR A LIST OF WORDS. WELL, I HAVE DRAWN THE UMBRELLA THERE TO HELP YOU UNDERSTAND BETTER MAIN IDEAS IN LISTS OF WORDS. LET'S PUT THE MAIN IDEA OF THE LIST OF WORDS ON THE UMBRELLA. Teacher writes *fruits* on the umbrella. CAN ANYONE HELP ME BY WRITING THE WORDS IN OUR LIST OF FRUITS UNDER THE UMBRELLA? Several students alternately write the words in the list under the umbrella. GOOD. NOW WE HAVE THE MAIN IDEA OF THE LIST OF WORDS ON THE UMBRELLA, AND ALL THE WORDS THAT GO WITH THE MAIN IDEA UNDER THE UMBRELLA. SO, JUST LIKE HOW AN UMBRELLA COVERS ALL THE PEOPLE WHO MIGHT STAND UNDERNEATH IT, THE MAIN IDEA ON THE UMBRELLA COVERS ALL THE WORDS IN A LIST THAT GO WITH IT. CAN ANYONE THINK OF ANOTHER WORD WE MIGHT ADD TO THIS LIST? Student responds *grapefruit*. YES, A *grapefruit* IS ANOTHER KIND OF FRUIT. WHY DON'T YOU GO UP TO THE CHART AND ADD *grapefruit* TO THE LIST OF FRUITS UNDER THE UMBRELLA. Student follows teacher's directions. WHAT IF I WANTED TO PUT *carrot* UNDERNEATH THE UMBRELLA? WOULD THAT BE ALL RIGHT? Student response. NO? WHY NOT? Student response. YES, YOU ARE CORRECT. A CARROT IS NOT A FRUIT; IT IS A VEGETABLE. The teacher continues in a similar manner with one or more additional lists of words until the teacher is convinced that the students have acquired the concept.

Teacher directed application. LOOK AT THE PAPER I AM PASSING OUT. Teacher distributes Group Exercise for "Main Ideas in Lists of Words" (Box 3). NOW YOU WILL HAVE A CHANCE TO TRY TO FIGURE OUT THE MAIN IDEA FOR SOME LISTS OF WORDS ALL BY YOURSELF. LOOK AT NUMBER 1. THERE YOU HAVE TWO LISTS OF WORDS WITH A BLANK ABOVE EACH LIST. READ THROUGH EACH LIST CAREFULLY, AND SEE IF YOU CAN FIGURE OUT THE MAIN IDEA. THEN WRITE WHAT YOU THINK THE MAIN IDEA OF EACH LIST IS IN THE BLANK. THINK ABOUT AN UMBRELLA IF THAT HELPS. DON'T WORRY ABOUT SPELLING. IF YOU AREN'T SURE HOW TO SPELL A WORD, JUST SPELL IT THE BEST YOU CAN. ALL RIGHT, BEGIN NOW AND TRY TO FIGURE OUT THE MAIN IDEA FOR EACH LIST. Students complete number 1 independently.

LET'S SEE HOW WELL YOU DID. WHO HAS THE ANSWER FOR THE FIRST ONE? Student responds *tools*. DOES ANYONE ELSE HAVE *tools* AS AN ANSWER? Student response. IT SEEMS AS THOUGH ALL OF YOU AGREE, SO *tools* MUST BE THE MAIN IDEA FOR THAT LIST OF WORDS, BECAUSE ALL THE WORDS IN THE LIST ARE TOOLS. HOW ABOUT THE SECOND LIST? Student responds, *balls*. LET'S TEST OUT *balls* AND SEE IF IT WORKS AS THE CORRECT ANSWER. IS A *football* A BALL? Student response. IS *baseball* A BALL? Student response. IS *swimming* A BALL? Student response. NO, *swimming* IS NOT A BALL, SO *balls* CAN'T BE THE CORRECT ANSWER

BECAUSE THE MAIN IDEA HAS TO COVER ALL THE WORDS IN THE LIST. DOES ANYONE HAVE A DIFFERENT ANSWER? Student responds *sports*. LET'S SEE IF *sports* WORKS BETTER. Teacher tests out *sports* for the students in a similar fashion.

Main Ideas in Lists of Words
Group Exercise

1. _____   _____

   hammer   football

   hoe   baseball

   rake   swimming

   shovel   tennis

   saw   golf

2. red   Coke   ear

   blue   7 Up   face

   colors   milk   nose

   yellow   juice   mouth

   brown   coffee   eye

   green   drinks   chin

3. ___school subjects___   _____money_____

   _____   _____

   _____   _____

   _____   _____

   _____   _____

Box 3

Baumann

The teacher works through numbers 2 and 3 in similar manner. In number 2, students are required to find and circle the main idea word within each list, and in number 3, students must write words that fit the main idea word. Upon completion, a guided discussion of the correct

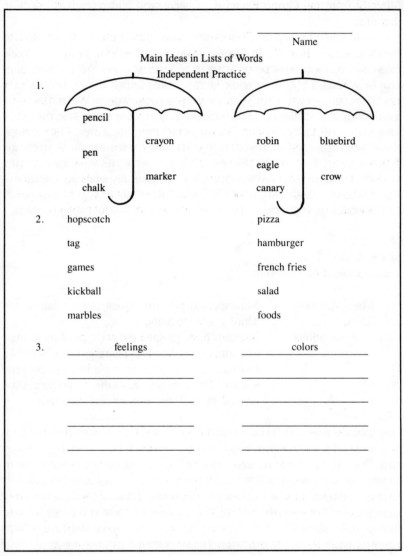

Name _____

Main Ideas in Lists of Words
Independent Practice

1.

    pencil

        crayon   robin   bluebird

   pen

                           eagle

        marker   crow

    chalk   canary

2.   hopscotch   pizza

        tag   hamburger

        games   french fries

        kickball   salad

        marbles   foods

3.   feelings   colors

Box 4

answers would occur. This provides the teacher feedback about the student's skill acquisition and provides the students feedback about their success in mastering main ideas in lists of words. If students demonstrate difficulty completing these exercises, the teacher would provide additional examples (directly from the Group Exercise, if necessary) and reteach the skill at that time.

Independent practice. GOOD WORK. NOW TURN YOUR PAPER OVER TO THE OTHER SIDE (see Box 4). PUT YOUR NAME ON THE BLANK. HERE ARE SOME EXERCISES YOU WILL NOW DO ON YOUR OWN. THEY ARE LIKE THE ONES WE JUST DID. IN NUMBER 1 YOU MUST LOOK AT THE WORDS UNDER THE UMBRELLA AND TRY TO FIGURE OUT WHAT THE MAIN IDEA IS FOR THOSE WORDS. WRITE THE MAIN IDEA INSIDE THE UMBRELLA. FOR NUMBER 2, YOU MUST LOOK FOR THE MAIN IDEA WITHIN THE LIST OF WORDS AND THEN CIRCLE THE MAIN IDEA. FOR NUMBER 3, YOU MUST THINK OF SOME WORDS THAT FIT UNDER THE MAIN IDEAS THAT ARE PRINTED THERE. THEN WRITE THE WORDS THAT GO WITH THE MAIN IDEAS IN THE BLANKS. DOES ANYONE HAVE A QUESTION? Teacher responds to questions. ALL RIGHT, GO AHEAD AND WORK CAREFULLY. REMEMBER, A MAIN IDEA FOR A LIST OF WORDS MUST COVER ALL THE WORDS IN THE LIST, NOT JUST SOME OF THEM.

Model Lesson 2
Background information.

Main idea task:	Main ideas and details in paragraphs—implicit.
Grade level:	Third grade students.
Assumptions:	Students have grasped the concept of main idea and supporting details in paragraphs and are able to find explicit paragraph main ideas (topic sentences). Students also have the decoding ability needed to read the instructional materials.

Introduction. IN OUR LAST LESSON, WE LEARNED HOW TO FIND MAIN IDEAS IN PARAGRAPHS WHEN THERE WAS A SINGLE SENTENCE THAT STATED THE MAIN IDEA. WE CALLED THIS MAIN IDEA SENTENCE A TOPIC SENTENCE. WE CALLED IT A TOPIC SENTENCE BECAUSE IT TOLD US WHAT THE WHOLE PARAGRAPH WAS ABOUT; THAT IS, THE MAIN IDEA OF THE WHOLE PARAGRAPH. TODAY WE WILL AGAIN FIND MAIN IDEAS IN PARAGRAPHS, BUT THE PARAGRAPHS WE LOOK AT TODAY WILL NOT HAVE A TOPIC SENTENCE. THE PARAGRAPHS WILL STILL HAVE MAIN IDEAS, BUT YOU WILL NEED TO FIGURE OUT WHAT THE MAIN IDEA IS BY LOOKING AT ALL THE DETAILS IN THE PARAGRAPH. MANY PARAGRAPHS YOU READ WILL NOT HAVE TOPIC

SENTENCES. THEREFORE, YOU WILL NEED TO FIGURE OUT ON YOUR OWN WHAT THE MAIN IDEA IS. BEING ABLE TO FIGURE OUT THE MAIN IDEA IS AN IMPORTANT READING SKILL BECAUSE KNOWING WHAT THE MAIN IDEA IS TELLS YOU WHAT THE WRITER MEANT TO BE THE MOST IMPORTANT INFORMATION IN A PARAGRAPH.

Example. LOOK AT THE PARAGRAPH I HAVE WRITTEN ON THIS CHART. Teacher points to chart (Box 5). FOLLOW ALONG WITH ME SILENTLY AS I READ THE PARAGRAPH ALOUD. Teacher reads paragraph. HERE IS AN EXAMPLE OF WHAT WE WILL LEARN TODAY. THERE IS NO TOPIC SENTENCE IN THIS PARAGRAPH. RATHER, THE WHOLE PARAGRAPH IS A LIST OF DETAILS. THAT DOES NOT MEAN THAT THERE IS NOT A MAIN IDEA FOR THIS PARAGRAPH, FOR THERE IS. BUT YOU MUST FIGURE OUT WHAT THAT MAIN IDEA IS BY LOOKING AT ALL THE DETAILS. THE MAIN IDEA OF THIS PARAGRAPH IS "HOW DOGS HELP PEOPLE" BECAUSE EACH OF THE SENTENCES TELLS US ABOUT HOW PEOPLE ARE HELPED BY DOGS.

Seeing eye dogs help protect blind people. Police dogs can chase and catch robbers and other criminals. Some dogs work on farms by rounding up cows or sheep or by keeping rats and mice away. Pet dogs are helpful simply because they are good friends to their owners.

Box 5

Direct instruction. IN OUR LAST LESSON WE LEARNED THAT THE MAIN IDEA OF A PARGRAPH CONSISTS OF THE TOPIC OF THE PARAGRAPH AND WHAT IS SAID ABOUT THE TOPIC. IT WAS FAIRLY EASY IN OUR LAST LESSON TO FIND THE MAIN IDEA OF A PARAGRAPH BECAUSE A SENTENCE IN THE PARAGRAPH TOLD US THE TOPIC AND WHAT WAS SAID ABOUT THE TOPIC: THE TOPIC SENTENCE. TODAY WE WILL HAVE TO LOOK AT ALL THE DETAILS IN PARAGRAPHS TO TRY TO FIGURE OUT WHAT THE MAIN IDEA IS.

LOOK AT THE PARAGRAPH I HAVE WRITTEN ON THIS CHART. Teacher points to chart (Box 6). READ ALONG SILENTLY AS I READ THIS PARAGRAPH ALOUD. Teacher reads paragraph. FIRST, LET'S FIGURE OUT WHAT THE TOPIC OF THE PARAGRAPH IS. CAN ANYONE TELL US? Student responds, *thunderstorms*. DOES EVERYONE AGREE THAT THE TOPIC OF THIS PARAGRAPH IS THUNDERSTORMS? Student response. ALL RIGHT, THAT WAS EASY, BUT NOW WE HAVE TO FIGURE OUT WHAT IS SAID ABOUT THUNDERSTORMS AND COME UP WITH A SENTENCE THAT TELLS US THE MAIN IDEA. TO HELP US COME UP WITH A MAIN IDEA SENTENCE, LET'S BEGIN BY MAKING A LIST OF ALL THE IDEAS IN THIS PARAGRAPH THAT TELL US ABOUT THUNDERSTORMS. WHO CAN HELP US BEGIN? Student responds, *Thunderstorms cause flooding*. The teacher writes this and the other three details in a numbered list on the chalkboard.

> Thunderstorms can cause flooding, and people have drowned because of thunderstorm floods. Lightning also happens during thunderstorms, and people can die if struck by lightning. Strong winds sometimes blow during thunderstorms, and some people have been knocked down or injured by blowing things. And, of course, tornadoes can happen with thunderstorms, and you know how dangerous they can be.

Box 6

VERY GOOD. THESE ARE THE IDEAS THAT TELL US ABOUT THUNDERSTORMS, AND WE LEARNED LAST TIME WE CALL THESE IDEAS SUPPORTING DETAILS. SINCE SUPPORTING DETAILS GO WITH A MAIN IDEA, LET'S INSPECT THESE DETAILS AND SEE IF WE CAN FIGURE OUT WHAT THE MAIN IDEA OF THIS PARAGRAPH IS. Teacher rereads the four supporting details on the board. NOW, WHAT WOULD BE A MAIN IDEA SENTENCE ABOUT THE TOPIC THUNDERSTORMS THAT TELLS US ABOUT ALL THESE DETAILS? REMEMBER, IT MUST COVER ALL THE DETAILS. Several students respond and teacher writes responses on the board. YES, THERE ARE SEVERAL DIFFERENT WAYS OF SAYING WHAT THE MAIN IDEA OF THIS PARAGRAPH IS. ONE OF YOU SAID "THUNDERSTORMS ARE DANGEROUS." SOMEONE ELSE SAID "THUNDERSTORMS CAN KILL PEOPLE." EITHER OF THESE STATEMENTS TELLS US THE MAIN IDEA, BECAUSE EACH OF THE SUPPORTING DETAILS TELLS US ABOUT HOW A THUNDERSTORM CAN BE DANGEROUS OR HOW IT CAN KILL PEOPLE.

NOW LOOK AT THIS NEXT CHART. Teacher points to chart (Box 7). WHO CAN TELL ME WHAT THIS IS? Student response. YES, IT IS A TABLE. LET'S USE THIS TABLE TO HELP US UNDERSTAND HOW MAIN IDEAS AND DETAILS GO TO-GETHER. JUST AS A TABLE IS SUPPORTED BY LEGS, SO TOO, A MAIN IDEA IS SUP-PORTED BY DETAILS. LET'S PUT THE MAIN IDEA ON THE TABLE TOP AND A SUPPORT-ING DETAIL ON EACH LEG OF THE TABLE. WHO CAN HELP US GET GOING? LET'S BEGIN WITH THE DETAILS ON THE LEGS. Students respond and the teacher writes the details on the table legs. ALL RIGHT, NOW LET'S PUT THE MAIN IDEA THAT GOES WITH THESE SUPPORTING DETAILS ON THE TABLE TOP. Teacher writes main idea on table top. JUST AS THE LEGS OF THIS TABLE SUPPORT THE MAIN IDEA OF THIS PARAGRAPH, SO TOO, THE DETAILS IN THE PARAGRAPH SUPPORT THE MAIN IDEA OF THE PARAGRAPH. WHEN YOU TRY TO FIGURE OUT THE MAIN IDEA OF A PARAGRAPH, THINK OF A TABLE AND LEGS TO HELP YOU UNDERSTAND HOW SUP-PORTING DETAILS AND MAIN IDEAS GO TOGETHER.

Box 7

Teacher directed application. I HAVE A WORK PAPER THAT WE WILL COM-PLETE TOGETHER. Teacher distributes Group Exercise for "Unstated Main Ideas and Details" (Box 8). LOOK AT THE PARAGRAPH AFTER NUMBER 1. READ THIS PARAGRAPH TO YOURSELF SILENTLY, AND THEN SEE IF YOU CAN FIGURE OUT THE MAIN IDEA FOR THAT PARAGRAPH. THERE IS NO TOPIC SENTENCE IN THIS PARAGRAPH, SO YOU WILL HAVE TO USE THE SUPPORTING DETAILS TO DETERMINE WHAT THE MAIN IDEA IS. THEN DARKEN THE LETTER THAT GOES WITH THE SEN-TENCE YOU THINK BEST STATES THE MAIN IDEA OF THIS PARAGRAPH. Students complete exercise 1.

ALL RIGHT, HOW DID YOU DO? WHO CAN TELL US WHAT THE MAIN IDEA IS? Student response. CORRECT, ANSWER CHOICE "C," "ANIMALS HELP PEOPLE IN DIFFERENT WAYS," IS THE MAIN IDEA. WHO CAN TELL US WHAT THE SUPPORTING DETAILS ARE FOR THIS MAIN IDEA? Student response. GOOD. WHY WOULDNT

UNSTATED MAIN IDEAS AND DETAILS IN PARAGRAPHS

Group Exercise

1. Horses can carry people. Mules pull heavy loads. Dogs lead blind people across streets. Sheep give us wool, and cows give people milk to drink.

   (a) Animals give us many different foods to eat.

   (b) Horses and mules do heavy work for people.

   (c) Animals help people in different ways.

   (d) Dogs and horses are good companions for people.

2. Tom Smith can lift a barbell that weighs over 500 pounds. Tom can take a thick telephone book and tear it in two with his hands. Tom can kick a football 70 yards, and he can hit a baseball 450 feet. Tom is so strong he has never lost a wrestling match at school.

   _____

3. Robins build nests in trees. Eagles build their nests in high rocky places. Pheasants build nests in fields or meadows. Sparrows and wrens like to build their nests in bird houses or under the eaves of people's houses. Penguins build their nests on rocky beaches.

   _____

4. In order to grow, plants need good rich soil that has lots of minerals. Plants also need a gas from the air called carbon dioxide. Without carbon dioxide, plants would die. And, of course, plants need water to grow and plenty of warm sunshine.

   _____

Box 8

Baumann

ANSWER CHOICE "A" BE THE CORRECT ANSWER? Student response. YES, ANSWER "A" TELLS US THAT ANIMALS GIVE US DIFFERENT FOODS TO EAT, BUT THE ONLY DETAIL IN THE PARAGRAPH THAT TELLS US ABOUT ANIMALS GIVING PEOPLE FOOD IS THE IDEA THAT COWS GIVE US MILK. SO, NOT ALL THE DETAILS GO WITH THE STATEMENT "ANIMALS GIVE US MANY DIFFERENT FOODS TO EAT."

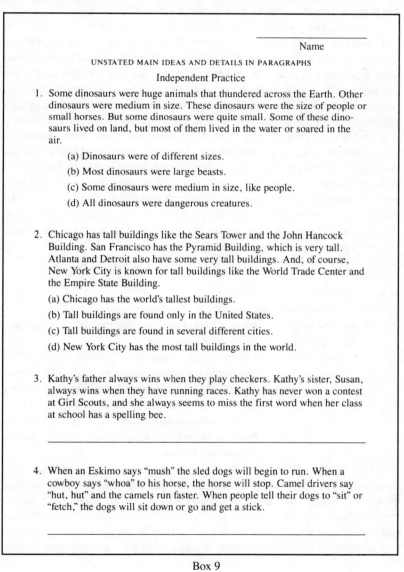

Name _____

UNSTATED MAIN IDEAS AND DETAILS IN PARAGRAPHS

Independent Practice

1. Some dinosaurs were huge animals that thundered across the Earth. Other dinosaurs were medium in size. These dinosaurs were the size of people or small horses. But some dinosaurs were quite small. Some of these dinosaurs lived on land, but most of them lived in the water or soared in the air.

   (a) Dinosaurs were of different sizes.

   (b) Most dinosaurs were large beasts.

   (c) Some dinosaurs were medium in size, like people.

   (d) All dinosaurs were dangerous creatures.

2. Chicago has tall buildings like the Sears Tower and the John Hancock Building. San Francisco has the Pyramid Building, which is very tall. Atlanta and Detroit also have some very tall buildings. And, of course, New York City is known for tall buildings like the World Trade Center and the Empire State Building.

   (a) Chicago has the world's tallest buildings.

   (b) Tall buildings are found only in the United States.

   (c) Tall buildings are found in several different cities.

   (d) New York City has the most tall buildings in the world.

3. Kathy's father always wins when they play checkers. Kathy's sister, Susan, always wins when they have running races. Kathy has never won a contest at Girl Scouts, and she always seems to miss the first word when her class at school has a spelling bee.

   _____

4. When an Eskimo says "mush" the sled dogs will begin to run. When a cowboy says "whoa" to his horse, the horse will stop. Camel drivers say "hut, hut" and the camels run faster. When people tell their dogs to "sit" or "fetch," the dogs will sit down or go and get a stick.

   _____

Box 9

NOW TRY NUMBER 2. READ THIS PARAGRAPH TO YOURSELF SILENTLY AND THEN WRITE WHAT YOU THINK THE MAIN IDEA OF THIS PARAGRAPH IS ON THE LINE BELOW THE PARAGRAPH. THINK OF THE TABLE AND LEGS IDEA TO HELP YOU. Students complete this and the other exercises, and the teacher leads a guided discussion of the correct answers. If students are having difficulty, the teacher provides feedback or reteaches the skill.

Independent practice. THE FINAL THING YOU WILL DO IN THIS LESSON IS TO COMPLETE A WORK PAPER ON YOU OWN. TURN YOUR PAPER OVER TO THE SIDE THAT SAYS "INDEPENDENT PRACTICE" (BOX 9). PUT YOUR NAME IN THE BLANK AT THE TOP OF THE PAGE. ON THIS PAPER THERE ARE PARAGRAPHS THAT HAVE UNSTATED MAIN IDEAS; THAT IS, YOU WILL NEED TO READ ALL THE DETAILS TO FIGURE OUT WHAT THE MAIN IDEAS ARE. NUMBERS 1 AND 2 HAVE YOU SELECT THE CORRECT MAIN IDEA STATEMENT FROM THOSE LISTED BELOW THE PARAGRAPH. SIMPLY DARKEN IN THE LETTER OF THE STATEMENT YOU THINK IS THE MAIN IDEA. FOR NUMBERS 3 AND 4 YOU MUST WRITE A SENTENCE THAT TELLS THE MAIN IDEA FOR EACH PARAGRAPH. DO YOU UNDERSTAND THE DIRECTIONS? Student response; teacher clarifies the directions if necessary. WHEN COMPLETING THESE EXERCISES, TRY TO REMEMBER HOW TO FIGURE OUT THE MAIN IDEA BY THINKING OF A STATEMENT THAT TELLS ABOUT ALL THE DETAILS IN THE PARAGRAPH; YOU ALSO MIGHT WANT TO USE THE TABLE AND LEGS IDEA TO HELP YOU. WORK CAREFULLY AND DO YOUR BEST.

Model Lesson 3
Background information.

Main idea task:	Main idea outlines for short passages—explicit.
Grade level:	Sixth grade students.
Assumptions:	Students have been taught to identify explicit and implicit main ideas in paragraphs. They have had some instruction in identifying explicit and implicit main ideas for short passages. (Three to five paragraphs in length). Finally, students have sufficient decoding ability to read the instructional materials.

Introduction. WE HAVE BEEN STUDYING MAIN IDEAS FOR SOME TIME. YOU HAVE LEARNED HOW TO FIND DIRECTLY STATED MAIN IDEAS IN PARAGRAPHS, WHICH WE CALLED TOPIC SENTENCES. YOU HAVE LEARNED HOW TO DETERMINE THE MAIN IDEA FOR PARAGRAPHS THAT DO NOT HAVE A STATED MAIN IDEA BY EXAMINING ALL THE DETAILS. AND YOU HAVE LEARNED THAT SHORT PASSAGES CAN HAVE MAIN IDEAS THAT COVER SEVERAL DIFFERENT PARAGRAPHS. TODAY

Baumann

YOU WILL CONTINUE TO LOOK AT MAIN IDEAS IN SHORT PASSAGES. YOU WILL LEARN HOW TO FIND AN OVERALL MAIN IDEA FOR A SHORT PASSAGE THAT IS DIRECTLY STATED AND HOW TO PUT OTHER MAIN IDEAS IN THE PASSAGE UNDER THIS BIGGER MAIN IDEA. TO HELP YOU UNDERSTAND HOW THESE TWO DIFFERENT TYPES OF MAIN IDEAS GO TOGETHER, YOU WILL LEARN HOW TO MAKE A MAIN IDEA OUTLINE FOR SHORT PASSAGES. KNOWING HOW TO MAKE MAIN IDEA OUTLINES IS IMPORTANT BECAUSE THEN WHEN YOU READ TEXTBOOKS IN SUBJECTS LIKE SCIENCE AND SOCIAL STUDIES, YOU WILL BE ABLE TO FIGURE OUT WHAT THE IMPORTANT INFORMATION IS, SO YOU WILL LEARN AND REMEMBER THE IMPORTANT IDEAS IN THESE SUBJECTS BETTER.

Example. HERE IS AN EXAMPLE OF WHAT WE WILL LEARN ABOUT TODAY. Teacher points to a wall chart (Box 10). READ THIS STORY SILENTLY AS I READ IT ALOUD. Teacher reads story aloud. THIS STORY HAS ONE BIG MAIN IDEA, AND THAT MAIN IDEA IS IN THE FIRST SENTENCE: "ANIMALS HELP PEOPLE IN SEVERAL DIFFERENT WAYS." SO THIS SENTENCE TELLS US THE MAIN IDEA FOR THE ENTIRE PASSAGE. TO PROVE THIS, LOOK WITHIN EACH OF THE PARAGRAPHS IN THE STORY. EACH PARAGRAPH TELLS ABOUT A DIFFERENT WAY ANIMALS HELP PEOPLE. THE FIRST PARAGRAPH TELLS ABOUT THE FOOD WE GET FROM ANIMALS; THE SECOND PARAGRAPH TELLS ABOUT HOW ANIMALS ARE HELPFUL IN WORK AND TRANSPORTATION; THE THIRD PARAGRAPH TELLS ABOUT OTHER PRODUCTS WE GET FROM ANIMALS; AND THE LAST PARAGRAPH TELLS ABOUT HOW ANIMALS HELP BY GIVING US ENJOYMENT.

Animals are helpful to people in several different ways. Animals give people food. For example, we get beef from cows, we get pork from hogs, and we get eggs from chickens.

Animals are helpful in work and transportation. Horses carry people and pull wagons. Mules can plow fields and carry loads. In some countries, elephants do work that humans would not be strong enough to do.

We get other products from animals. All the leather we use for coats, belts, purses, and sports equipment comes from animals like cows, pigs, and even kangaroos. Soap is made from animals, and many chemicals we use in foods and medicines come from animals.

Animals also help by giving people enjoyment. Riding horses is very much fun. Fishing is a sport many people enjoy, and, of course, many people enjoy their pet dogs, cats, fish, or birds.

Box 10

LOOK AT THIS NEXT CHART. Teacher uncovers chart (Box 11). HERE WE SEE OUR OLD FAMILIAR TABLE AND LEGS, BUT THIS TIME I HAVE THE WHOLE

PASSAGE MAIN IDEA ON THE TABLE AND THE INDIVIDUAL PARAGRAPH MAIN IDEAS ON THE LEGS. SO JUST LIKE THE DETAILS IN A PARAGRAPH SUPPORTED THE MAIN IDEA FOR THAT PARAGRAPH, NOW THE MAIN IDEAS WITHIN A PASSAGE SUPPORT THE OVERALL MAIN IDEA FOR THAT PASSAGE. WHAT YOU WILL LEARN ABOUT IS HOW TO FIND A SENTENCE IN A SHORT PASSAGE THAT TELLS THE MAIN IDEAS FOR THE ENTIRE PASSAGE. YOU WILL LEARN THIS BY LOOKING AT PASSAGES AND MAKING OUTLINES IN WHICH THE PASSAGE MAIN IDEA IS ON TOP OF THE OUTLINE AND THE PARAGRAPH MAIN IDEAS THAT SUPPORT IT ARE UNDERNEATH THE PASSAGE MAIN IDEA.

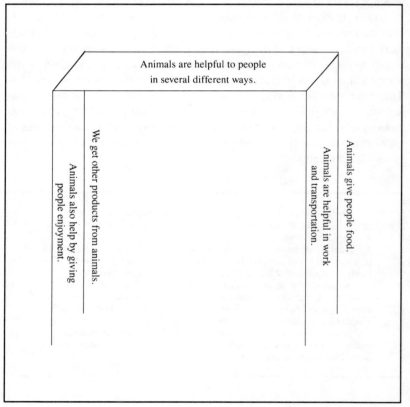

Box 11

Baumann

Electricity can be produced in several different ways. Some electricity is made in generating plants that burn coal, oil, or natural gas. This produces steam, which turns a generator and makes the electricity. Coal, oil, and gas generating plants are the most common ways to make electricity.

Nuclear power plants are also used to produce electricity. Nuclear fuel gives off heat. This heat then produces steam, which turns a generator and makes the electricity, just like in a plant that uses coal, oil, or gas. Nuclear plants work well, but some people think they are dangerous and should be closed.

Falling water can also be used to make electricity. Water that is held behind a dam goes through large pipes into huge water wheels. The falling water turns the wheels, which are connected to a generator. Generating plants that use water are nice because they are clean and safe.

Sunlight and wind can also be used to make electricity. Solar collectors can heat water, which is used to make electricity. Blades on huge windmills can be connected to generators to produce electricity. Electricity made from wind or sunlight is a good idea because the wind and sun are "free" to everyone.

Box 12

Direct instruction. LOOK AT THE PASSAGE I HAVE ON THIS CHART. Teacher displays chart (Box 12). COULD I HAVE A VOLUNTEER READ THROUGH THIS PASSAGE FOR ME? Kim volunteers. READ ALONG SILENTLY AS KIM READS THIS PASSAGE ALOUD FOR US, BUT AS YOU READ, TRY TO FIGURE OUT THE MAIN IDEA OF THE WHOLE PASSAGE AND THE MAIN IDEAS WITHIN THE PASSAGE THAT SUPPORT THIS BIG IDEA. REMEMBER, THINK OF A TABLE TOP AND TABLE LEGS. Student reads passage.

GOOD. NOW LET'S SEE IF WE CAN DETERMINE HOW THIS PASSAGE IS ORGANIZED. FIRST, WHAT IS THE TOPIC OF THIS PASSAGE? Student response. YES, IT IS CLEAR THAT THIS PASSAGE IS ABOUT *electricity*. NOW, WE HAVE TO FIGURE OUT WHAT IS SAID ABOUT THE TOPIC *electricity*. REMEMBER, WE ARE LOOKING FOR TWO KINDS OF MAIN IDEAS: THE MAIN IDEA THAT COVERS EVERYTHING IN THE STORY AND MAIN IDEAS FOR PARTS OF THE PASSAGE. DOES ANYONE THINK HE OR SHE HAS THE MAIN IDEA FOR THE WHOLE PASSAGE? Jenny responds. HOW MANY AGREE WITH JENNY THAT THE FIRST SENTENCE IS THE MAIN IDEA OF THE WHOLE PASSAGE? Students respond. IT SEEMS AS THOUGH MOST OF YOU DO AGREE AND THINK THAT "ELECTRICITY CAN BE PRODUCED IN SEVERAL DIFFERENT WAYS" IS THE PASSAGE MAIN IDEA. JENNY, WHY DON'T YOU GO UP TO THE CHART AND DRAW A CIRCLE AROUND THIS SENTENCE TO SHOW THAT IT TELLS THE MAIN IDEA OF THE ENTIRE PASSAGE. Student response. NOW, WHAT ARE THE MAIN IDEAS WITHIN THE PASSAGE? THAT IS, WHAT WOULD BE THE IDEAS THAT WE WOULD PUT ON THE LEGS OF THE TABLE TO SUPPORT THE TABLE TOP? Students respond.

IT SEEMS LIKE MOST OF YOU AGREE THAT THERE ARE TOPIC SENTENCES IN EACH OF THESE PARAGRAPHS. IN PARAGRAPH 1 IT IS THE SECOND SENTENCE, AND IN PARAGRAPHS 2, 3, AND 4, IT IS THE FIRST SENTENCE. SO, WE HAVE LEARNED THAT THE OVERALL MAIN IDEA OF THE PASSAGE IS THAT ELECTRICITY CAN BE PRODUCED IN SEVERAL WAYS. THEN, THE MAIN IDEAS WITHIN THE PASSAGE TELL US THAT IT CAN BE PRODUCED BY BURNING COAL, OIL, OR NATURAL GAS; BY USING NUCLEAR POWER; BY FALLING WATER; AND BY USING SUNLIGHT OR WIND. COULD SOMEONE GO UP TO THE CHART AND UNDERLINE EACH OF THE MAIN IDEAS WITHIN THE PASSAGE? Student responds.

WELL, LETS MAKE OUR OUTLINE NOW. LOOK AT THIS NEXT CHART. Teacher uncovers chart (Box 13). HERE I HAVE AN OUTLINE WE CAN USE FOR THIS PASSAGE. NOTICE THAT AT THE TOP IT SAYS "MAIN IDEA OF THE PASSAGE" AND A BLANK FOLLOWS IT. BELOW THIS BLANK IS ANOTHER TITLE THAT SAYS "MAIN IDEAS IN THE PASSAGE," AND FOUR NUMBERED BLANKS FOLLOW. WHAT WE WILL DO HERE IS TO WRITE THE PASSAGE MAIN IDEA IN THE FIRST BLANK AND THE MAIN IDEAS WITHIN THE PASSAGE IN THE OTHER BLANKS. COULD I HAVE SOME HELPERS TO DO THIS? Students volunteer and complete the passage outline.

Main idea *of* the passage *Electricity can be produced in several different ways.*

Main ideas *in* the passage

1. *Some electricity is made in generating plants that burn coal, oil, or gas.*
2. *Nuclear power plants are also used to produce electricity.*
3. *Falling water can also be used to make electricity.*
4. *Sunlight and wind can also be used to make electricity.*

Box 13

Baumann

GOOD. NOW WE HAVE AN OUTLINE FOR THIS PASSAGE. ACTUALLY, THIS OUTLINE IS A SUMMARY OF THE WHOLE PASSAGE. A SUMMARY, IN CASE YOU ARE NOT FAMILIAR WITH THAT WORD, TELLS THE MAJOR OR MAIN POINTS IN A PASSAGE, LEAVING OUT MOST OF THE DETAILS. WELL, LOOK AT OUR OUTLINE AND SEE IF IT MAKES A GOOD SUMMARY. IT SAYS THAT THE MAIN IDEA OF THE WHOLE PASSAGE IS THAT THERE ARE DIFFERENT WAYS IN WHICH ELECTRICITY CAN BE PRODUCED. THE WAYS THAT ARE DISCUSSED IN THE PASSAGE INCLUDE BURNING THINGS SUCH AS COAL, OIL, OR NATURAL GAS; USING NUCLEAR ENERGY; USING FALLING WATER; OR HARNESSING ENERGY FROM THE SUN OR WIND. DOES THAT TELL US THE IMPORTANT IDEAS IN THE PASSAGE? Student response. YES, I AGREE. THOSE ARE THE MAIN IDEAS OF THE PASSAGE AND THAT WAS A PRETTY GOOD SUMMARY OF THE PASSAGE. WHAT ABOUT IDEAS SUCH AS "NUCLEAR FUEL GIVES OFF HEAT" OR "WATER THAT IS HELD BEHIND A DAM GOES THROUGH LARGE PIPES AND INTO HUGE WATER WHEELS?" Teacher points to those sentences as they are stated. ARE THOSE MAIN IDEAS? Student response. YOU ARE CORRECT. THOSE ARE NOT MAIN IDEAS. THEY ARE DETAILS THAT SUPPORT THE MAIN IDEAS OF THE PASSAGE. THE DETAILS ARE NECESSARY FOR A PASSAGE, AND IT ISN'T AS THOUGH WE SHOULD IGNORE THEM OR FORGET THEM, BUT THEY ONLY SUPPORT THE MAIN IDEAS OF THE PASSAGE.

THE PASSAGE ABOUT ELECTRICITY WAS FAIRLY EASY BECAUSE NOT ONLY WAS THE PASSAGE MAIN IDEA STATED DIRECTLY, BUT EACH OF THE MAIN IDEAS WITHIN THE PASSAGE WAS STATED DIRECTLY. WRITERS DON'T ALWAYS WRITE THAT WAY, HOWEVER. LET'S LOOK AT THIS NEXT PASSAGE (teacher points to another chart; Box 14) AND SEE IF WE CAN FIGURE OUT THE PASSAGE MAIN IDEA AND THE MAIN IDEAS WITHIN THE PASSAGE. Teacher proceeds in a manner similar to the passage on electricity, only this time, the teacher guides the students to identify an explicit passage main idea that comes at the *end* of the passage ("So, goods can be transported from placd to place by land, air, or sea.").

Teacher directed application. GOOD WORK. NOW, LET'S WORK THROUGH ONE OF THESE OUTLINES FOR PASSAGES TOGETHER. TAKE A LOOK AT THIS PAPER I AM PASSING OUT. Teacher distributes Group Exercise "Main Idea Outlines for Short Passages" (Box 15). READ THROUGH THIS PASSAGE AND SEE IF YOU CAN FIGURE OUT ON YOUR OWN BOTH THE MAIN IDEA OF THE WHOLE PASSAGE AND THE MAIN IDEAS WITHIN THE PASSAGE; THAT IS, FIND THE STATEMENT THAT WOULD GO ON THE TABLE TOP AND THE STATEMENTS THAT WOULD GO ON THE TABLE LEGS. USE THE OUTLINE FORM AT THE BOTTOM OF THE PAGE TO WRITE YOUR ANSWERS. Students complete the exercise independently. When they are finished, the teacher leads them in a guided discussion of the correct

> Many goods are transported by ground. For example, big and small trucks carry goods and materials of all sizes and shapes. Trains carry extremely heavy or bulky items from one place to another.
>
> Transport planes carry air cargo. Businesses use air cargo because it is very quick; however, air cargo is very expensive. Helicopters are also used to carry goods by air, and in some places, hot air balloons or blimps are used to carry goods.
>
> Ships, barges, and other boats are frequently used to move goods across bodies of water like lakes, rivers, canals, and oceans. Bulk materials like coal, oil, and grain are frequently transported by water. So, goods can be transported from place to place by land, air, or sea.
>
> Main idea *of* the passage *So goods can be transported by land, sea, or air.*
>
> Main ideas *in* the passage
>
> 1. *Many goods are transported by ground.*
> 2. *Some goods are transported by air.*
> 3. *Some goods are transported by water.*

Box 14

answers, providing the teacher with feedback about the students' performance and about the teacher's success in teaching main idea outlines. Corrective feedback and additional instruction follow when necessary.

Independent practice. GOOD WORK AGAIN. THE LAST THING I WILL HAVE YOU DO IN THIS LESSON IS TO COMPLETE ONE OF THE PASSAGE MAIN IDEA OUTLINES ON YOUR OWN. TURN YOUR PAPER OVER TO THE OTHER SIDE (BOX 16) THAT SAYS "INDEPENDENT PRACTICE" AND WRITE YOUR NAME IN THE BLANK AT THE TOP. COMPLETE THIS PAGE EXACTLY LIKE THE ONE WE JUST DID; THAT IS, FIND THE MAIN IDEA OF THE WHOLE PASSAGE AND THE MAIN IDEAS IN THE PASSAGE. DOES EVERYONE UNDERSTAND WHAT YOU ARE TO DO? Student response. ALL RIGHT, BEGIN WORKING. WORK CAREFULLY AND REMEMBER THAT THE MAIN IDEA OF THE PASSAGE COVERS ALL THE IDEAS WITHIN THE PASSAGE AND THE MAIN IDEA IN THE PASSAGE TELLS THE MAIN IDEAS THAT SUPPORT THE PASSAGE MAIN IDEA. Students complete exercise independently.

Group Exercise

There are a number of reasons for world food problems. One of the problems is related to climate. Recent droughts, long periods of time without rainfall, occurred in many parts of the world. When the rains did not come, streams dried up and the soil hardened or became dust. Many people died of starvation.

Another world food problem is due to subsistence farming. Subsistence farming is when farmers grow just enough food for the family with no extra for emergencies. If a drought, a flood, or another disaster comes along, there is no extra food to live on.

The growth of towns and cities has added to food problems. More and more people are moving to cities. Land used for towns and cities cannot be used for growing crops or herding animals. Offices and factories are being built on what was once farmland. With the decreased farmland, less food can then be grown.

Main Idea *of* the Passage _____

_____

Main Ideas *in* the Passage

1. _____

_____

2. _____

_____

3. _____

_____

Box 15

Independent Practice

Geothermal, plant, and wind energy are good replacements for oil and gas energy.

Geothermal energy is a good replacement for oil and gas energy. Geothermal energy comes from the heat in the earth's mantle. When water trapped underground reaches hot areas, it turns to steam. Sometimes this steam can be tapped and used to generate electricity.

Plants absorb the sun's energy. This energy is used by plants to make food. Some plants can also be processed into liquid alcohol. Brazil, for example, is trying to replace some petroleum with alcohol. Therefore, plant energy is another good replacement for oil and gas energy.

Wind is another possible replacement for oil and gas energy. If all winds blew at a speed of 21 miles per hour, the energy produced would be 7,000 times the electricity produced by Hoover Dam in one year. Windmills can be used to convert wind energy into electrical power all over the world.

Main Idea *of* the Passage _____

_____

Main Ideas *in* the Passage _____

1. _____

_____

2. _____

_____

3. _____

_____

Box 16

Baumann

Adapting Existing Instructional Materials to Include More Direct Instruction on Main Ideas

The previous lessons were called model lessons for a specific purpose: They were intended to provide a stereotype—that is, a model—of what the application of direct instruction principles would result in when original main idea lessons are constructed. This information may be of direct value to curriculum specialists in public schools or authors of reading instructional materials for commercial publishers, as well as to teachers.

Few classroom teachers, however, have the time to construct original reading skill lessons, and doing so, perhaps, would not be an efficient use of preparation time given the numerous demands on a classroom teacher. Rather than writing original materials, teachers rely on the skill lessons within the commerical materials they use, which, in most cases, are basal readers. Indeed, using prepared materials is sensible and efficient.

However, basal readers have been criticized for lacking a rigorous comprehension instructional component (Durkin, 1981). Durkin found that the preponderance of procedures related to comprehension were not directly instructional but instead involved asssessment or practice of comprehension abilities. Although current basal programs are superior to the materials Durkin evaluated (the basal readers she inspected had 1978 and 1979 copyrights) in both the quantity and quality of comprehension instruction, the limitations she noted are still present to some degree; that is, teachers do not always find in basal manuals complete, coherent, comprehension lessons that are truly *instructional*.

What follows is an example of how a teacher can adapt a basal lesson to include more features of the direct instruction strategy presented in this chapter. A skill lesson on main ideas which is representative of current, popular basal programs is selected and analyzed. Then, suggestions are presented about how this lesson can be adapted or modified to include more of the features of the direct instruction strategy. The lesson is taken from a fourth grade basal reader (*Barefoot Island,* of the Ginn Reading Program, Clymer & Venezky, 1982). Figure 1 reprints the skill lesson section from the *Barefoot Island, Teacher's Edition* (pp. 155-156). Figure 2 presents an exercise page from the *Skillpack;* an additional practice exercise from the *Studybook* also accompanies the lesson, although it is not reproduced here.

COMPREHENSION

Main idea: Identifying the main idea of a paragraph (Practice)

Ask pupils:

What is the difference between the main idea sentence and the other sentences in a paragraph? (The main idea is a general statement that tells what the whole paragraph is about. The other sentences in the paragraph are usually specific details that exemplify or illustrate the main idea.)

Explain that writers do not include a main idea statement in every paragraph. When the main idea is not stated, readers should ask themselves, "What is the point? What is the author saying?" Then say:

Listen as I read aloud this paragraph. Try to figure out the unstated main idea.

Bob and Maria earn money by raking leaves. Carmen gives clown shows and birthday parties. Several families in town call Bruce their "number-one baby-sitter."

Read aloud these main idea statements and have pupils identify the one that best describes the whole paragraph.

1. Bruce is a popular baby-sitter. (supporting detail)
2. Children have a hard time finding work today. (contradictory main idea)
3. Young people earn money in many ways. (main idea)

Ask pupils to explain why the second statement is not the correct choice. Be sure pupils understand that even though it is a main idea statement it contradicts the ideas in the paragraph.

To provide practice with main ideas, distribute Skillpack page 43. This page is in the format used on the Unit Tests. When pupils have finished, go over the answers with them. Have pupils explain why some of the answer choices are not main idea statements. (wrong answer choices are stated or unstated details)

Studybook page 45 also provides practice with main ideas.

Figure 1. Main idea comprehension instruction in a basal reader manual.
From Teacher's Edition of *Barefoot Island* of the Ginn Reading Program by Theodore Clymer et al. Copyright © 1982 by Ginn and Company (Xerox Corporation). Used with permission.

This lesson is not the first lesson on main idea in his fourth grade basal reader. This lesson—which involves practice of prior instruction—was preceded by a very elaborate initial lesson on main idea (Teacher's Edition, pp. 146-147). This lesson was quite complete when examined for elements

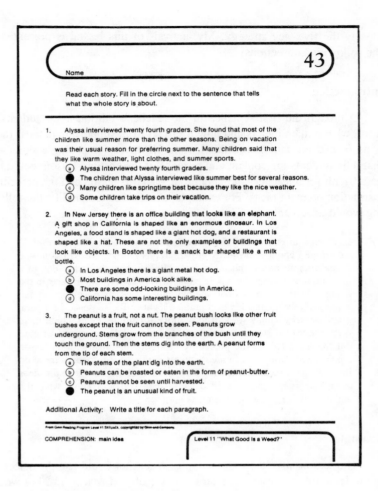

Figure 2. Workbook page accompanying a basal reader skill lesson.

From Teacher's Edition of (Skillpack) *Barefoot Island* of the Ginn Reading Program by Theodore Clymer et al. Copyright © 1982 by Ginn and Company (Xerox Corporation). Used with permission.

of the five-step, direct instruction strategy. Given this context, the reader is encouraged at this point to inspect Figures 1 and 2 to determine if this lesson contains the features of direct instruction articulated in the five-step direct instruction strategy presented in this chapter. This reader then might determine how this lesson could be adapted so that it approximates more closely the five-step strategy. My analysis of this lesson is presented in the following subsections.

Introduction

Although the first sentence in the teacher's edition asks students to recall what a main idea is and how it differs from supporting details, there is no formal introduction to this lesson. However composing a statement that tells students the content and purpose of the ensuing lesson would not be difficult for a teacher who is familiar with this lesson and the preceding instruction on main ideas. For example, a simple statement like the following would adequately introduce this lesson:

> Last week after we read the story "Last Days of Brightness, Part 2" we learned about main ideas in paragraphs. Today, we will continue to learn about paragraph main ideas. Remember, the main idea of a paragraph tells what the whole papagraph is about. Other ideas in the paragraph go with or support the main idea. Last time we learned that sometimes the main idea is contained right in the sentence in a paragraph or story; today we will look more at paragraphs in which there is no main idea stated in the story, and you, the reader, must figure out the main idea. [The preceding "Introductory Instruction" lesson emphasized explicit main ideas, whereas this lesson focuses more on implicit main ideas.] Knowing how to find or figure out main ideas is an important reading skill because then you will know what the author's major points or big ideas are.

Example

The lesson also lacks an example, A teacher could use the selection in the lesson that is used for instruction ("Bob and Maria..."), but would probably want to save it for the direct instruction part of the lesson. A teacher could write a short paragraph to provide the students an example of what they will learn about, but doing so is not an efficient use of time. A simple option would be to have the students look back at prior instructional materials in either the *Skillpack* or *Studybook*. For example, a teacher could make the following statement to provide the example part of the five-step strategy.

> Turn to page 39 of your *Skillpack*. This was one of the exercises we did last week when we learned about main ideas. Look at the first paragraph there. Read it to yourself as I read it aloud. (Teacher reads

the paragraph.) What is the main idea sentence for that paragraph? (Student responds.) Yes, the main idea sentence is "Food is important for growth and energy." What we will learn about today is how to figure out main ideas for paragraphs like this one.

Direct Instruction

The paragraph in the teacher's edition that begins "Explain that writers do not..." through the paragraph that ends "...it contradicts the ideas in the paragraph" provides some nice direct instruction on constructing an implicit main idea. Obviously, the teacher should use this instruction. What would improve the instruction, however, would be to have the sample paragraph ("Bob and Maria...") displayed for the students on either a wall chart or a transparency. It is far easier to teach about reading comprehension when students can actually see and read the instructional texts as opposed to when they may only listen to passages. If additional texts are needed to instruct students, the teacher may need to prepare an extra sample text or two. Another more efficient option would be to select a text or two from those found in the *Skillpack* or *Studybook* exercises that accompany this lesson. The disadvantage in using several of these texts, however, is that fewer exercises are available for teacher directed application and independent practice steps of instruction.

Teacher Directed Application

The second to the last paragraph in the teacher's edition ("To provide practice with main ideas...") directs the teacher to have students complete *Skillpack* page 43 (Figure 2). Further, the teacher is directed to review correct and incorrect answers with the students after they have completed the exercise. This is a form of teacher directed application; however, feedback and correction is not provided until the students have completed the entire page. To provide more immediate feedback to students about their ability to acquire the main idea skill that has been taught, a teacher could work through *Skillpack* page 43 in the manner demonstrated in the model lessons in this chapter; that is, have the students complete one or two exercises, correct them, provide feedback, and then move on to the remaining exercises. Working through an exercise page in this manner provides the students immediate feedback about their success in skill acquisition and informs the teacher whether added instruction at this point is necessary.

Independent Practice

Studybook page 45 (an exercise similar to Figure 2) would be an exercise the students could complete independently to practice their ability to determine the main idea for a paragraph.

What about the many ancillary materials on main idea that come in the form of workbooks, black line masters, kits, games, filmstrips, computer software, and the like? How can instruction using these materials be adaped or modified so that more direct teaching of main idea comprehension occurs? First, evaluate the intended purpose and use of the materials. If a set of black line masters is intended to be purely supplemental *practice and reinforcement* of prior main idea instruction, then perhaps no modification is in order. If, however, you intend to use ancillary materials to *teach* one or more main idea comprehension skills, then an analysis similar to the preceding one for basal readers is required. For example, if you wish to rely on a kit that includes main idea instruction as an integral part of the reading comprehension program, first determine if any teacher directed instruction is included. If instruction is deficient or lacking, then you will need to elaborate on the existing instructional component. As with basal readers, the areas of introduction/example, direct instruction, and teacher directed application are the areas in which most breakdowns occur, so be prepared to develop, augment, or elaborate on whatever main idea instructional support the kit provides. In summary, if ancillary materials are intended to be truly instructional, then you must evaluate the effectiveness of the instruction that is present and then expand upon that instructional component when necessary.

Conclusions

The five-step direct instruction strategy for teaching main ideas presented in this chapter should not be viewed as the only or best way to teach main idea comprehension ability. No single strategy or technique should ever be considered definitive. Indeed, other contributors to this volume have recommended alternate strategies and techniques for main idea instruction.

What the strategy does present, however, is one way a teacher can systematically and intensively teach main idea comprehension. The power of the approach is that it is based upon what is known empirically about effective classroom instruction. When using the direct instruction strategy to design original lessons or when using it to evaluate and then modify existing lessons on main idea, the goal should not be to follow the technique explicitly. There are no scripts for this approach to direct instruction. Rather, the goal should be to design or modify lessons such that the teacher becomes the critical factor in instruction. That is, the teacher tells the students what the lesson will be about; the teacher provides an example; the teacher actually teaches the lesson; then, gradually, the teacher releases responsibility for learning to the students through guided application exercises and then by providing independent practice. In other words, the spirit of the direct instruction strategy is most important, not the explicit nature of the five steps that are recommended.

Finally, although it has not been stated directly, the five-step strategy is generalizable to other reading comprehension skills. The five-step strategy has been found to be effective not only for teaching main idea comprehension (Baumann, 1984b) but also in teaching students to comprehend anaphoric relationships (Baumann, 1986). Other reading comprehension skills (e.g., cause/effect, sequence, characterization, predicting outcomes, figurative language, drawing conclusions) could be taught effectively using this same approach.

References

Alexander, C.F. Strategies for finding the main idea. *Journal of Reading*, 1976, *19*, 299-301.

Anderson, L., Evertson, C., and Brophy, J. An experimental study of effective teaching in first grade reading groups. *Elementary School Journal*, 1979, *79*, 193-223.

Anderson, L., Evertson, C., and Brophy, J. *Principles of small group instruction in elementary reading*. Occasional Paper No. 58. East Lansing, MI: Institute for Research on Teaching, Michigan State University, 1982.

Aulls, M.W. *Developmental and remedial reading in the middle grades*. Boston: Allyn & Bacon, 1978.

Axelrod, J. Getting the main idea is still the main idea. *Journal of Reading*, 1975, *18*, 383-387.

Baumann, J.F. A generic comprehension instructional strategy. *Reading World*, 1983, *22*, 284-294.

Baumann, J.F. Implications for reading instruction from the research on teacher and school effectivness. *Journal of Reading*, 1984a, *28*, 109-115.

Baumann, J.F. The effectiveness of a direct instruction paradigm for teaching main idea comprehension. *Reading Research Quarterly*, 1984b, *20*, 93-115.

Baumann, J.F. Teaching third grade students to comprehend anaphoric relationships: The application of a direct instruction model. *Reading Research Quarterly*, 1986, *21*, 70-90.

Baumann, J.F., and Serra, J.K. The frequency and placement of main ideas in children's social studies textbooks: A modified replication of Braddock's research on topic sentences. *Journal of Reading Behavior,* 1984 *16,* 27-40.

Becker, W.C. Teaching reading and language to the disadvantaged—what we have here learned from the research. *Harvard Educational Review,* 1977, *47,* 518-543.

Becker, W.C., and Carnine, D.W. Direct instruction: An effective approach to educational intervention with the disadvantaged and low performers. In B.B. Lahey and A.E. Kazdin (Eds.), *Advances in clinical child psychology,* vol. 3. New York: Plenum, 1980, 429-473.

Berliner, D.C. Academic learning time and reading achievement. In J.T. Guthrie (Ed.,) *Comprehension and teaching: Research reviews.* Newark, DE: International Reading Association, 1981, 203-226.

Berliner, D.C., and Rosenshine, B.V. The acquisition of knowledge in the classroom. In R.C. Anderson, R.J. Spiro, and W.E. Montague (Eds.), *Schooling and the acquisition of knowledge.* Hillsdale, NJ: Erlbaum, 1977, 375-396.

Bridge, C.A., Belmore S.M., Moskow, S.P., Cohen, S.S. & Matthews, P.D. Topicalization and memory for main ideas in prose. *Journal of Reading Behavior,* 1984, *16,* 61-80.

Brookover, W.B., and Lezotte, L.W. *Changes in school characteristics coincident with changes in student achievement.* Occasional Paper No. 17. East Lansing, MI: Institute for Research on Teaching, Michigan State University, 1979.

Brophy, J. Teacher behavior and student learning. *Educational Leadership,* 1979, *37,* 33-38.

Brophy, J., and Evertson, C.M. *Process-product correlations in the Texas teacher effectiveness study: Final report.* Report No. 4004. Austin, TX: Research and Development Center for Teacher Education, University of Texas at Austin, 1974.

Brophy, J. and Evertson, C.M. *Learning from teaching: A developmental perspective.* Boston, MA: Allyn and Bacon, 1976.

Brophy, J., and Good, T.L. Teacher behavior and student achievement. In M.C. Wittrock (Ed.), *Third handbook of research on teaching.* New York: Macmillan, 1985.

Brown, A.L. and Day, J.D. *Macrorules for summarizing texts: The development of expertise.* Technical Report No. 270. Champaign, IL: University of Illinois, Center for the Study of Reading, 1983.

Clymer, T., and Venezky, R.L. *Ginn Reading Program.* Lexington, MA: Ginn, 1982.

Dishner, E.K., and Readence, J.E. A systematic procedure for teaching main idea. *Reading World,* 1977, *16,* 292-298.

Doctorow, M., Wittrock, M.C., and Marks, C. Generative processes in reading comprehension. *Journal of Educational Psychology,* 1978, *70,* 109-118.

Donlan, D. Locating main ideas in history textbooks. *Journal of Reading,* 1980 *24,* 135-140.

Duffy, G.G. Teacher effectiveness research: Implications for the reading profession. In M.L. Kamil (Ed.), *Directions in reading: Research and instruction.* Thirtieth yearbook of the National Reading Conference. Washington, D.C.: National Reading Conference, 1981, 113-136.

Duffy, G.G. Fighting off the alligators: What research in real classrooms has to say about reading instruction. *Journal of Reading Behavior,* 1982, *14,* 357-373.

Duffy, G.G., and Roehler, L.F. Direct instruction of comprehension: What does it really mean? *Reading Horizons,* 1982, *23,* 35-40.

Durkin, D.D. What classroom observations reveal about reading instruction. *Reading Research Quarterly,* 1978-1979, *14,* 481-533.

Durkin, D.D. Reading comprehension instruction in five basal reader series. *Reading Research Quarterly,* 1981, *16,* 515-544.

Emmer, E., Evertson, C., and Anderson, L. Effective classroom management at the beginning of the school year. *Elementary School Journal*, 1980, *80*, 219-231.

Engelmann, S., and Bruner, E.D. *DISTAR reading: An instructional system*. Chicago: Science Research Associates, 1969.

Fisher, C.W., Filby, N.N., Marliave, R., Cahen, L.S., Dishaw, M.M., Moore, J.E., and Berliner, D.C. *Teaching behaviors, academic learning time, and student achievement: Final report phase III-B, beginning teacher evaluation study*. San Francisco: Far West Educational Laboratory for Educational Research and Development, 1978.

Fitzgerald, J., and Speigel, D.L. Enhancing children's reading comprehension through instruction in narrative structure. *Journal of Reading Behavior*, 1983, *15*, 19-36.

Good, T.L. Research on classroom teaching. In Lee S. Shulman and G. Sykes (Eds.), *Handbook of teaching and policy*. New York: Longman, 1983.

Good, T.L. Teacher effectiveness in the elementary school: What we know about it now. *Journal of Teacher Education*, 1979, *30*, 52-64.

Hansen, J. The effects of inference training and practice on young children's reading comprehension. *Reading Research Quarterly*, 1981, *16*, 391-417.

Hansen, J., and Pearson, P.D. An instructional study: Improving the inferential comprehension of fourth grade good and poor readers. *Journal of Educational Psychology*, 1983, *79*, 821-829.

Hoffman, J.V., and Rutherford, W.L. Effective reading programs: A critical review of outlier studies. *Reading Research Quarterly*, 1984, *20*, 79-92.

Johnson, D.D., and Pearson, P.D. *Teaching reading vocabulary* (2nd ed.). New York: Holt, Rinehart & Winston, 1984.

Jolly, H.B. Determining main ideas: A basic study skill. In L.E. Hafner (Ed.), *Improving reading in secondary schools: Selected readings*. New York: Macmillan, 1967, 181-190.

Kean, M.H., Summers, A.A., Raivetz, M.J., and Farber, I.J. *What works in reading?* Philadelphia: School District or Philadelphia, 1979.

McDonald, F.J., and Ellias, P. *The effects of teaching performance on pupil learning: Final report, volume 1, beginning teacher evaluation study, phase II, 1974-1976*. Princeton, NJ: Educational Testing Service, 1976.

Patching, W., Kameenui, E., Carnine, D., Gersten, R., and Colvin, G. Direct instruction in critical reading skills. *Reading Research Quarterly*, 1983, *18*, 406-418.

Pearson, P.D. Changing the face of reading comprehension instruction. *Reading Teacher*, 1985, *38*, 724-738.

Pearson, P.D., and Gallagher, M.C. The instruction of reading comprehension. *Contemporary Educational Psychology*, 1983, *8*, 317-344.

Pearson, P.D., and Johnson, D.D. *Teaching reading comprehension*. New York: Holt, Rinehart & Winston, 1978.

Raphael, T., and McKinney, J. An examination of fifth and eighth grade children's question-answering behavior: An instructional study in metacognition. *Journal of Reading Behavior*, 1983, *15*, 67-86.

Raphael, T., and Pearson, P.D. *The effect of metacognitive training on children's question-answering behavior*. Technical Report No. 238. Champaign, IL: University of Illinois, Center for the Study of Reading, 1982.

Reis, R., and Spekman, N.J. The detection of reader-based versus text-based inconsistencies and the effects of direct training of comprehension monitoring among upper-grade poor comprehenders. *Journal of Reading Behavior*, 1983, *15*, 49-60.

Rosenshine, B. Classroom instruction. In N.L. Gage (Ed.), *The psychology of teaching methods*. Seventy-fifth yearbook of the National Society for the Study of Education. Chicago: University of Chicago Press, 1976.

Rosenshine, B.V. Content, time, and direct instruction. In H. Walberg and P. Peterson (Eds.), *Research on teaching: Concepts, findings, and implications*. Berkeley, CA: McCutchan, 1979.

Rosenshine, B.V., and Berliner, D.C. Academic engaged time. *British Journal of Teacher Education*, 1978, *4*, 3-16.

Rosenshine, B.V., and Stevens, R. Classroom instruction in reading. In P.D. Pearson (Ed.), *Handbook of reading research*. New York: Longman, 1984, 745-798.

Rutter, M., Maughan, B., Martimore, P., Ouston, J., and Smith, A. *Fifteen thousand hours: Secondary schools and their effects on children*. Cambridge, MA: Harvard University Press, 1979.

Samuels, S.J. Characteristics of exemplary reading programs. In John T. Guthrie (Ed.), *Comprehension and teaching: Research reviews*. Newark, DE: International Reading Association, 1981, 255-273.

Smith, M.L. and Glass, G.V. Meta-analysis of research on class size and its relation to attitudes and instruction. *American Educational Research Journal*, 1980, *17*, 419-434.

Soar, R.S. *Follow-through classroom process measurement and pupil growth (1970-71): Final report*. Gainesville, FL: College of Education, University of Florida, 1973.

Solomon, D., and Kendall A.J. *Children in classrooms*. New York: Praeger, 1979.

Stallings, J., Cory, R., Fairweather, J., and Needles, M. *Early childhood education classroom evaluation*. Menlo Park, CA: Stanford Research Institute, 1977.

Stallings, J., and Kaskowitz, D. *Follow through classroom observation evaluation 1972-1973*. Project URU-7370). Menlo Park, CA: Stanford Research Institute, Stanford University, 1974.

Stallings, J., Needles, M., and Stayrook, N. *How to change the process of teaching basic reading skills in secondary schools*. Menlo Park, CA: Stanford Center for Research and Development in Teaching, 1979.

Taylor, B.M., and Berkowitz, S. Facilitating children's comprehension of content material. In M.L. Kamil and A.J. Moe (Eds.), *Perspectives in reading research and instruction*. Twenty-ninth yearbook of the National Reading Conference. Clemson, SC: National Reading Conference, 1980, 64-68.

Tharp, R.G. The effective instruction of comprehension: Results and description of the Kamehameha Early Education Program. *Reading Research Quarterly*, 1982, *17*, 507-527.

Tierney, R.J., and Bridge, C.A. The functions of inferences: An extended examination of discourse comprehension. In M.L. Kamil and A.J. Moe (Eds.), *Reading research: Studies and applications*. Twenty-eighth yearbook of the National Reading Conference. Clemson, SC: National Reading Conference, 1979, 129-133.

Tikunofff, W., Berliner, D.C., and Rist, R.C. *An ethnographic study of the forty classrooms of the beginning teacher evaluation study known sample*. Technical Report No. 75-10-5. San Francisco: Far West Laboratory for Educational Research and Development, 1975.

Venezky, R.L., and Winfield, L. *Schools that succeed beyond expectations in teaching reading*. Technical Report No. 1. Newark, DE: Department of Educational Studies, University of Delaware, 1979.

Winograd, P.N. Strategic difficulties in summarizing texts. *Reading Research Quarterly*, 1984, *19*, 404-425.

7

Teaching Students Main Idea Comprehension: Alternatives to Repeated Exposures

Victoria Chou Hare
Adelaide Bates Bingham

In this chapter, Victoria Chou Hare and Adelaide Bates Bingham argue that too often students are provided only practice activities instead of real instruction on main idea comprehension. To supply the need for actual instruction, the authors provide a series of discovery lessons and direct instruction lessons on main idea comprehension. The discovery lessons lead students to understand hierarchically important information in narratives and to understand main ideas in exposition through the use of text structure cues. The direct instruction lessons teach students information about main ideas in a direct, systematic manner. Hare and Bingham end their chapter with suggestions about how basal reader lessons can be restructured to improve main idea instruction.

Reading researchers are now documenting what reading teachers have known for a long time. That is, defining main ideas (Cunningham & Moore, Chapter 1, this volume) and teaching readers to find main ideas (Winograd & Bridge, Chapter 2, this volume) have been inappropriately characterized as simple activities. Main idea has been traditionally identified as the most important idea or statement in a text; however, many now believe that all top level ideas in a hierarchy of text ideas should be called *main* ideas (Meyer, 1975). A hierarchy of text ideas certainly seems truer to complex, real life texts.

Children have been directed to practice finding the main idea; they have not been taught to find the main idea. Thus, typical main idea activities have always been fairly easy to execute. Consider the usual instructional practice of having students read brief stories and then having them select a suitable main idea (sometimes title) from a list of choices (Hare & Milligan, 1984; Winograd & Brennan, 1983). Students are told, "The main idea is what the story is about" or "The main idea is the most important idea." Those students who have trouble picking out the correct answer are exhorted to try and try again on another story until, presumably, they achieve success. Duffy and Roehler (1982) contend that this "repeated exposures" model of instruction reduces teaching to directing a series of practice sessions. We have always felt that repeated practice with very easy exercises as a means of helping students identify main ideas is inadequate, but until very recently, few alternatives for teaching have been available to teachers.

Fortunately, we can use the results from recent main idea studies to design lessons for teaching main idea comprehension. (We suspect Durkin's, 1978-1979, evaluation of current comprehension instruction practices provided the impetus for many of these studies.) The instructional lessons described in this chapter focus on the critical, how-to aspects of main idea understanding. Taken as a set, we see these lessons as offering teachers a sensible alternative to repeated exposures for helping students find main ideas in texts.

We have divided our lessons into two sections. The first section consists of three lessons to be taught according to a discovery approach, whereas lessons in the second section are taught by way of direct instruction. We expect most school children to have had experiences with text forms, particularly narratives. When possible, we would prefer to capitalize upon the knowledge acquired about stories and other texts as a result of these experiences. By using a discovery approach, known to be compatible with problem solving objectives (Peterson, 1979), we can urge students to use their existing knowledge to help them formulate their own ideas about main idea comprehension. We believe, nevertheless, that certain important information is best conveyed directly by teachers to students. Hence, we recommend instruction combining discovery and direct approaches to maximize students' understanding of importance in text. All the lessons may be adapted to any grade level and can be used at any stage in the instructional sequence. Furthermore, the lessons are not tied to a particular commercial program. In the subsequent discussion, we explain the discovery lessons in greater detail, for we have observed that it can take longer to lead students to induce their own principles for comprehension than to tell them directly how to comprehend (Hare & Borchardt, 1984).

Hare and Bingham

Discovery Lessons

We anticipate that students will actively induce three major concepts from these lessons. First, they will recognize that a one-to-one correspondence between main ideas and texts does not always exist; that is, they will become aware that texts have hierarchies of ideas and that top level ideas are considered important or main ideas. Second, they may begin to recognize the distinction between textual and contextual relevance (Adler & Van Doren, 1972; van Dijk, 1979). *Textual relevance* refers to the reader's assignment of relevance on the basis of structural grounds. At the microstructure level, relevance is described in terms of "information distribution concepts" such as topic and comment; at the macrostructure level, relevance is described in terms of major topics. Textual relevance is signaled by graphic, phonological, syntactic, lexical, semantic, and other cues. *Contextual relevance,* on the other hand, refers to the reader's assignment of relevance on the basis of his/her personal cognitive and social context, including characteristics such as interest, attention, knowledge, and wishes. van Dijk (1979, p. 125) refers to contextual relevance as "what the actual reader finds important now." Third, students will begin to understand how systematic structural differences between narrative and expository texts influence the selection of important ideas. The three discovery lessons follow.

Lesson 1. Develop a blueprint for understanding the structure of important ideas in narratives (stories).

Students already possess tacit knowledge of story organization when they come to school (Stein & Glenn, 1979). We can take advantage of this knowledge to help them recognize that many important ideas comprise a story, and thereby rid them of the erroneous notion that every story has one and only one main idea. The importance blueprint in Figure 1 illustrates component parts of narratives with which most children are already familiar, and the relationship of the parts to the generation of important ideas. Using this blueprint with the discovery method takes advantage of children's implicit knowledge of story parts.

The importance blueprint for narratives lends itself to a variety of discovery teaching techniques. We have developed one instructional task analysis to accompany the blueprint, based on our classroom teaching experiences. Task analysis is a technique appropriate to problem solving or the discovery method.

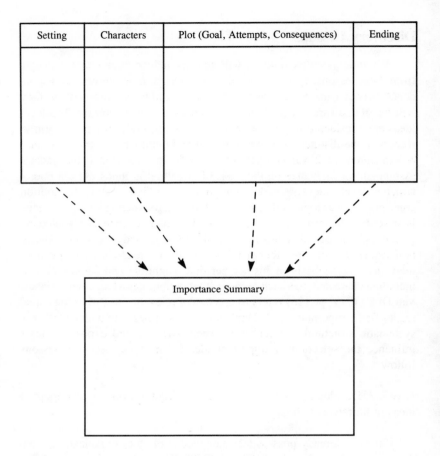

Setting	Characters	Plot (Goal, Attempts, Consequences)	Ending

Importance Summary

Figure 1. Blueprint for locating importance in narratives.

Task Analysis for Developing a Blueprint for Importance in Narratives

I. INTRODUCTION

A. Display the blueprint on the chalkboard or on chart paper. You could distribute copies of the blueprint to children.

B. Discuss each category in the blueprint. Ask students to tell what they think each category means, and provide corrective feedback. Select examples from familiar stories for each category except the importance summary. Well known fairy tales are good selections; stories which the whole class has recently heard are also suitable.

C. Write the category examples on the blueprint.

Hare and Bingham

II. INSTRUCTION

A. *Directions*

1. Have students look at the importance blueprint, and tell them the story that they are now going to read follows this blueprint.
2. Explain that after reading the story, they will help match the parts of the story to the blueprint.
3. Provide appropriate background for the story and then have the students read the story.

B. *Teacher/Student Interaction Sequence*

1. Ask for volunteers to describe the story, and jot their ideas on the chalkboard.
2. Ask clarifying questions if necessary. Encourage thinking aloud.
3. Select one of the student's ideas and write it in the appropriate category on a display blueprint, or ask a student to categorize the idea.
4. Ask for reasons why the idea was placed in that category.
5. Continue this procedure until children's ideas are placed in all the categories. Elicit relevant discussion and justification for category placements during this procedure.
6. Have children examine the completed blueprint categories.
7. Next, without necessarily referring to the blueprint, ask children for the most important ideas and the reasons for their choices. Encourage alternate important ideas.
8. Discuss the reasons and explicitly point out any divergence of opinions about important ideas.
9. Match the important ideas to the categories and/or focus on ideas from specific categories which contribute to the most important ideas.
10. Write the most important ideas in the importance summary. Tell students to read the importance summary to themselves, and to see if it makes sense.
11. Elicit conclusions, for example, strategies that students used in locating importance in stories. When possible, students should try to identify their own strategies and information learned.

During the teacher/student interaction sequence, the children should observe that what is important for one student may not be important for another student. They should hypothesize about why this may be so.

Developmental/instructional effects may mediate students' selection of important ideas in stories. For example, Bingham, Rembold, and Yussen (in press) noted that children's selections of main idea statements for stories were quite consistently different from adults' selections. Brown and Smiley (1977) also found developmental/instructional effects in sensitivity to structural importance. Teachers can help students recognize situations when assignments of relevance are dictated by personal interests as opposed to relevance assignments on the basis of structural characteristics. They may also help students discuss and think about the appropriateness of either kind of relevance assignment on the basis of particular situations.

Developing an importance blueprint for narratives can be used as an independent or group activity once the children are familiar with the process. Students can also teach their discovery or problem solving methods to other children.

Lesson 2. Develop a blueprint for understanding the structure of important ideas in comparison/contrast expository text.

Because the universe of possible expository text types is larger than the one for narrative text types, and because many students are insensitive to expository structure (McGee, 1982), we recommend dealing with only one expository text type at a time. The comparison/contrast structure is illustrated here. Comparison/contrast exposition may be borrowed from, but not limited to, passages in content textbooks or commercial materials such as Barnell Loft's *Specific Skills Series*. Local news or weather stories or television programs also supply possible examples of comparison/contrast exposition. As is true for stories, the more familiar the content and the more relevant the comparison/contrast selection, the more adept students will be at locating important ideas. The blueprint for the comparison/contrast structure appears in Figure 2.

The concepts of *comparison* and *contrast* may be unfamiliar to some students. Therefore, explicitly relate the concepts *same/comparison* and *different/contrast* for the readers. In the discovery method, it is effective to have students provide examples illustrating these concepts. Students should see that two or more clusters of information are related either by their similarities or by their differences on various attributes (Bartlett, 1980).

The importance blueprint for the comparison/contrast structure can also be used with a variety of discovery teaching techniques. Our experiences again suggested a task analysis to accompany this blueprint.

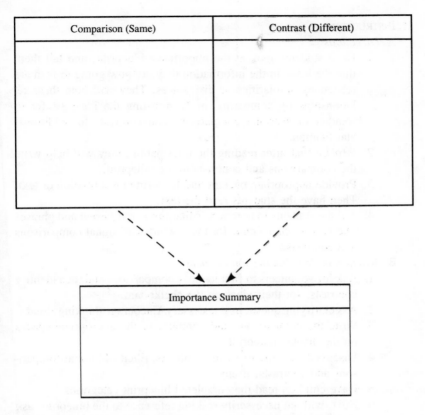

Comparison (Same)	Contrast (Different)

Importance Summary

Figure 2. Blueprint for locating importance in a comparison/contrast structure.

Task Analysis for Developing a Blueprint for Importance in a Comparison/Contrast Structure

I. INTRODUCTION
  A. Display the blueprint on the chalkboard or on chart paper. You could distribute copies of the blueprint to children.
  B. Discuss both concept categories in the blueprint. Be sure to include the *same* and *different* relationships. Provide written examples from content texts or newspapers. Have children generate additional examples.

II. INSTRUCTION

A. *Directions*

1. Have students look at the importance blueprint, and tell them that the ideas in the information they are now going to read are related by similarities or differences. They will note these relationships by comparing and contrasting the ideas. Refer to weather or seasonal comparisons and contrasts for additional clarification.
2. Explain that after reading the information, they will help write the comparisons and contrasts in the blueprint.
3. Provide appropriate background for written information or text. Then have the students read the text.
4. Tell the students to note words like *same* or *different* and phrases like *on the other hand,* for these words can signal comparisons and contrasts.

B. *Teacher/Student Interaction Sequence*

1. Ask for volunteers to first identify comparisons and then identify contrasts. Jot their ideas on the chalkboard.
2. Ask clarifying questions if necessary. Encourage thinking aloud.
3. Write the comparisons and contrasts in the appropriate spaces on the display blueprint.
4. Discuss the comparisons and contrasts. Elicit additional comparisons and contrasts, if any.
5. Have children read the completed blueprint categories.
6. Next, without necessarily making reference to the blueprint, ask children for the most important ideas and the reasons for their choices.
7. Discuss the reasons and explicitly point out any differences of opinions about important ideas.
8. Write the most important ideas in the importance summary. Tell students to read the summary to themselves and to see if it makes sense.
9. Compare the important ideas selected by children with the ideas in the comparison and contrast categories.
10. Discuss the usefulness of employing the blueprint to understand important ideas.
11. Elicit conclusions, for example, strategies that were used in locating importance in textual information. Also, elicit what students believe they have learned from the process.

Because students are less familiar with expository text structures, at times, teachers may need to think aloud (see Afflerbach & Johnston, Chapter 3, this volume) for students the process of determining important ideas for the comparison/contrast blueprint. Think alouds by proficient comprehenders can serve as models for less proficient readers. Main ideas—especially implicit ones—are often hard to comprehend, even for experts (Afflerbach & Johnston, Chapter 3, this volume; Brown & Day, 1983; Hare & Borchardt, 1984). Describing why certain ideas seem more important than others is extremely difficult; indeed, expert readers find it difficult to explain how they arrived at their main idea decisions (Campione & Armbruster, 1985). However, the discovery process facilitates students' ability to describe their reasoning. Younger and/or less proficient students may, however, initially benefit from explicit how-to advice in these lessons.

Again, developmental/instructional effects may influence students' assignments of importance. For example, Meyer, Brandt, and Bluth (1980) suggest that use of text structures may develop in the following sequence: 1) stories, 2) description, 3) antecedent/consequent, 4) problem/solution, and 5) comparison. Also, Winograd (1984) found that eighth grade students were more likely to recall interesting, highly visual bits of information than they were to recall information rated important by adults. In other words, they had not yet separated the concepts of textual relevance and contextual relevance. This finding emphasizes the need to teach students to think about their reasons for locating importance. It may be that the reasons are related to either textual or contextual relevance, that is, characteristics of the text and characteristics of the reader.

The comparison/contrast blueprint can also be used as an independent or group activity once the children are familiar with the process. Blueprints for additional expository text structures and task analyses can be designed and implemented in a similar manner.

Lesson 3. Provide students with additional opportunities to practice using narrative and expository blueprints for identifying important ideas.

This lesson should be presented after students have acquired a working understanding of both narrative and expository structures. In this lesson, students receive practice in classifying information into either narrative or expository blueprint categories. Have students listen to or read selected portions of stories and informational texts presented one at a time. Clear exemplars as well as less clear exemplars should be presented (e.g., expository texts containing implicit main ideas, short stories of the kind found in early basal reader main idea exercises). Students must decide whether the information belongs with the narrative or expository blueprint, or to both. They must then justify their responses by making reference to the information itself and to particular structural categories within the relevant blueprint. In this way, students may learn about main idea comprehension from one another, and teachers may learn where students lack understanding. During this activity, teachers must be careful to evaluate students' understanding of text structures correctly, to sequence teaching activities appropriately, and to choose reading materials carefully. Other sequences for extending understanding of importance blueprints may be planned according to group or individual needs.

Direct Instruction Lessons

The following lessons contain information that must be taught directly to students. These lessons apply primarily to, but are not limited to, expository texts.

Lesson 1. Familiarize students with unknown concepts and information in text.

Consider the following text:

> Because the within-subjects design really does allow the "all else being equal" assumption in interpretation, one should not expect as much variability within subjects as exists between them. However, one can expect effects which are less contaminated by extraneous variables. Furthermore, the number of observations involved in the within-subject side of this study is three times that for the between-subjects side. Since the analysis is consequently less likely to "overfit" the data (that is, repeated samples are likely to yield very similar findings), the variables tend to explain less dramatic but more reliable proportions of variance. (Johnston, 1984, p. 226)

Searching for main ideas in this passage could be frustrating, if the reader were unfamiliar with experimental design and analyses. Young readers frequently experience the same frustration when the concepts and information in text are unfamiliar to them. All ideas seem equally important or unimportant. Therefore, evaluate students' prior knowledge, and where prior knowledge is insufficient, provide the necessary experiences. Advance organizers (Ausubel, 1978) are useful techniques for preparing students to read text which contains unfamiliar ideas or information. Advance organizers can define concepts or generalizations. They can also make use of analogies that compare new information with known information. For example, a social studies unit on the Louisiana Territory might include living on haciendas, or large estates. Known features of cattle ranches could be used to compare haciendas to ranches. Advance organizers can take a linguistic form, like the one just given, or they can be presented in a graphic form such as a structured overview.

Lesson 2. Teach students to recognize different text structures with their idiosyncratic main ideas.

Because students often are not familiar with structures for expository texts, which is not the case for stories, we consider it necessary to teach students directly about different expository text structures. Bartlett (1980) suggests discussing the general topic of patterns in organizing texts before discussing the specifics of typical expository structures. He and others have identified major text structures (called macrostructures) such as problem/solution, cause/effect, comparison/contrast, and enumeration or listing. Students then apply this specific knowledge in seeking the presence of given structures in texts. Where structure is perceived to be absent, students can be encouraged to provide an implicit structure. Of course, this procedure applies best to well written texts. Providing students with a map of the hierarchy of text should enable them to recognize top level ideas. For instance, given a problem/solution text, students can be taught to seek the sentence or sentences which explicitly summarize both the problem and the solution. Or, when main ideas are implied, students can formulate their own statements of the perceived problem and solution. Students who already intuitively discriminate among different macrostructures may be urged to apply their knowledge to finding main ideas (Barnett, 1984).

Lesson 3. Judiciously encourage students to use the intuitive "Aha-So What" test for determining main ideas in expository materials.

Pearson and Johnson (1978) suggest if an idea seems to provide some general rule or way of looking at the world ("a meaningful conclusion, generalization, or rule about an event, type of event, or kind of behavior," p.91), then students might accord the idea an *Aha* rating. If, on the other hand, the idea seems relatively unimportant, then they might award the *So what* rating. We endorse teaching students this test because it breaks students away from the belief that every single printed idea is meaningful. However, if students possess markedly different notions of importance than adults' notions of importance, or if students have insufficient prerequisite background knowledge for understanding the text, the strategy will not be effective. Readers need to be aware of the previously mentioned distinction between textual and contextual importance, as well as possess the necessary prior knowledge for adequate text comprehension, before applying the Aha/ So What test. Because development may be involved in children's determinations of importance, however, this test may be more suitable for older or more proficient readers.

Lesson 4. Show older students how to find main ideas in real world passages.

Main idea comprehension instruction needs to consider unpredictable text structures as well as predictable text structures. Telling students how to transfer a strategy is absolutely necessary (Belmont & Butterfield, 1977). In school, students usually demonstrate proficiency with locating main ideas in predictable text structures, as in the following four sentence text, of which the first sentence is a topic sentence summary of the next three example sentences:

> There are so many kinds of balls. One kind is a basketball. Another kind is a football. Still another is a ping-pong ball.

Following simple activities of this sort, have students refer to their social studies or science textbooks which have less predictable text structures, turn to a random passage, and together discuss how to locate main ideas for that passage. The second task greatly differs from the first task. A teacher cannot fairly evaluate the adequacy of prior main idea comprehension instruction without including functional reading activities. Students will quickly discover those painfully long stretches of text which have nothing important to say but which endlessly chain details, or they will confront texts with no clear structure, explicit or implicit. Readers may also find texts which combine several structures. In these events, teachers can suggest or model additional hints in applying strategies developed for contrived texts to real school texts.

Restructuring Basal Main Idea Lessons

We wish to present one additional set of guidelines related to restructuring basal reader main idea lessons to students' advantage. We believe it is important to mention these guidelines, because main idea instruction as it exists in basal reader manuals is the prevalent way of informing students about main idea comprehension. We believe instruction can be improved in at least five ways.

First, mass or teach together haphazardly spaced main idea lessons to provide sufficient explanation and review of explanation (Baumann, 1984). Surprisingly few main idea related explanations are appropriate for teaching in basal reader manuals (Hare & Milligan, 1984), which contain infrequent review opportunities. Children who miss a lesson or two may have to wait until the following year before main idea explanations occur again. Teaching several basal lessons together as a unit may enhance students' understanding. Concomitantly, checking for students' maintenance of main idea skills should take place regularly.

Second, favor generation over recognition activities. Most main idea exercises in basal reader manuals and workbooks are recognition activities; that is, students are asked to read a text and then select the main idea of the text from a list of alternatives. From our experience, poor comprehenders are especially inclined to use a meaningless process of elimination to make a best guess. Sometimes, the main idea appears in the text as a topic sentence and appears again as a multiple choice alternative. In these instances, you should disregard the superfluous multiple choices. Instead of using the multiple choice recognition tasks as presented in the basal, cover the choices and force students to generate their own main ideas for texts. Not only does main idea generation more closely approximate functional tasks, but researchers note that generation leads to significantly better memory for text than does rating the understandability of text (Bridge et al., 1984). Students should know that reasonable variation in their main idea responses is acceptable and may even be preferred to the uniformity of response required by a recognition activity. In addition, generation activities are more likely to reveal students' thinking processes for teachers.

Third, recognize camouflaged main idea questions for what they are not. All basal reader manuals provide questions that accompany stories and articles. Commonly, these questions are labeled by skill, e.g., "'What did So-and-So vow never to do again?' (main idea)." By interspersing questions such as this one before, during, and after text reading, we can be deluded into thinking we have taught main ideas, when we actually have not. Unless connections are made explictly with the term *main ideas,* students who answer camouflaged main idea questions will be no more able to apply this knowledge to other main idea identification assignments than students who have not answered such questions.

Fourth, be on guard for misleading or unhelpful advice which will leave students feeling confused. Inaccurate information will not help students comprehend main ideas. For example, it is frequently suggested that a topic sentence is usually the first sentence in a paragraph, although Baumann and Serra (1984) demonstrated that only 27 percent of all the paragraphs they examined in second, fourth, sixth, and eighth grade social studies textbooks began with an explicitly stated main idea. Similar inaccurate comments will frustrate students. Many explanations for finding implicit main ideas are examples of unhelpful advice. These explanations are inadequate because they describe practices, not processes. Comments such as, "Think about the meaning of the piece to yourself," are not only worthless, but may needlessly instill a sense of discouragement in students who do not know what "the meaning" refers to.

Finally, be wary of teaching students that titles express main ideas. At best, titles will denote topics, not main ideas (see Aulls, Chapter 5, this volume). In addition, using titles to infer importance in narratives and expository texts can be risky. People who choose titles for texts hope to entice others to read their texts; therefore, considerations such as catchiness may enter into selecting a title. Main ideas can hardly be inferred from titles like "The Mud Ponies."

Many of these same guidelines apply when using other commercial materials on main idea such as black line masters, workbooks, kits, games, and computer software. In other words, when feasible and possible, we recommend that users of such ancillary materials: 1) mass such lessons or activities so students receive a sufficient quantity of material on main idea; 2) require students to generate responses—as opposed to simply recognize responses—whenever possible; 3) adapt or extend any main idea questions so they are effective instructional tools; 4) omit, revise, or adapt misleading instruction or advice; and 5) be cautious when using titles in teaching main ideas and inform students that titles usually specify only the topic of a passage and not the main idea.

Conclusion

In this chapter, we have presented lessons for teaching readers to understand importance in text. The lessons reflect the results of recent main idea research. For example, our lessons incorporate the evidence for a hierarchy of text ideas, as well as the strong relationship between importance in text and the structure of text. Discovery lessons, including blueprints and task analyses, and direct instruction lessons were presented, for we believe methodology should match readers' and teachers' needs and goals. The lessons were designed to be flexible; therefore, they can be used in a variety of sequences, with different classroom organizational plans and with a range of proficiency levels. These lessons and the guidelines for restructuring basal reader main idea lessons, we believe, can be used to expand existing main idea comprehension instructional programs.

References

Adler, M.J., and Van Doren, C. *How to read a book,* revised. New York: Simon and Schuster, 1972.

Ausubel, D.P. In defense of advance organizers: A reply to the critics. *Review of Educational Research,* 1978, *48,* 251-257.

Barnett, J.E. Facilitating retention through instruction about text structure. *Journal of Reading Bahavior,* 1984, *16,* 1-13.

Bartlett, B.J. *So this is the main idea: Where use of an author's top-level structure helps a reader.* Paper presented at the Eighth World Congress in Reading, Manila, Philippines, August 1980.

Baumann, J.F. The effectiveness of a direct instruction paradigm for teaching main idea comprehension. *Reading Research Quarterly,* 1984, *20,* 93-115.

Baumann, J.F., and Serra, J.K. The frequency and placement of main ideas in children's social studies textbooks: A modified replication of Braddock's research on topic sentences. *Journal of Reading Behavior,* 1984, *16,* 27-40.

Belmont, J.M., and Butterfield, E.C. The instructional approach to developmental cognitive research. In R.V. Kail, Jr., and J.W. Hagen (Eds.), *Perspectives on the development of memory and cognition.* Hillsdale, NJ: Erlbaum, 1977, 437-481.

Bingham, A.B., Rembold, K.L., and Yussen, S.R., Developmental change in identifying main ideas in picture stories. *Applied Developmental Psychology,* in press.

Boning, R.A. *Specific skills series.* Baldwin, NY: Barnell Loft, 1976.

Bridge, C.A., Belmore, S.M., Moskow, S.P., Cohen, S., and Matthews, P.D. Topicalization and memory for main ideas in prose. *Journal of Reading Behavior,* 1984, *16,* 61-80.

Brown, A.L., and Day, J.D. Macrorules for summarizing texts: The development of expertise. *Journal of Verbal Learning and Verbal Behavior,* 1983, *22,* 1-14.

Brown, A.L., and Smiley, S.S. Rating the importance of structural units of prose passages: A problem of metacognitive development. *Child Development,* 1977, *48,* 1-8.

Campione, J.C., and Armbruster, B.B. Acquiring information from texts: An analysis of four approaches. In J. Segal, S. Chipman, and R. Glaser (Eds.), *Thinking and learning skills: Relating instruction to research.* Hillsdale, NJ: Erlbaum, 1985, 317-359.

Duffy, G.G., and Roehler, L.R. Commentary: The illusion of instruction. *Reading Research Quarterly,* 1982, *17,* 438-445.

Durkin, D. What classroom observations reveal about reading comprehension instruction. *Reading Research Quarterly,* 1978-1979, *14,* 481-533.

Hare, V.C., and Borchardt, K.M. Direct instruction of summarization skills. *Reading Research Quarterly,* 1984, *20,* 62-78.

Hare, V.C., and Milligan, B. Main idea identification: Instructional explanations in four basal reader series. *Journal of Reading Behavior,* 1984, *16,* 189-204.

Johnston, P. Prior knowledge and reading comprehension test bias. *Reading Research Quarterly,* 1984, *19,* 219-239.

McGee, L.M. Awareness of text structure: Effects on children's recall of expository text. *Reading Research Quarterly,* 1982, *17,* 581-590.

Meyer, B.J.F. *The organization of prose and its effects on memory.* Amsterdam: North-Holland Publishing, 1975.

Meyer, B.J.F., Brandt, D.M., and Bluth, G.J. Use of top level structure in text: Key for reading comprehension of ninth grade students. *Reading Research Quarterly,* 1980, *16,* 72-103.

Pearson, P.D., and Johnson, D.D. *Teaching reading comprehension.* New York: Holt, Rinehart and Winston, 1978.

Peterson, P.L. Direct instruction reconsidered. In P.L. Peterson and H.J. Walberg (Eds.), *Research on teaching: Concepts, findings, and implications.* Berkeley, CA: McCutchan, 1979, 57-69.

Stein, N.L., and Glenn, C.G. An analysis of story comprehension in elementary school children. In R.O. Freedle (Ed.), *Advances in discourse processes, vol. 2: New directions in discourse processing.* Norwood, NJ: Ablex, 1979, 53-120.

van Dijk, T.A. Relevance assignment in discourse comprehension. *Discourse Processes,* 1979, *2,* 113-126.

Winograd, P.N. Strategic difficulties in summarizing text. *Reading Research Quarterly,* 1984, *19,* 404-425.

Winograd, P.N., and Brennan, S. Main idea instruction in the basal readers. In J.A. Niles and L.A. Harris (Eds.), *Searches for meaning in reading/language processing and instruction.* Rochester, NY: National Reading Conference, 1983, 80-86.

8

Teaching Middle Grade Students to Summarize Content Textbook Material

Barbara M. Taylor

In this chapter, Barbara Taylor focuses on the need for middle grade students to comprehend important information in content textbook material. After discussing how textbook material ought to be read, the author documents the difficulty middle grade students have in summarizing (stating the main points concisely) textbook passages. Given the need for instruction in summarization ability, Taylor presents three techniques for teaching students to summarize textbook material: hierarchical summarizing, cooperative summarizing, and mapping. She explains and describes each strategy and provides empirical support for its effectiveness.

The title of this chapter suggests that we should be teaching students in grades five through eight how to summarize content textbook material. Since middle grade students typically receive little reading instruction during content area lessons (see Durkin, 1978-1979) and generally are not taught how to summarize textbook selections, one might ask why we should teach middle grade students this skill.

How Textbook Material Ought to Be Read

Students will need to summarize throughout their formal schooling. After reading informative text, students should be able to form a gist of important ideas. Readers obviously cannot remember everything they read at any one time but should comprehend and be able to remember the important ideas. According to van Dijk and Kintsch (1983), who have studied text comprehension extensively, skilled readers do, in fact, form a gist of important information after reading and studying text. In other words, if skilled adult readers, such as college students, read three pages in a textbook and are asked to summarize what they have read, they will tend to remember the important ideas constituting a gist of the three pages (see Afflerbach & Johnston, Chapter 3, this volume). For example, after reading about Turkey or Israel in a social studies book, undergraduate students enrolled in a reading/language arts methods course wrote summaries similar to the following two examples (important information is italicized):

> *Turkey. The nation of Turkey, a country of the middle lands, was once part of the large Ottoman Empire.* The city of Istanbul still reveals its past greatness by the ancient buildings in its modern skyline. *The Turkish Empire began to lose strength in the 19th century. The real modernization of Turkey began after World War I under the rule of Mustafa.*
>
> *Mustafa stressed Westernization and modernization of Turkey and hoped one day to see it become a democracy. Today Turkey shows many of the attributes of a modern nation.* Its resources, if utilized properly, could potentially make Turkey even stronger. *Agriculture in many areas of Turkey still lags far behind. With government help, however, this too may soon see modernization.*

> *Israel. Israel is the only country in the Middle East where there's enough schooling for everyone.* Israel is developing industries, but they need capital, *so people from all over the world are donating money to help. Eighty-five percent of the people live in the cities.*
>
> *Israel doesn't have much farmland, yet its farmers are able to produce most of the food necessary to feed its population. Israel is reclaiming land from the Jordan valley swamplands, the desert, and by terracing hillsides.* Israel is also working on turning seawater into fresh water which can be used for irrigation.
>
> *Israel became a nation in 1948 but since then has been fighting with the Palestinians over the land. In 1978 a peace treaty was established, but many are still not happy with it.*

The above summaries reflect the mental gist two undergraduate students formed after reading and studying several pages from a social studies textbook. In general, the summaries contain important ideas, not trivial details.

Middle Grade Students' Difficulty in Summarizing

Unlike experienced adult readers, however, students in the middle grades generally are not skilled comprehenders of textbook material (Baumann, 1983; Taylor et al., 1985) and specifically are not skilled in summarizing textbook selections (Brown & Day, 1983). Many middle grade students form almost no mental gist, even of unimportant information, after reading several pages in a textbook. Consequently, these students are unable to write or tell much at all when asked to summarize the important ideas of what they have just read. Many other middle grade students form a gist comprising unconnected ideas and unimportant details as opposed to important information.

To illustrate children's difficulty with summarizing, sixteen sixth grade students reading on or above grade level were asked to read, study, and then immediately summarize four pages on Turkey from their social studies book. (The same passage on Turkey was read by the college students discussed above.) The passage discussed the Ottoman empire, the founding of modern Turkey, and life in modern Turkey. Ten of the sixteen students included three ideas or less in their summaries. The remaining six students averaged eight ideas in their summaries, but only three of these ideas, on the average, were considered important. Similarly, a different group of sixteen sixth grade students from the same school, also reading on or above grade level, were asked to read, study, and summarize a three page section from their textbook on Israel (the same passage read by the college students). The passage discussed cities in Israel, farming in Israel, and Israel's military problems. Five of the sixteen students wrote three ideas or less in their summaries. The remaining eleven students averaged six ideas in their summaries, but only four important ideas.

Typical summaries by the sixth graders of the two passages are presented below. Both summaries were written by students reading at a high level (96th to 98th national percentile), as measured by the Iowa Test of Basic Skills.

Student A
Ataturk was a ruler. He made many changes in the Turkish ways. Turks used to write from right to left. *He passed a law that the Turkish people had to write from left to right.* He prohibited newspapers so they would not ridicule and criticize government ways. He put people in jail who expressed their opinion about him. He was cruel to others.

The village of Constantinople's roads had inns every 18 miles. That's how far a caravan can go. Over a million acres of Turkey's land is either too wet, too dry, or has too much trash on it to farm.

Student B
Israel is one of the few countries that educates all of its children. Israel is located just off the Mediterranean.
One million acres of Israel is dry land that swamps, lakes, rivers, and marshes are irrigating for farming.
For many years there was a war about who should inhabit Israel. In 1970 they passed a peace treaty. But there are still problems.

Important ideas in the previous summaries are italicized. (Important ideas were identified on the basis of judgments from three adult judges. The nonitalicized ideas that appear important resulted from students' background knowledge instead of from the text.) As you can see, particularly in comparison with the college students, the two sixth grade students have included relatively little important information in their summaries. The summaries suggest that the two students did not comprehend the passages very well or completely.

A number of possible reasons may account for middle grade students' difficulty summarizing textbook material. Students may read a textbook selection as a series of unconnected sentences instead of as a coherent whole (Taylor & Samuels, 1983). Or students may remember details because the details are more concrete or of higher imagery value than many of the main ideas. Alternatively, students simply may not have been taught that one purpose of textbook reading is to comprehend and remember important information. Or, they may not have been taught how to read for important information.

If middle grade students are taught one or more strategies for summarizing textbook material, they should learn in the process that a common goal of textbook reading is to understand and to remember important ideas in the material they have read. Additionally, by learning a strategy for summarizing textbook material, students should learn *how* to read for important information.

I hope you are convinced that summarizing textbook material is an important reading skill, and that middle grade students are not very good at this skill and so need instruction in summarizing. In the remainder of the chapter, I will present several summarization strategies which I have found to be effective in improving middle grade students' ability to comprehend and remember important ideas after reading content textbook selections.

The Need for Direct Instruction in Summarizing

We cannot expect students to acquire summarization skills on their own, nor simply tell them to summarize to themselves what they have read. Research has demonstrated that simply telling students to use a particular study strategy, such as outlining or underlining, is not effective; students must be taught to use a particular study strategy (Anderson & Armbruster, 1984). Therefore, we must provide students with direct, explicit instruction in summarizing textbook material and with opportunity for practice. This instruction might occur during time set aside for reading or during a content class like social studies, science, or health.

Hierarchical Summarizing

One effective summarizing technique is hierarchical summarizing. A hierarchical summary is like an outline in appearance. However, the approach to creating a hierarchical summary is somewhat different from that of outlining. An example is presented below.

A Hierarchical Summary for a Social
Studies Textbook Selection on Egypt

A. *Egypt depends on the Nile.*
  1. The Aswan High Dam is important because it provides water for irrigation and electricity.
  2. Most of the people of Egypt live in the Nile Valley.
B. *Cairo is a mixture of the old and new.*
  1. It is one of the largest cities in the Mideast.
  2. It has tall buildings, new factories, and people in Western dress.
  3. It also has people in ancient dress, an old marketplace, and ancient crafts.
C. *Farm families live and work in ways similar to ancient times although modernization is taking place.*
  1. People live in mud huts and often use animals instead of machines.
  2. Some changes are taking place like use of machines, electricity, and farmer ownership of land.
D. *Egypt leaders are working on Egypt problems.*
  1. Both Nasser and Sadat wanted Egypt to be independent of foreign control and influence.
  2. A big problem being worked on is that Egypt does not have enough food.
  3. Egypt is developing as an industrial nation.

Explanation of the technique. The hierarchical summary technique is most useful with textbook material organized according to headings. Students first skim three to four pages, reading the headings contained in the section. They make a skeleton outline using a capital letter for every subsection designated by a heading, leaving space for three or four sentences between capital letters. Then, students read the material, subsection by subsection. They should read a subsection more than once because summarizing a text is hard after one reading (van Dijk and Kintsch, 1983). For every subsection, students select two or three words from the heading, but no more than two or three words, that reflect the topic of the subsection. They turn the two or three words into a main idea sentence that reflects the most important idea about the topic, and they underline this main idea sentence. Then, they write two or three detail sentences that tell more about the main idea and are important to remember. Tell students to write no more than two or three important detail sentences so they are selective. Otherwise, many will write down almost everything in a subsection.

Also tell students to write main idea and important detail sentences in their own words. In fact, stress that students are not to copy from the book. Although looking back at the book is certainly permissible, students might be told to close their books whenever they are going to write a sentence on their skeleton outline to help them avoid the temptation to copy.

Generating sentences, as opposed to copying, is important in terms of enhanced reading comprehension (Bridge et al., 1984; Doctorow, Wittrock, & Marks, 1978; Taylor & Berkowitz, 1980). Students are more likely to understand better and, hopefully, remember better what they have read if they have come up with main idea and important detail sentences in their own words.

After reading and summarizing one subsection, students should go on to the next subsection and repeat the above procedure. At the end, they are to write one or two sentences at the top of the page which reflect the main idea of the entire section.

Upon completing their hierarchical summary, students must study it. To give students a purpose for "practicing" studying, I have found having students study with a partner to be effective. After reading over their summaries several times and saying to themselves what they have written, students can tell a partner the important ideas they have read about, as included on their summary. The partner can point out any omitted ideas. Then, roles can be reversed.

Hierarchical summarizing should not be seen as something students do, at least in written form, every time they read several pages in a textbook.

By teaching them to summarize in this manner, however, we are showing them one effective way to read and study textbook material in which they pick out important information. They might practice summarizing in this way in their heads when they read in their textbooks. For particularly difficult or unfamiliar material, they might actually take the time to write out a hierarchical summary.

Suggestions for instruction. I have explained in some detail the steps to follow to write and study a hierarchical summary. Next I will provide a few suggestions for teaching this technique to students. When introducing the hierarchical summary technique, present a sample of a hierarchical summary for a textbook selection which the students recently read. Explain 1) *what* the hierarchical summary is (about 10 or 12 sentences reflecting the most important ideas in a three to four page section in the textbook); 2) *why* the technique is useful (to teach students how to read for and remember the important ideas in their textbooks); and 3) *when* they might use the technique (with a particularly difficult textbook selection, or mentally after becoming skilled at the technique).

Then demonstrate, or model, for the students how to make and study a hierarchical summary according to the steps presented above. Along with good main idea statements, present poor main idea statements for contrast. Also contrast important with unimportant details.

For subsequent lessons, work with students to make several hierarchical summaries for textbook selections. Each time, do a little less with the students and have them do a little more on their own. Then, review what students have done on their own in a group discussion. For example, volunteers could read what they put down for main ideas or important details for subsections, and the appropriateness of these ideas could be discussed. Students could also compare their hierarchical summaries to one you prepared on an overhead transparency.

I have found that a minimum of five or six one hour sessions is necessary to get fifth and sixth grade students to the point where they can make adequate hierarchical summaries on their own. Beyond this, they still have room for improvement. Nevertheless, in a relatively short period of time, you can teach middle grade students a rather complex reading study strategy. After the initial set of lessons, periodically ask students to write and study hierarchical summaries for textbook sections currently being covered to help them maintain this study strategy.

Research support. The hierarchical summarizing procedure has been found to be effective in several studies. Taylor (1982) worked closely with four fifth grade teachers who either taught their students how to summarize and study sections in their health textbook or worked with them on answering questions and studying their questions and answers. After either making and studying a hierarchical summary or answering and studying practice questions, students who learned the hierarchical summary procedure reasonably well after seven one hour sessions had better recall of health material and equally good scores on short answer test questions as students who had answered and studied practice questions for seven sessions. The same effect was found to transfer to social studies material.

In a second study Taylor and Beach (1984) worked closely with two seventh grade teachers who taught one-third of their students to summarize and study sections in a social studies textbook. The other students either received instruction in how to answer questions on the social studies material and study the questions and answers or received no special instruction in studying. Results indicated that the hierarchical summary procedure enhanced students' recall for relatively unfamiliar social studies material. The same effect was not found, however, with material judged by the students to be relatively familiar.

Preinstruction and postinstruction examples of students' performance in summarizing. In addition to the research support just cited, the following examples illustrate gains in summarizing which middle grade students made in a relatively short period of time. Sixth grade students in a suburban Minneapolis elementary school were asked to read and study a four page section on Egypt from their social studies book. They were asked to summarize the material in paragraph form the following day. (An example of a summary was presented to the students.) Following five one hour sessions in the hierarchical summary procedure, the students were asked to make and study a hierarchical summary after reading a four page section on London in their social studies book. The students again were asked to summarize the material in paragraph form the following day.

Summaries of the passages on Egypt and London written by Students C and D follow. The summaries of the Egypt passage were written before instruction; the summaries for the London passage were written after students had received instruction in summarizing. The passage on Egypt discussed the Aswan High Dam and the Nile River, life in Cairo, life in the country, and Egypt's problems. The passage on London discussed London as a large business center, the Thames River, the people of London, and the expansion of London within and outside the city limits. Student C was reading on a 6.6 grade level and perceived the contents of both passages to be relatively unfamiliar. Student D was reading on an 8.7

grade level and perceived the contents of both passages to be somewhat familiar. Important information is italicized.

Student C

Egypt Summary

Egypt is an Arab country growing fast. For quite some time people were invading and trying to conquer and rule, but finally they got their independence back. Cairo, their capital city, is located on the Red Sea.

The Suez Canal is in Egypt.

I remember something about a city danger by rising water and making higher dams to save the city.

London Summary

London has a big part in stocks and bonds. Most people do thousands of dollars during the day. Then at dinner time they also do some business. Some do billions of dollars.

One river that runs through London is the Thames. It has many famous sites on it like the Clock Tower which houses Big Ben, London's famous timekeeper. *Another famous site is Westminster Abbey.*

There are many different nationalities. *People live there from all over the world like India and Africa.* But this causes one of their many problems over population.

The government is starting new towns outside the green belt. The green belt is a long strip of land just outside London which is nothing else except green grass, and the government wants to preserve it.

Old London never had many tall buildings until now. *There is a new skyscraper right next to St. Paul's Cathedral.* So they are trying to grow up instead of out.

Student D

Egypt Summary

Egypt is very, very old. In Egypt there are pyramids that are very old. Egypt is sometimes known for its government. A man named Nasser was elected and he died in 1970.

Egypt has many old statues. Lots and lots of people live in Egypt. Egypt is a very hot and dry place to live. Egypt doesn't get much rain.

Egypt is located in Africa. Egypt is a very beautiful place and it's very well known.

London is one of the world's largest cities. It is a capital city three times over. More than 1/6 of England's people live in London. *London has changed a great deal in the past few years. Now people of many nationalities live in London.* London's people built many tall buildings and changed London's skyline a great deal. London is still changing. *London is also known for its very clean air. The people of London also cleaned up the once polluted Thames River.* London has many fine foods and drink. Many people come from all over the world to see London.

Comparisons of these two sets of summaries written before and after instruction clearly reveal improvements in both students' ability to read for, remember, and write down important information from sections in their social studies book. In fact, neither student recalled any important information from the passage on Egypt as determined by three adult judges. Both students did include, however, a fair number of important ideas in their summaries of the passage on London.

Their post instruction summaries could have been more complete and contained less unimportant information. Nevertheless, the important point is that some improvement in the difficult skill of summarizing appears to have been made after only five instructional sessions dealing with the hierarchical summary procedure.

Cooperative Summarizing

Cooperative summarizing is a variation of the hierarchical summary procedure. As the name suggests, cooperative summarizing involves working together on a learning task; that is, it involves cooperative learning. Although underused in our classrooms, cooperative learning has been found to be a powerful approach to learning (R. Johnson & Johnson, 1983). In fact, students have been found to make greater gains in achievement when involved in cooperative learning tasks than when involved in competitive or individualistic learning tasks (Johnson et al., 1981).

D. Johnson and Johnson (1983, p. 146) reason that "the discussion process in cooperative groups promotes the discovery and development of higher quality cognitive strategies for learning than does the individual reasoning found in competitive and individualistic learning situation." Group reasoning and discussion can be a powerful asset in the preparation of a hierarchical summary.

Explanation of the technique. In a cooperative learning task, students work together, take turns and listen to one another, share ideas, praise and help each other, and make sure that everyone participates. Cooperative learning can be applied to the hierarchical summary procedure in the following manner.

Students are divided into heterogeneous groups of three. They take turns reading aloud the subsections from a three to four page segment of their content textbook. As one reads a subsection, the other two follow along. Then, students as a group select two or three words from the heading of the subsection that they feel represent the topic. They take turns giving a main idea sentence on the topic and then together come up with one best main idea sentence in their own words for the subsection. Everyone in the group writes this down. They each suggest two details from the subsection which they feel elaborate on the main idea and are important to remember. As a group, they decide on two or three sentences, again in their own words, which they feel best reflect important ideas. Everyone in the group writes this on a skeleton outline. The same procedure is repeated for every subsection in the reading selection. At the end, the group comes up with one or two sentences which best reflect the main idea of the entire selection. Students then study their hierarchical summaries and take turns reciting this information and giving feedback to one another on omitted information.

Suggestions for instruction. In cooperative learning tasks, all students must participate, work together, and help each other. Situations in which one student does all the work for the group or in which students sit together in a group and are free to talk but do their own work are not cooperative groups (R. Johnson & Johnson, 1983). So, when engaged in cooperative summarizing, all members of the group must offer their ideas, discuss these ideas, and help each other come up with what they feel are the best main idea and important detail statements for subsections of text.

In addition to giving students feedback about the quality of their hierarchical summaries, the teacher must give them feedback about their performance in cooperative groups. Basic cooperative behaviors need to be specified and monitored, and the extent to which these behaviors are being used needs to be discussed. More detail on setting up cooperative learning tasks and on structuring cooperative groups can be found in Johnson and Johnson (1975) and Johnson and Johnson (1982).

Mapping

Mapping is another approach to summarizing which has been found to be effective (Berkowitz, 1982). A map is different from a hierarchical summary in that it is composed of important key words instead of main idea and important detail sentences. Although it is less similar to the mental gist a reader should form while reading informative text, an advantage of a map is that it involves less writing. Therefore, a map will take less time for students to make and use. Also, the technique has been designed for use with informative text which is not organized according to headings. An example of a map is presented in Figure 1. This map presents information from a social studies textbook selection on Egypt.

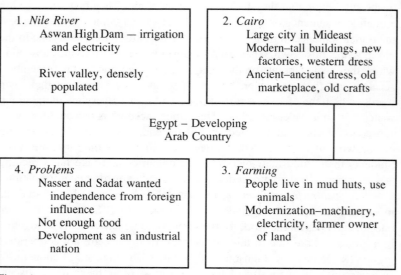

Figure 1. A map for a social studies textbook selection on Egypt.

Explanation of the technique. To make a map, students first read a three to four page selection in their content textbook. They write the title of the selection in a box in the middle of a blank sheet of paper turned so that the long sides are along the top and bottom. Then, students skim the selection to pick out what they feel are the main topics. The topics, numbered and underlined, are written in a clockwise direction around the center box. Then, students skim the selection again to pick out from two to four details on each topic which they feel are important to remember. They write these details in phrases instead of complete sentences to minimize the amount of writing. A box is drawn around each topic and its important details.

After making a map, students are instructed to study it. To do this, they are told to read each topic and the information under it. Then they are to say the information to themselves and look back to see if they remembered the ideas correctly. After studying, pairs of students take turns telling one another all they can remember from reading the textbook selection and studying their maps.

Suggestions for instruction. As with the hierarchical summary procedure, the teacher needs to explain *what* the mapping technique consists of, *why* it is useful, and *when* to use it. When introducing the technique, the teacher should model for students *how* to make and study a map. On subsequent lessons, the teacher and students should make several maps together. Each time the teacher should do less with the students and have them do more of the mapping, perhaps providing a sample map to which students can compare their own maps. However, the teacher should stress that no two maps will look exactly the same so that students don't get frustrated when their maps don't look like the sample map provided by the teacher.

Research support. Berkowitz (1982) conducted a study on mapping with four fifth grade teachers. The teachers worked with their students in one of the following conditions using social studies textbook material: making and studying a map, studying a teacher made map, answering questions, rereading. After six one hour sessions, students who received instruction in making and studying maps had better recall for social studies material when using the mapping technique than students in the other conditions. The results in this particular study, however, were limited to a passage judged by adults to be particularly easy to map because it was organized according to several explicit categories. The same results were not found with a passage judged to be less easy to map due to the fact that the organization of the passage was less clear.

With more practice, middle grade students might be able to successfully map textbook selections which were not particularly well organized. Also, the mapping technique, like the hierarchical summary procedure, could be used with textbook material organized according to headings. Used in this manner, maps should be easier to make than when used with material containing no headings.

Summary

Teaching middle grade students to summarize textbook material is just one of a number of ways to help them better comprehend and remember what they have read in their textbooks. Other study strategies, such as self questionings (Andre & Anderson, 1978-1979), reciprocal teaching (Palincsar, 1982), and networking (Dansereau, 1979) have also been found to be effective (see Anderson & Armbruster, 1984, for a review).

One advantage of a study strategy like summarizing is that it focuses readers' attention on important information. While learning to summarize, middle grade students may realize that one common goal of textbook reading is to pick out and remember important information. Many middle grade students appear to read their textbooks as if they are unaware of this goal. By learning one of the summarizing strategies presented in this chapter, students will have an explicit procedure to follow to help them read textbook material for important information.

References

Anderson, T.H., and Armbruster, B.B. *Studying*. In P.D. Pearson (Ed.), *Handbook of reading research*. New York: Longman, 1984, 657-679.

Andre, M.E.D.A., and Anderson, T.H. The development and evaluation of a self-questioning study technique. *Reading Research Quarterly*, 1978-1979, *14*, 605-623.

Baumann, J.F. Childrens ability to comprehend main ideas in content textbooks. *Reading World*, 1983, *22*, 322-331.

Berkowitz, S.J. *The effects of instruction in text organization on middle school students' memory for expository reading*. Unpublished doctoral dissertation, University of Minnesota, 1982.

Bridge, C.A., Belmore, S.M., Moskow, S.P., Cohen, S.S., and Matthews, P.D. Topicalization and memory for main ideas in prose. *Journal of Reading Behavior*, 1984, *16*, 61-80.

Brown, A.L., and Day, J.D. Macrorules for summarizing texts: The development of expertise. *Journal of Verbal Learning and Verbal Behavior*, 1983, *22*, 1-14.

Dansereau, D.F. Development and evaluation of a learning strategy training program. *Journal of Educational Psychology*, 1979, *71*, 64-73.

Doctorow, M., Wittrock, M.C., and Marks, C. Generative processes in reading comprehension. *Journal of Educational Psychology*, 1978, *70*, 109-118.

Durkin, D. What classroom observations reveal about reading comprehension instruction. *Reading Research Quarterly*, 1978-1979, *14*, 481-533.

Johnson, D.W., and Johnson, F. *Joining together: Group theory and group skills*, second edition. Englewood Cliffs, NJ: Prentice-Hall, 1982.

Johnson, D.W., and Johnson, R.T. *Learning together and alone: Cooperation, competition, and individualization*. Englewood Cliffs, NJ: Prentice-Hall, 1975.

Johnson, D.W., and Johnson, R.T. The socialization and achievement crisis: Are cooperative learning experiences the solution? In L.Bickman (Ed.), *Applied social psychology annual 4*. Beverly Hills, CA: Sage Publications, 1983, 119-164.

Johnson, D.W., Maruyama, G.M., Johnson, R.T., Nelson, D., and Skon, L. Effects of cooperative, competitive, and individualistic goal structures on achievement: A meta-analysis. *Psychological Bulletin*, 1981, *89*, 47-62.

Johnson, R.T., and Johnson, D.W. *Cooperation in learning: Ignored but powerful.* Unpublished paper, University of Minnesota, 1983.

Palincsar, A. *Improving the reading comprehension of junior high students through the reciprocal teaching of comprehensive-monitoring strategies.* Unpublished doctoral dissertation, University of Illinois, 1982.

Taylor, B.M. Text structure and children's comprehension and memory for expository material. *Journal of Educational Psychology,* 1982, *74,* 323-340.

Taylor, B.M., and Beach, R.W. The effects of text structure instruction on middle grade students' comprehension and production of expository text. *Reading Research Quarterly,* 1984, *19,* 134-146.

Taylor, B.M., and Berkowitz, S.B. Facilitating children's comprehension of content material. In M.L. Kamil and A.J. Moe (Eds.), *Perspectives in reading research and instruction.* Clemson, SC: National Reading Conference, 1980, 64-68.

Taylor, B.M., Olsen, V., Prenn, M., Rybczynski, M., and Zakaluk, B. A comparison of students' ability to read for main ideas in social studies textbooks and to complete main idea worksheet. *Reading World,* 1985, *24,* 10-15.

Taylor, B.M., and Samuels, S.J. Children's use of text structure in the recall of expository material. *American Educational Research Journal,* 1983, *20,* 517-528.

van Dijk, T.A., and Kintsch, W. *Strategies of discourse comprehension.* New York: Academic, 1983.

9

Graphic Organizers: Cuing Devices for Comprehending and Remembering Main Ideas

Donna E. Alvermann

To help middle grade and secondary students comprehend main ideas in content textbook material, Donna Alvermann recommends the use of a graphic organizer: a visual device that cues the relationship between superordinate and subordinate information in a passage. After providing a rationale for the use of graphic organizers, Alvermann describes and presents examples of three different types of graphic organizers: a restructuring organizer, a lookback organizer, and an organizer plus summarizing. She also discusses extensions of graphic organizers—lesson organizers and thematic organizers.

A prerequisite for teaching students how to study and learn from text is specific instruction in identifying important ideas. It is quite obvious, for instance, as Brown and Smiley (1977) observed, that "children who have difficulty determining the keypoints of a passage can hardly be expected to select them for intensive study" (p. 7). The problem for most teachers lies not in accepting the obvious, but rather, in locating appropriate strategies for helping students distinguish differences among important and less important ideas.

According to Durkin's research (1981), teacher manuals that accompany basal reader programs offer few such strategies. Perhaps the manuals tend to focus on main idea *practice* at the expense of main idea *instruction* for the simple reason that educators themselves cannot agree on what it means to get the main idea (cf., Harris & Hodges, 1981; Moore & Cunningham, Chapter 1, this volume; Pearson & Johnson, 1978). Not surprisingly, evidence suggests that this general lack of agreement is reflected in students' conceptions of the main idea (Moore, Cunningham, & Rudisill, 1983).

While this chapter does not purport to offer a solution (assuming one exists) to the several problems besetting main idea instruction (Baumann & Serra, 1984; Winograd & Brennan, 1983), it does offer some practical guidance to teachers who are interested in helping students use the structure of their texts to separate important from less important ideas. As Brown and Smiley (1977) noted, that is an important first step. The procedure presented in this chapter for improving students' main idea comprehension ability is the *graphic organizer*, which is a device for cuing the reader about the relation of superordinate (more important) to subordinate (less important) textual information.

Getting Started

The graphic organizer in Figure 1 illustrates how the information in this chapter will be presented. Study it carefully, noting the relationship of superordinate to subordinate information. Then try to state in one sentence what you think this chapter *mainly* will be about.

The intent of the foregoing activity was twofold. First, it seemed a natural way to introduce the concept of a prereading graphic organizer, sometimes referred to as a *structured overview,* and second, it provided an opportunity to illustrate different interpretations of what it means to get the main idea. For instance, if you said the chapter would be mainly about

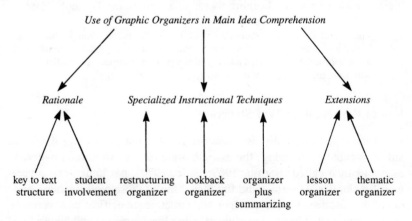

Figure 1. Graphic organizer for Chapter 9.

how to use graphic organizers in main idea comprehension, your interpretation of getting the main idea would resemble what Moore and others (1983) have defined as a *topic main idea*. On the other hand, if you said the chapter would be mostly about developing a rationale for applying specialized graphic organizers and their extensions to main idea comprehension, you would have interpreted getting the main idea to mean what they defined as a *gist main idea*. Either or both of these interpretations would be correct, although finding the main idea is an activity more commonly associated with paragraph length material than with an entire chapter. (Refer to Chapter 1 of this volume for a comprehensive discussion of the varying definitions of main idea.)

Graphic Organizers and Main Idea Comprehension: A Rationale

A variety of adjunct aids can help students learn from text. Among those that have received most of the attention in the research literature are questioning (Anderson & Biddle, 1975; Frase, 1967) and the use of advance organizers (Ausubel, 1963; Luiten, Ames, & Ackerson, 1980). Closely related to the concept of an advance organizer is the graphic organizer. The two differ in that the advance organizer uses prose while the graphic organizer, like Hanf's mapping strategy (1971), arranges information in hierarchical order while keeping words to a minimum. To quote Hanf:

> The effect is that of perceptual comprehension rather than verbal. Instead of reading the information, one *sees* it. The gestalt, seeing the whole and all its related parts, yields a powerful impact, immediate comprehension and easy retention. (p. 226)

Key to Representing Text Structure

Developed originally as a teacher constructed prereading device to aid in vocabulary learning, the graphic organizer, or structured overview as it was then called (Barron, 1969; Earle, 1970), has undergone several modifications in its format and function. One of those modifications grew out of the past decade of research on text structure. Specifically, Alvermann (1981) constructed graphic organizers using lines, arrows, and hierarchical ordering of ideas to represent a text's organizational structure. At least four organizational structures are commonly found in subject matter textbooks. These include simple listing (a series of subordinate ideas related to a superordinate idea but not themselves ordered according to importance or consequence), time ordering, comparison/contrast, and cause/effect (Herber, 1978; Meyer, 1979; Niles, 1965).

To illustrate how a graphic organizer can serve as a cuing device for helping readers distinguish differences among important and less important ideas in text, consider the following passage from *The Making of Our America* (1974, pp. 238-241), a fourth grade social studies textbook. Figure 2 then presents a graphic organizer constructed to reflect the passage's simple listing organizational structure.

Farmers Come to the Plains*

Before the Transcontinental Railroad was finished the United States government made a law about the unsettled land. The law said a person who lived on some land and farmed it for five years could own the land. The government gave the land to the farmer.

The people knew that pioneering on the Great Plains would be different from pioneering in the other regions. This did not make them give up. They had the pioneer spirit. They thought they could conquer the Plains as they had conquered the woodlands. And they did. Thousands of pioneers went to the Plains to claim the free land....

Since they had no wood, these pioneers built their houses of earth. Wherever the grass grew, the earth was very tough. The roots of the grass held the earth together. This covering of grass and earth was called sod. To build homes, the pioneers cut big chunks of sod. Then they piled the sod up like bricks.... Most pioneers hung buffalo skins over the doorways. They made their roofs of sod.

Getting fuel was a big problem. Some pioneers tied grass into tight bundles and burned it. Others used buffalo chips. These chips were the dried droppings of buffalo. Later, when most of the buffalo were killed off, the pioneers grew sunflowers. Their wood stems made good fuel....

Water was the biggest problem on the Great Plains. You know how much water your family uses every day. What if you had to go several miles to a stream every time you needed water? That is what the Plains pioneers had to do. When it rained, pioneers put all their pots and pans outside to catch the drops.

The settlers dug wells as soon as they could. Sometimes they had to dig hundreds of feet into dry earth before they struck water. Windmills were used for power to pump the water out of the wells.

*From *Concepts and Inquiry: The Educational Research Council Social Science Program/The Making of Our America*, Learner-Verified Edition II. Copyright © 1974 by the Educational Research Council of America. Reprinted with permission of Allyn and Bacon, Inc., the publisher.

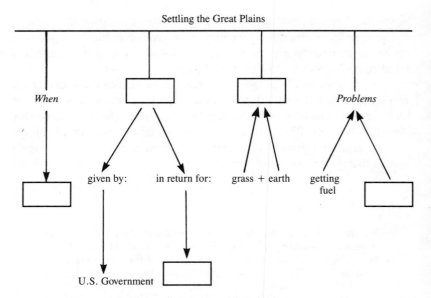

Figure 2. Modified (cloze type) graphic organizer.

Student Involvement

Note that the graphic organizer in Figure 2 is only partially complete. The organizer's missing pieces of information are represented by empty slots which are joined by lines and arrows and arranged spatially to indicate how superordinate and subordinate ideas are related. Students study a partially completed organizer before reading the corresponding portion of their textbook in order to see how the author has structured the information. Then, during or immediately after reading students fill in the missing information. In effect, this procedure is a type of cloze activity not unlike the one Gordon and Braun (1983) developed for helping students understand the structure of narrative prose.

This type of graphic organizer is appealing for several reasons. In addition to actively involving readers in a search for missing superordinate/subordinate information, the cloze graphic organizer, with its paucity of words, has special motivational appeal for less skilled readers. This type of organizer also has the potential to increase recall for what is read. For example, in Figure 2, remembering that "getting fuel" was one of the problems Plains farmers faced would likely trigger recall of the second

Alvermann

problem, "getting water." Finally, if teachers construct cloze graphic organizers with a view to helping students remember what is important in text (and if they test accordingly), the completed organizers will greatly simplify the studying process.

Specialized Graphic Organizers and Main Idea Comprehension

Before describing some of the more specialized types of graphic organizers, I should point out that the effectiveness of graphic organizer instruction is based on a limited number of studies, the results of which are mixed (e.g., Moore & Readence, 1980, 1983). But even with these limitations some classroom implications are worth noting.

First, the length of time devoted to organizer instruction appears to make a difference in young children's ability to perform well on a transfer task. Alvermann, Boothby, and Wolfe (1984), for example, found that fourth graders who received instruction in how to use graphic organizers with their social studies text for 14 consecutive school days recalled significantly more main ideas on a transfer passage than did similar groups of students who received either seven days of training or none at all. Researchers also generally report greater effects for graphic organizers that students construct (as opposed to teachers) after reading (as opposed to before reading) (Bean et al., 1983; Moore & Readence, 1980). One final note of caution pertains to the generalizability of these findings to text other than exposition. Almost without exception, graphic organizers have been used with informative, textbook passages rather than with narrative material. If, therefore, as Aulls (1978, Chapter 5, this volume) and others contend, there are major differences in identifying main ideas in expository and narrative texts, one would not expect the effects of graphic organizers used with expository texts to be the same as those used with narrative texts.

What follows is a three part overview of graphic organizers thought to be particularly useful in fostering students' ability to distinguish differences among important and less important ideas. Excerpts from the textbook passages used in the respective studies, or in some cases the full passage, are included with each organizer to provide you the text needed to interpret each organizer. A complete set of directions for constructing a cloze graphic organizer is also included, but only for the first organizer study.

Restructuring Organizer

The idea for a graphic organizer that would help students restructure text written in a poorly organized manner grew out of three dissertation studies (Alvermann, 1980; Bartlett, 1979; Brandt, 1978). Working from the premise that students should be able to recall superordinate information written in a comparison/contrast structure more easily than that written in a simple list fashion, Alvermann (1982) constructed a cloze graphic organizer which encouraged students to restructure the author's original organizational plan. An example of this organizer (see Figure 3), including directions for its construction, can be found following the passage, "Loss of Body Water." As you read this passage, pay particular attention to its simple listing organizational structure; that is, note how a series of subordinate ideas, listed in random order, are related to a superordinate idea but not to one another.

Loss of Body Water*

Several aspects of the loss of body water will be discussed in this article. First, the loss of body water is frequently required by athletic coaches of wrestlers, boxers, judo contestants, karate contestants, and 150-pound football team members so that they will reach specified body weights. These specified weights are a lot less than the athletes' normal weights. Second, loss of body water for athletes is strongly condemned by the doctors of America each year. Third, loss of body water hurts the body. More specifically, a loss of three percent of body water hurts physical performance and a loss of five percent results in heat exhaustion. Moreover, a loss of seven percent of body water causes hallucinations. Losses of ten percent or more of body water result in heat stroke, deep coma, and convulsions; if not treated, death will result.

The procedure used to construct the graphic organizer for the preceding passage is as follows:

1. "Loss of Body Water" was examined to determine if the author had used a simple listing organizational plan in writing it. That is, was a general statement supported by a number of less important statements listed in no particular order?
2. All important words related to the topic (loss of body water in athletes) were written on separate index cards. These were then arranged and

*This passage was adapted from one used by Brandt (1978) and Meyer (1977).

rearranged a number of times until a comparison/contrast structure emerged.
3. Certain words were omitted, and empty slots were substituted in their place. Choosing which words to replace with empty slots was a matter of personal preference once the following guidelines were satisfied.
   a) The topic (loss of body water in athletes) had to remain intact.
   b) Empty boxes were substituted for words that were parallel to each other. For example, the term *doctors* was replaced by an empty box because it was parallel to *coaches* (see Figure 3).
4. The completed organizer was then transferred from index cards to an overhead transparency from which individual copies were made for students.
5. Before reading the passage, the students were told the purpose of the organizer (to help them distinguish among important and less important ideas). They were also told that keeping the graphic organizer's comparison/contrast organizational plan in mind would help them identify and later recall important information from the passage.
6. After students filled in the missing information, they discussed the graphic organizer. A statement of the main idea was derived from the completed organizer: Coaches and doctors disagree about the loss of body water in athletes.

The thirty tenth grade subjects in the study that involved the above passage and organizer were assigned randomly to one of the two treatment groups (fifteen used the graphic organizer and fifteen did not). An assistant who trained the graphic organizer group in the strategy followed steps 1 to 6. Students in the no graphic organizer group were engaged in the usual pre and postreading activities of their regular class. The results suggested that students' recall of important information was positively influenced by the restructuring activity. Evidence suggested that the superimposed comparison/contrast structure may have served to cue students' memory; for example, remembering what the coaches found helpful about loss of body water appeared to trigger students' recall of what doctors found harmful.

Although the usefulness of the restructuring organizer outside an experimental setting is still being tested, several suggestions seem warranted. As soon as possible, teachers need to involve students in the construction of their own graphic organizers. Initially, this might mean asking students to supply the words in Step 2 of the procedure outlined. Through their

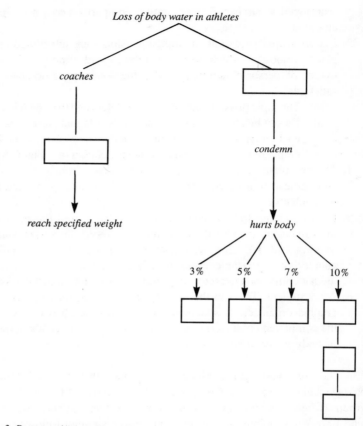

Figure 3. Restructuring graphic organizer.

responses, a teacher may gain a better understanding of what is or is not known about a particular topic. As students take on more and more of the responsibility for constructing their own organizers, the teacher may suggest that they pair up and trade graphic organizers so that each student tests the other's organizer. In addition to its motivational effect, this type of activity would seem to demonstrate to students that graphic organizers can make the textbook a viable source of personal learning.

Lookback Organizer

The lookback organizer, as its name would suggest, is concerned with inducing intentional rereadings of segments of text for the purpose of locating answers to questions (the questions may be generated by teacher or student). Though seemingly a simple strategy, lookback behavior is not employed evenly across different age and ability groups. Research has shown, for instance, that older proficient readers engage in lookback behaviors more frequently than younger readers (Garner & Reis, 1981), and good comprehenders employ lookbacks more often than poorer comprehenders (Garner et al., 1984). What is encouraging about the lookback strategy is that it has been shown to have facilitative effects on studying (Alessi, Anderson, & Goetz, 1979). Also, Garner and her colleagues (Garner & Reis, 1981; Garner et al., 1984) have shown repeatedly that lookback behaviors can be increased significantly with training.

This latter research finding — success in training students to use lookbacks — prompted Alvermann and VanArnam (1984) to explore the feasibility of using the graphic organizer to help high school students locate important ideas once read but not remembered. The results of this study suggested that low ability comprehenders (but not high ability comprehenders) who received graphic organizer instruction performed significantly better on a multiple choice posttest than did subjects in the control group. Excerpts from the 998 word historical essay used in the experiment are presented below. Figure 4 presents the lookback organizer that corresponds to this passage.

In order to understand the nature of the lookback organizer and its function in helping students distinguish among the important and less important ideas in text, it helps to think of this particular type of graphic organizer as being a kind of road map. That is, students should be told to use the lookback organizer to guide their search for answers to questions over material once read but subsequently forgotten. Emphasize its useful-

---

LOUIS XIV: THE ANATOMY OF ABSOLUTISM

In 1643, at the age of five, Louis XIV became King of France. In 1661, Cardinal Mazarin, Louis' chief minister, died, and the king took control of the affairs of the state....

Like other absolute rulers, Louis thought of the nation as his personal estate and its inhabitants as his obedient children....

Louis' clothing — flowing cloaks, high heeled shoes, and broadbrimmed hats with waving ostrich plumes — emphasized his regality. He wore wigs made of dark hair with rows of curls falling over the shoulders. The sun, source of light and life, became Louis' personal emblem. Flatterers called him the "Sun King," and they said he strongly resembled Apollo, the Greek god of the sun...

page 1

Socially, Louis surrounded himself with the aristocracy. But the key to his political success lay in the bourgeoisie. To run his government, the king selected men from the wealthy middle class who depended on him for social and political advancement....

The king used a number of committees as an aid in running the government. These committees held frequent meetings which the king usually led. But though committee members discussed policy and gave advice, they never voted. Louis alone made the final decisions. Then his royal ministers sent these decisions to provincial administrators called intendants. Because the intendants represented the royal will and reported to the king, they had full power over local officials. Town councils and nobles, who claimed political rights given them by ancient charters and tradition, were helpless against them. This total control of the state by the king characterized seventeenth century absolutism....

Jean Baptiste Colbert, Louis' most important minister, was a member of the bourgeoisie. Colbert adopted the economic policies of mercantilism and reorganized the economic life of France to serve the state. To achieve the main goal of mercantilism—filling the royal treasury—Colbert had to make France economically self-sufficient. He developed new industries which were protected by tariffs and strictly regulated....

page 2

Louis poured the income brought in by Colbert's policies into the glitter of Versailles and into the building of a modern army and navy. The French army numbered 100,000 in peacetime, the largest in the seventeenth century, and it reached four times that size during Louis' wars....

Alarmed at his expansion, England led the opposition to Louis. The fighting spread beyond Europe to the English and French colonies in Asia, the West Indies, and North America. Louis' extremism, his ambition, and his self-infatuation led him to wage war on such a grand scale that he eventually exhausted his mighty army as well as his overflowing treasury....

page 3

Excerpted by permission from *The Shaping of Western Society: An Inquiry Approach*, by Edwin Fenton and John M. Good. Copyright © 1974 by Holt, Rinehart and Winston, Publishers. All rights reserved.

ness as a study strategy for pinpointing important, as opposed to less important, ideas. Finally, it is desirable to introduce this type of organizer to a class using an overhead transparency made up of several overlays that correspond with several *pages* of poorly signaled text. In short, the lookback organizer should not be used with paragraph length material or with text that already contains sufficient signaling (e.g., text segmented by numerous headings and subheadings). Both of the criteria for using a lookback graphic organizer are met in the historical essay on Louis XIV (Fenton & Good, 1974).

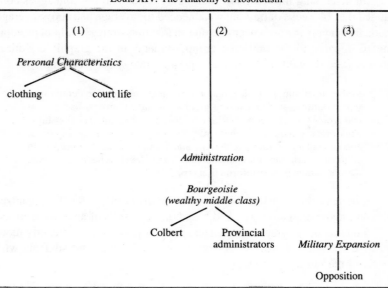

Louis XIV: The Anatomy of Absolutism

      (1)   (2)   (3)

Personal Characteristics

clothing   court life

Administration

Bourgeoisie
(wealthy middle class)

Colbert   Provincial
administrators   *Military Expansion*

Opposition

Key:
(1) Refers to overhead transparency overlay that accompanied page 1 of the passage.
(2) Refers to overhead transparency overlay that accompanied page 2 of the passage.
(3) Refers to overhead transparency overlay that accompanied page 3 of the passage.

Figure 4. Lookback organizer.

Organizer Plus Summarizing

Another variation on the graphic organizer theme—organizer plus summarizing—was explored by Bean and others (1983). They compared the effect of outlining instruction versus graphic organizer instruction on tenth graders' comprehension of a world history text. In addition, they compared students' attitudes toward the two types of instruction, paying particular attention to whether students expressed a desire to use either of the two strategies in other classes.

Their study called for students to construct graphic organizers. In the first step of the procedure, students selected a topic sentence that tied together subordinately stated ideas. Step two required students to construct their own graphic organizers in a manner that reflected how they believed important and less important ideas were related.[1] Finally, step three involved summarizing; that is, students were expected to derive a main idea or summary statement based on the information displayed in their graphic organizers.

In discussing the results of their study, Bean and his colleagues concluded that 14 weeks of training were needed for average and above average students to apply the organizer plus summarization strategy without prompting. Compared to the outlining group, students in the graphic organizer groups were thought to develop a superior strategy for studying:

> Rather than simply listing major ideas and subordinate details in a linear outline, students in the graphic organizer groups had to sort and reconstruct text concepts in order to depict their interrelationships. This process required higher order thinking and, as a consequence, encouraged integration, retention, and retrieval of text concepts. In contrast, outlining may encourage lower level rehearsal or rote memorization of text information. (p. 20)

The researchers also found a modest transfer effect for the organizer plus summarization strategy. And based on the results of an attitude measure, students in the graphic organizer group displayed a significantly more positive attitude toward the strategy they learned than did students who received the outlining strategy.

Extensions of the Graphic Organizer Concept

A variety of instructional strategies exists under the rubric organizer. Two that seem to hold particular appeal for educators concerned with the teaching of main idea comprehension are the lesson organizer and the thematic organizer. A summary of both of these organizers concludes the present chapter

Lesson Organizer

Not surprisingly, when teachers make the relationships among the different parts of a lesson explicit, students' achievement is positively affected. Kallison's research (1984) supports this notion and provides support for the idea that a lesson organizer might produce similar effects if used in conjunction with whole class discussion.

Specifically, a graphic organizer (which incorporated the major points a teacher wanted to cover in a discussion of previously assigned material) might focus students' attention on important information, thus lessening the chances of their becoming mired in the details. And, if the information in this lesson organizer were to be formatted in a manner similar to that of the graphic organizer developed by Bean et al. (1983), students would be privy both to the direction of the discussion and to the teacher's thinking on what is important. Figure 5 provides an example of a lesson organizer that might accompany a discussion on Louis XIV: The Anatomy of Absolutism.

Thematic Organizer

Although numerous researchers have investigated the effectiveness of various prereading instructional strategies on students' ability to learn from text, none have developed a strategy with more useful applications to remedial reading than Risko and Alvarez (1983; Alvarez and Risko, 1984). Their work with the thematic organizer has spanned a wide range of ages among poor readers — fourth through sixth graders, junior high school students, and college age students. In almost every instance, their findings suggest that thematic organizers do facilitate and expand conceptual learning of expository texts.

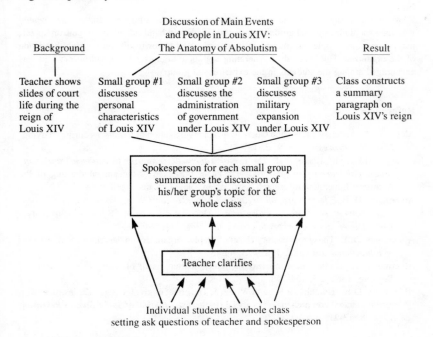

Figure 5. Lesson organizer.

Directions for constructing a thematic organizer, unlike those of its predecessor the advance organizer, have been clearly defined. Designed to activate students' prior knowledge about a specific concept and to relate this knowledge to the central theme of a passage, a thematic organizer consists of two parts. The first part contains several paragraphs that define the implied concept and relate this concept to a reader's background of experiences. The second part contains a set of statements written on the interpretive level. Readers are expected to indicate their agreement (or lack of agreement) with each of the statements during or after reading a related passage.

In summary, the thematic organizer, like each of the other organizers presented in this chapter, can be easily adapted for use in a variety of settings. However, the focus of the present chapter has been on the versatility of organizers within a specific setting, that is, classrooms in which teachers are primarily concerned with helping readers distinguish among important and less important ideas in expository text.

Note

[1] An interesting side note is the fact that the teacher in Bean's research group experimented with the idea of placing background information on the left hand side of the graphic organizer, main events and people information in the middle, and major results on the right hand side of the organizer. This method of generating a graphic organizer for world history text was encouraged among the students in the experimental group.

References

Alessi, S.M., Anderson, T.H., and Goetz, E.T. An investigation of lookbacks during studying. *Discourse Processes*, 1979, *2*, 197-212.

Alvarez, M.C., and Risko, V.J. *The use of a thematic organizer to enhance transfer of conceptual learning in poor readers*. Paper presented at the annual meeting of the American Educational Research Association, New Orleans, April 1984.

Alvermann, D. E. *Effects of graphic organizers, textual organization, and reading comprehension level on recall of expository prose*. Doctoral dissertation, Syracuse University, 1980. *Dissertation Abstracts International*, 1980, *41*, 3963A.

Alvermann, D. E. The compensatory effect of graphic organizers on descriptive text. *Journal of Educational Research*, 1981, *75*, 44-48.

Alvermann, D. E. Restructuring text facilitates written recall of main ideas. *Journal of Reading*, 1982, *25*, 754-758.

Alvermann, D.E., Boothby, P.R., and Wolfe, J. The effect of graphic organizer instruction on fourth graders' comprehension of social studies text. *Journal of Social Studies Research*, 1984, *8*, 13-21.

Alvermann, D.E., and Van Arnam, S. *Effects of spontaneous and induced lookbacks on self-perceived high and low ability comprehenders.* Paper presented at the annual meeting of the American Educational Research Association, New Orleans, April 1984.

Anderson, R.C., and Biddle, W.B. On asking people questions about what they are reading. In G.H. Bower (Ed.), *The psychology of learning and motivation*, vol. 9. New York: Academic Press. 1975.

Aulls, M. W. *Developmental and remedial reading in the middle grades.* Boston: Allyn and Bacon, 1978.

Ausubel, D. P. *The psychology of meaningful verbal learning.* New York: Grune and Stratton, 1963.

Barron, R.F. The use of vocabulary as an advance organizer. In H.L. Herber and P.L. Sanders (Eds.), *Research in reading in the content areas: First year report.* Syracuse, NY: Syracuse University, Reading and Language Arts Center, 1969.

Bartlett, B. J. *Top-level structure as an organizational strategy for recall of classroom text.* Doctoral dissertation, Arizona State University, 1978. *Dissertation Abstracts International,* 1979, *39,* 6641A.

Baumann, J. F., and Serra, J. K. The frequency and placement of main ideas in children's social studies textbooks: A modified replication of Braddock's research on topic sentences. *Journal of Reading Behavior,* 1984, *16,* 27-40.

Bean, T.W., Singer, H., Sorter, J., and Frazee, C. *Direct instruction in metacognitive strategies: Cumulative instruction in summarization and graphic organizer construction vs. graphic organizer alone vs. an outlining strategy in tenth grade world history.* Technical Report No. 6. Fullerton, CA: California State University, 1983.

Brandt, D. M. *Prior knowledge of the author's schema and the comprehension of prose.* Unpublished doctoral dissertation, Arizona State University, Tempe, 1978.

Brown, A. L., and Smiley, S. S. Rating the importance of structural units of prose passages: A problem of metacognitive development. *Child Development,* 1977, *48,* 1-8.

Durkin, D. Reading comprehension instruction in five basal reader series. *Reading Research Quarterly,* 1981, *16,* 515-544.

Earle, R. A. *The use of vocabulary as a structured overview in seventh grade mathematics.* Unpublished doctoral dissertation, Syracuse University, 1970.

Fenton, E., and Good, J. M. *The shaping of western society: An inquiry approach.* New York: Holt, Rinehart, and Winston, 1974.

Frase, L. T. Learning from prose material: Length of passage, knowledge of results, and position of questions. *Journal of Educational Psychology,* 1967, *58,* 266-272.

Garner, R., Hare, V. C., Alexander, P., Haynes, J., and Winograd, P. N. Inducing use of text lookback strategy among unsuccessful readers. *American Educational Research Journal,* 1984, *21,* 789-798.

Garner, R., and Reis, R. Monitoring and resolving comprehension obstacles: An investigation of spontaneous text lookbacks among uppergrade good and poor comprehenders. *Reading Research Quarterly,* 1981, *16,* 569-582.

Gordon, C. J., and Braun, C. *Teaching story schema: Metatextual aid to reading and writing.* Paper presented at the American Educational Research Association, Montreal, April 1983.

Hanf, M. B. Mapping: A technique for translating reading into thinking. *Journal of Reading,* 1971, *14,* 225-230.

Harris, T. L., and Hodges, R. E. (Eds.). *A dictionary of reading and related terms*. Newark, DE: International Reading Association, 1981.

Herber, H. L. *Teaching reading in content areas*, second edition. Englewood Cliffs, NJ: Prentice-Hall, 1978.

Kallison, J. M. Organization of the lesson as it affects student achievement. Paper presented at the annual meeting of the American Educational Research Association, New Orleans, April 1984.

Luiten, J., Ames, W., and Ackerson, G. A meta-analysis of the effects of advance organizers on learning and retention. *American Educational Research Journal*, 1980, *17*, 211-218.

Meyer, B.J.F. The structure of prose: Effects on learning and memory and implications for educational practice. In R. C. Anderson, R. Spiro, and W. E. Montague (Eds.), *Schooling and the acquisition of knowledge*. Hillsdale, NJ: Erlbaum, 1977.

Meyer, B.J.F. *Structure of prose: Implications for teachers of reading*. Research Report No. 3, prose learning series. Tempe: Arizona State University, Department of Educational Psychology, 1979.

Moore, D.W., Cunningham, J.W., and Rudisill, N.J. Readers' conceptions of the main idea. In J.A. Niles and L.A. Harris (Eds.), *Searches for meaning in reading/language processing and instruction*. Thirty-second yearbook of the National Reading Conference. Rochester, NY: National Reading Conference, 1983, 202-206.

Moore, D.W., and Readence, J. E. A meta-analysis of the effect of graphic organizers on learning from text. In M.L. Kamil and A.J. Moe (Eds.), *Perspectives on reading research and instruction*. Twenty-ninth yearbook of the National Reading Conference. Washington, DC: National Reading Conference, 1980, 213-218.

Moore, D.W., and Readence, J.E. *A quantitative and qualitative review of graphic organizer research*. Paper presented at the annual meeting of the American Educational Research Association, Montreal, April 1983.

Niles, O.S. Organization perceived. In H. L. Herber (Ed.), *Developing study skills in secondary schools*. Newark, DE: International Reading Association, 1965.

Pearson, P. D., and Johnson, D. D. *Teaching reading comprehension*. New York: Holt, Rinehart, and Winston, 1978.

Risko, V. J., and Alvarez, M. C. Thematic organizers: Application to remedial reading. In G.H. McNinch (Ed.), *Reading research to reading practice*, third yearbook of the American Reading Forum. Carrollton, GA: West Georgia College, 1983, 85-87.

The making of our America. Boston, MA: Allyn and Bacon, 1974.

Winograd, P.N., and Brennan, S. Main idea instruction in the basal readers. In J.A. Niles and L.A. Harris (Eds.), *Searches for meaning in reading/language processing and instruction*. Thirty-second yearbook of the National Reading Conference. Rochester, NY: National Reading Conference, 1983, 80-86.

Alvermann

10

Getting the Main Idea of the Main Idea: A Writing/Reading Process

James Flood
Diane Lapp

James Flood and Diane Lapp recommend that teachers capitalize on the relationship between reading and writing to help students comprehend (and compose) main ideas more effectively. After documenting the rationale and the need for a reading/writing perspective in main idea comprehension, the authors present a composing approach to main idea comprehension. This approach entails a four step procedure: 1) prewriting, in which students generate a topic; 2) theme composing, in which students write a theme statement or main idea sentence based upon the topic; 3) elaboration on the theme, in which students provide details that prove, expand, or elucidate their main idea theme statement; and 4) feedback, rewriting, and editing, in which students refine and polish their composition.

T eachers and researchers have been offered a variety of explanations for the difficulties children have when they are asked to read for the main idea of an expository text (see Winograd and Bridge, Chapter 2, this volume). Some theorists suggest that reading for main idea is a difficult task because authors fail to include an explicit main idea in their texts, or they conceal main ideas in inappropriate places in the text (Baumann & Serra, 1984). Other theorists have suggested that the writer is not the sole cause of the difficulty in reading for main idea; some readers are unable to understand main ideas because they lack prerequisite skills in reasoning, synthesizing, paraphrasing, and summarizing (Flood & Menyuk, 1983; Winograd, 1984).

A third group has argued that failure to extract main ideas from texts is situation-specific; a reader may have the necessary cognitive and linguistic prerequisites for dealing with main idea in one text but may fail to apply those skills with another text (Squire, 1983; Lapp & Flood, 1983a). This third group further argues that scores on main idea assessments will differ with varying testing modes (e.g., choosing the main idea from a list of possible choices versus generating a main idea by oneself) and the content of the material.

One comprehensive theory to explain all the difficulties that children encounter when trying to extract a main idea is unavailable at the present time because the texts that children are asked to read are extremely diverse. Three examples will demonstrate some obvious differences in texts that make reading for main idea a simple task in some instances and a far more difficult task in others.

The first passage is an example of a text that causes little difficulty for most students who are developing at normal rates. It may serve as a starting point for students who are unable to deal with main idea. It is taken from the Stanford Diagnostic Reading Test (Karlsen, Madden, & Gardner, 1976), Brown Level, Form A, p. 10:*

> Dust is a serious problem in industry. When workers breathe the dust-filled air, some of the dust remains in their lungs. Although breathing any kind of dust may make workers ill, the most dangerous kinds of dust are those that come from irritating substances, such as lead or asbestos. Coal miners can get "black lung" from years of breathing coal dust. To make matters worse, the most common way of removing coal dust from the air is "rockdusting" — spreading the coal surfaces with powdered limestone.
>
> A government report has suggested several ways of removing dust from the air that workers breathe: Hoods should be built over dust-producing machines; as much dust as possible should be removed by fans, vacuum cleaners, and water sprays; and workers should use masks or other devices that will protect them from the dust. All these may help to solve the problems that dust causes.

The testing situation asks students to choose the explicitly stated main idea from the following choices:*

> e) Dust is a problem in industry.
> f) The government makes good suggestions.
> g) "Black lung" is very serious.
> h) Factory work is unhealthy.

Flood and Lapp

Many studies have provided evidence that students can successfully read these types of texts containing a standard organizational structure with an explicitly stated main idea in the first sentence, followed by complementary supporting details (e.g., Bridge et al., 1984; Flood, 1978; Kieras, 1978).

However, students do less well when texts are not written clearly (Hasan, 1984); when they contain unfamiliar, unpracticed, or hybrid organizational structures (Meyer, 1984; Schallert & Tierney, 1982); when explicitly stated main ideas are followed by contradictory or irrelevant information (Flood, 1978); when main ideas are not explicitly included in the text (Baumann, 1984; Williams, Taylor, & Ganger, 1981); and when ideas that are directly unrelated to the main idea are included far more often than related ideas (Mohr, Glover, & Ronning, 1984).

A second passage is included as an example of a text that may be difficult for students because it does not contain an explicitly stated main idea. While this is a cohesive text that may not be difficult for children to understand, they may have difficulty with the testing task of answering "What is the main idea?" because they have not been trained to synthesize several pieces of information into a single summary statement. The passage is also taken from the Stanford Diagnostic Reading Test (Karlsen, Madden, & Gardner, 1976), Brown Level, Form A, p. 8:*

> The number of fish gathered from ocean fisheries has been rising rapidly and doubles about every ten years. However, we could get even more food from our oceans if we had as much experience in this field as we do in farming the land. For example, fencing has long been used on land to keep herds of animals together. It is only recently that this idea has been tried in the sea. Sardine fisheries in Maine are using "bubble fences" to keep fish within certain boundaries. These fences are made by forcing air through holes in pipes to form bubbles around the fish. However, because no one country owns the open seas, such fish farming is not likely to become widespread. While we are developing new forms of aquaculture, we must also find ways to share the wealth of the seas in peace and harmony.

The task of reading the text and answering a multiple choice item that requires synthesizing many pieces of information into a single item and matching it to the choices provided is a more difficult task than that required for the dust passage because the main idea, applying land experience to the sea, is not explicitly stated. The text itself, however, is probably no more difficult for students to process than the dust text, but generating a main idea becomes more difficult when students cannot depend upon their ability to recognize an explicit statement from the text. Since these types of text are the rule and not the exception (Baumann & Serra, 1984), children need direct instruction in reading for main idea in order to be able to deal with them. This is best done through an integrated, repeated reading/writing program which will be explained in a later section in this chapter.

A third passage exemplifies a poorly written text that is extremely difficult for students because it contains more information that is unrelated to the main idea than related information. It has been altered slightly from a science basal text to protect author/publisher anonymity.

> The human skeletal system protects and supports the organs of the body. Its 206 separate bones support the body and serve as a framework for the attachment of muscles. The skeleton makes up about 18% of a person's body weight. Bones in a skeleton are held together by strands of tough tissue called ligaments. Ligaments stretch easily to allow the bones to move. The point at which two bones move against one another is called a joint. Shoulder and hip joints are examples of ball and socket joints. Hinge joints are those found in knees, elbows, and toes. The skeleton supports the heart and kidneys.

While the main idea of this passage seems to be explicitly stated in the first sentence, a great deal of extraneous information is presented in the remainder of the paragraph that does not support the thesis of the first sentence. If asked the main idea, students may have difficulty synthesizing the information and determining its relation to the main idea. This is an example of the kind of text Anderson and Armbruster (1984) refer to as inconsiderate.

Reading/Writing Relationships: Implications for Main Idea Instruction

While these three texts show some of the most obvious difficulties students encounter, they only hint at the complexity of the problem of understanding main idea. Because this volume has presented the most current viewpoints on the complexity of dealing with main idea, we will not restate varying theories in this chapter; rather, we will present a set of procedures for instructing students in recognizing and generating main ideas in reading and writing. These procedures, emanating from the current research on the relations between reading and writing, assume that the reader must understand the organization of the text to improve reading comprehension (Meyer, 1984; Lapp & Flood, 1983a).

In understanding the organization of a text, the reader understands the way in which a writer thinks. In order to fully comprehend how a writer writes, the student must begin as a writer, trying to organize information into a cohesive whole that is comprehensible to a reader (Flood, 1984). In attempting to write an expository text, students see the need for organization and the need for using the conventions of writing to display their organization. When students do not organize their information, they realize quickly that their audience cannot understand them. In turn, when they are reading, they realize that the writer has attempted to organize information, and their task then is to recognize previously learned organizational schemes (if they are present) or to generate organizational schemes that make sense of the information (if organization is not present).

Recently, researchers have provided a strong rationale for teaching reading and writing together by explaining the relations between reading and writing. Squire (1983) argued that reading and writing are two complementary, reciprocal processes. Table 1 presents Squire's view of the similarities of the processes of reading and writing.

In synthesizing the research on reading/writing relations, Stotsky (1983) found that most studies were correlational and examined the influence of writing on the development of reading. These studies consistently indicated that 1) better writers tend to be better readers; 2) better writers tend to read more than poorer writers; and 3) better readers tend to produce more syntactically mature writing than poorer readers.

In examining studies specifically designed to improve writing by providing reading experiences in lieu of grammar study or additional writing practice, Stotsky found that reading experiences were more beneficial than either grammar study or extra writing practice on students' writing performance. She also found that studies using literary models as examples of good writing proved effective in writing growth. As a result of her investigations, she concluded: 1) writing instruction can enhance reading development, and 2) reading experience may be as critical a factor in developing writing ability as writing instruction itself.

Wittrock (1983) also discussed the close relations between reading comprehension and effective writing in explaining his model of generative reading comprehension. Based on an analogy between reading with com-

Table 1
A PERSPECTIVE ON THE RELATIONSHIP
BETWEEN READING AND WRITING*

Before Writing: Securing ideas
Organizing ideas
Determining point of view
Considering audience

Before Reading: Preparing to comprehend
Relating to prior experience
Establishing purpose
Looking for the author's stance

During Reading or Writing: Composing or comprehending
Actively engaged emotionally
and intellectually

After Writing: Evaluating
Editing and revising
Applying outside standards or correctness

After Reading: Evaluating
Studying parts in relation to whole
Analyzing how effects are achieved
Applying independent judgments
(preferences, ethics, aesthetics)

From "Composing and Comprehending: Two Sides of the Same Basic Process" by J.R. Squire, 1983, *Language Arts, 60*, 586. Copyright © 1983 by the National Council of Teachers of English. Reprinted by permission of the publisher.

prehension and writing, speaking, and listening with understanding, he suggested that good reading, like effective writing, involves generative cognitive processes that create meaning by building relationships between the text and what the reader knows, believes, and experiences. He argued that when people read, they generate meaning by relating parts of the text to one another and to prior knowledge. He further argued that learning to read with comprehension involves acquiring and using some of the same generative skills needed to learn to write.

Flood and Lapp

In his analysis of the relationship between reading and writing, Squire (1983) stated: "Composing and comprehending are process-oriented thinking skills which are basically interrelated. Our failure to teach composing and comprehending as process impedes our efforts not only to teach children to read and write, but our efforts to teach them how to think" (p. 581). Squire further states that classroom strategies for regenerating ideas are essential to teaching and comprehending and children require instruction in all important modes of rhetoric if they are to comprehend and compose these varied forms and functions.

Main Idea Instruction: A Composing Approach

Although many researchers have argued that students need to be taught about main idea through a reading/writing curriculum, there is still uncertainty about the most effective ways of doing this. The first step in dealing with main idea formation in reading is direct instruction in paraphrasing and summarizing skills; however, a full analysis of these skills is beyond the scope of this chapter (see Taylor, Chapter 8, this volume). Rather, we will present a procedure for teaching students to read for main idea by writing main ideas and by learning how authors organize their ideas in writing. In a previous article, we stated:

> The best way to help students understand their responsibilities as active readers is to encourage them to be writers who write for a specific audience. The two language arts, reading and writing, when taught together, enhance each other and serve to strengthen the child's ability in both areas. (Lapp and Flood, 1983b, p. 236)

This statement will serve as the rationale for the procedures we will present. A primary assumption of these procedures is that students often confuse topic with main idea (theme). When asked "What is the main idea of passage X?," teachers will often receive topic responses rather than appropriate main idea responses; for example, children might answer in the following way for each of the pasasages cited previously:

Text #1. Dust
Text #2. Ocean Fisheries
Text #3. Human Skeleton System

The procedures we are suggesting deal directly with this confusion. Teachers are often told to teach language as process, but they are rarely given guidelines or sets of procedures for doing this. Instead of exhorting teachers again to teach process, we will present a set of procedures that will result in teaching language as process.

The procedures follow the Writing-Process model, with emphasis on the prewriting stage. In this chapter we will present procedures that deal with only one type of writing (exposition) in one form (major idea followed by supporting details). The presentation of a single type of writing does not suggest that children should not be taught many different forms; rather, it is presented as an initial step in teaching children to learn that writers need to organize their thoughts so that the pieces of a text fit together. Although main ideas are not frequently explicitly stated in texts (Baumann & Serra, 1984), in this procedure children will be asked to generate texts with explicit main ideas as a starting point for understanding that well written texts do have a main idea that holds the text together whether they are explicitly stated or not.

Step 1: Prewriting

As a first step, students generate a topic for their writing through an oral and written interview. For example, when a child tells the teacher that he or she wants to write about motorcycles, the teacher probes: "Tell me some things that you know about motorcycles. Do you have a motorcycle? Is your brother's motorcycle faster than a Kawasaki? Is it bigger than a Honda? Does he race with it?"

After students have talked out the facts they know about their topic, ask them to fill in the first part of the prewriting interview form (see Table 2). After students have done this, ask them to collect other facts about their topic from reference materials, teachers, librarians, parents, or knowledgeable adults/children.

Step 2: Theme Composing

After they have collected sufficient information on the topic, students select from their Prewriting Form the most important information they have acquired. Next, ask students to synthesize the information into a single main idea that encompasses all of that information. The students then write this main idea sentence or topic sentence on a Theme Composing Form (see Table 3). For example, the student writing about motorcycles might write, "The Kawasaki is the fastest motorcycle on the market today."

Table 2

PREWRITING INTERVIEW FORM

Topic_____

Facts I already knew about the topic
1._____
2._____
3._____
4._____
5._____

Facts I have learned about the topic

SOURCE	FACT
1. (reference material, e.g., encyclopedia)_____	1._____
2. (reference material)_____	2._____
3. (teacher)_____	3._____
4. (other informed adult or child)_____	4._____
5. (miscellaneous)_____	5._____

Table 3

THEME COMPOSING FORM

Theme or Main Idea

_____

_____

Supporting Details
1._____
2._____
3._____
4._____
5._____

Step 3: Elaboration on the Theme

Ask students to complete the Theme Composing Form by giving details that prove, expand, or elucidate their main idea. For example, the student writing about motorcycles might come up with the following paragraph:

> The Kawasaki is the fastest motorcycle on the market today. It has been driven at speeds exceeding 150 mph in two separate professional races. No other motorcycle has been driven at a speed of more than 140 mph in a professional race. *Consumer Reports* rates the Kawasaki as the fastest motorcycle among the leading motorcycles sold in America.

Step 4: Feedback, Rewriting, Editing

After the students have filled in the main idea portion of the form, guide them through the other steps in the writing process: feedback, rewriting, editing.

This procedure has been used in many classrooms with students at several different grade/age levels. Even as early as first and second grade, children generate language experience charts that reflect understanding of the difference between topic and main idea after they have received instruction in these procedures. For example, second grade children with their teacher's help produced the following text.

Animals That Live in the Zoo

There are many different kinds of animals that live in the zoo.
Gorillas live in the zoo.
Elephants live in the zoo.
Monkeys live in the zoo.
Giraffes live in the zoo.

Again, this is only one type of text; use the procedure flexibly. You will need to expand it to teach children to write many different types of texts. For example, children can compose texts that do not include explicitly stated main ideas from the information they have gathered for the *Topic* portion of the Prewriting Form.

The procedure is intended to help children understand that good texts have an underlying organizational scheme and that authors have a main idea that holds various pieces of information together whether it is stated or implied. In generating texts with explicitly stated main ideas, students will grow in their awareness of an underlying organization that holds information together in writing and in their ability to recognize explicitly stated main ideas. Children also need to be given opportunities to read texts with and without explicitly stated main ideas. In both cases, children should be taught to generate the main idea, paraphrasing those that are explicitly stated, and generating main ideas from texts in which main ideas are missing or not explicitly stated.

References

Anderson, T.H., and Armbruster, B. B. Content area textbooks. In R. C. Anderson, J. Osborn, and R. J. Tierney (Eds.), *Learning to read in American schools: Basal readers and content texts*. Hillsdale, NJ: Erlbaum, 1984, 193-226.

Baumann, J.F. The effectiveness of a direct instruction paradigm for teaching main idea comprehension. *Reading Research Quarterly*, 1984, *20*, 93-115.

Baumann, J. F., and J. Serra. The frequency and placement of main ideas in childrten's social studies textbooks: A modified replication of Braddock's research on topic sentences. *Journal of Reading Behavior*, 1984, *16*, 27-40.

Bridge, C., S. Belmore, S. Moskow, S. Cohen, and P. Matthews. Topicalization and memory for main ideas in prose. *Journal of Reading Behavior*, 1984, *16*, 61-80.

Flood, J. Introduction to understanding reading comprehension. In J. Flood (Ed.), *Understanding reading comprehension*. Newark, DE: International Reading Association, 1984, 7-9.

Flood, J. The effects of first sentences on readers' expectations in prose passages. *Reading World*, 1978, *17*, 306-315.

Flood, J., and P. Menyuk. The development of metalinguistic awareness and its relation to reading achievement. *Journal of Applied Developmental Psychology*, 1983, 65-80.

Hasan, R. Coherence and cohesive harmony. In J. Flood (Ed.), *Understanding reading comprehension*. Newark, DE International Reading Association, 1984, 181-219.

Karlsen, B., R. Madden, and E. Gardner. *Stanford diagnostic reading test, brown level, form a*. New York: Harcourt, Brace, Jovanovich, 1976.

Kieras, D. E. Good and bad structure in simple paragraphs: Effects on apparent theme, reading time, and recall. *Journal of Verbal Learning and Verbal Behavior*, 1978, *17*, 13-28.

Lapp, D., and J. Flood. Reading comprehension instruction: What has been and what might be. *Forty-seventh yearbook of the Claremont Reading Conference*, 1983b, 230-238

Lapp, D., and J. Flood. *Teaching reading to every child*, second edition. New York: Macmillan, 1983a.

Meyer, B. Organizational aspects of texts: Effects of reading comprehension and applications for the classroom. In J. Flood (Ed.), *Promoting reading comprehension*. Newark, DE: International Reading Association, 1984, 113-138.

Mohr, P., J. Glover, and R. Ronning. The effect of related and unrelated details on the recall of major ideas in prose. *Journal of Reading Behavior*, 1984, *16*, 97-108.

Schallert, D., and R. Tierney. *Learning from expository texts: The interaction of text structure with reader characteristics*. Final report, NIE G 79 0167, 1982.

Squire, J. R. Composing and comprehending: Two sides of the same basic process. *Language Arts*, 1983, *60*, 581-589.

Stotsky, S. Research on reading/writing relationships: A synthesis and suggested direction. *Language Arts*, 1983, *60*, 627-642.

Williams, J.P., Taylor, M.B., and Ganger, S. Text variations at the level of the individual sentence and the comprehension of simple expository paragraphs. *Journal of Educational Psychology*, 1981, *73*, 851-865.

Winograd, P. Strategic difficulties in summarizing texts. *Reading Research Quarterly*, 1984, *19*, 404-425.

Wittrock, M.C. Writing and the teaching of reading. *Language Arts*, 1983, *60*, 600-606.

Flood and Lapp

11
Main Idea Instruction for Low Performers: A Direct Instruction Analysis

Edward J. Kameenui

In contrast to Baumann's teacher behavior view of direct instruction (see Chapter 6), Kameenui presents a design of instruction analysis for teaching low performing children to comprehend main ideas. Following the design of instruction perspective, Kameenui analyzes the knowledge, content, and curriculum of main idea to produce structured, systematic lessons. Each lesson consists of 1) a set up, which specifies the materials to be used in instruction; 2) a modeled set of examples, in which the student is provided examples and nonexamples of the main idea skill under consideration according to specific teacher wording; and, 3) a series of test examples. Kameenui provides several sample lessons that employ this design of instruction approach to main idea comprehension at beginning, intermediate, and advanced levels.

A s Baumann (1984) points out, "teaching and testing main idea is a pervasive educational practice" (p. 94). Although this particular practice appears to be widespread, exactly what is meant by the skill of main idea comprehension continues to bewilder educators (Hare & Milligan, 1984; Cunningham & Moore, Chapter 1, this volume; Williams, Taylor, & Jarin, 1983). In spite of the lack of operational definitions of main idea, practitioners and researchers do not appear to be deterred from proposing and promoting a variety of instructional strategies for finding, identifying, or getting the main idea (Alexander, 1976; Baumann, 1984; Dishner & Readence, 1977; Donlan, 1980; Hare & Milligan, 1984; Isakson, Miller, & O'Hara, 1979; Williams, Taylor, & Jarin, 1983). Given the elasticity and apparent elusiveness of the skill identified as getting the main idea (Cunningham & Moore, Chapter 1, this volume), coupled with the range of recommended instructional strategies for teaching learners how to get the main idea, the challenge facing any book primarily concerned with main idea instruction is clear and straightforward. Will Axelrod's characterization (1975) of main idea as the "hub in the wheel of reading comprehension" (p. 383) finally benefit from a design of instruction technology that will provide an operational definition of main idea and detailed procedures for designing instructional sequences to teach main idea? This challenge takes on even more profound dimensions when learning disabled children, low performing children, and children who have failed repeatedly are drawn into the instructional province.

The purpose of this chapter is to specify an analysis of main idea and a set of strategies that could be used to teach children for whom the traditional strategies for main idea instruction have not worked. The first section describes briefly an instructional model (the Direct Instruction Model) that has been effective in improving classroom practices and the achievement level of low performing children. The second section describes the major components of the instructional episode and the assumptions that underlie those components. The third section of the chapter specifies the design of instruction analysis and principles of the Direct Instruction Model. The final section of the chapter provides several Direct Instruction teaching sequences for main idea instruction.

The Direct Instruction Model

Rosenshine's application (1976) of the term *direct instruction* coupled with the results of the National Follow Through Project (Becker, 1977; Bereiter & Kurland, 1981; Guthrie, 1977; House et al., 1978; Kennedy, 1978; Singer & Balow, 1981; Stebbins, 1976; Stebbins et al., 1977) set the stage for a variety of subsequent teaching innovations that have embraced direct instruction. These varying conceptualizations of direct instruction range from Zohorik and Kritek's conception (1983) of direct instruction as consisting of twenty-one elements that include "available materials," "lecturing," "small step tasks," "small bit content," and "warm climate" to Baumann's emphasis (1983) on teacher directiveness and active teaching (see Baumann, Chapter 6, this volume). Similarly, Duffy and Roehler (1982) define direct instruction as meaning "an academic focus, precise sequencing of content, high pupil engagement, careful teacher monitoring and specific corrective feedback to students" (p. 35).

While Rosenshine's conceptualization of direct instruction is the most prevalent, he was neither the only nor the first person to use the term. The Direct Instruction Follow Through Project came into being in 1967. This model, originated by Siefried Engelmann and Wesley Becker, trained teachers and paraprofessionals to teach reading, language, and mathematics to economically disadvantaged students. However, the Direct Instruction Model went beyond merely training teachers in specific teaching techniques. This comprehensive educational model includes 1) a specific curriculum, 2) a specific way of teaching (rapidly paced small group instruction), 3) a specified program of inservice education, and 4) a system for monitoring both student and teacher performance (Gersten & Carnine, 1984). The model specifies a set of principles for making decisions about how to design teaching sequences, as well as a set of assumptions about the learner, the teacher, and the curriculum. The model, as Gersten and Carnine (1984) point out, is "a synthesis of learning theory, behavioral technology, and Engelmann's principles of instructional design" (p. 396). In this chapter, main idea instruction will be analyzed in accordance with this Direct Instruction Model. (A more detailed discussion of the Direct Instruction Model appears in Becker and Carnine, 1980, and specific instructional strategies in reading comprehension can be found in Carnine and Silbert, 1979.)

Direct Instruction:
Learner, Teacher, and Content Interaction

An *instructional episode* is an event or series of actions that takes place every time a teacher makes an attempt to pass information to the learner. For example, pointing out that the proper way for learners to sit in a small reading group is to have their eyes on the teacher and voices quiet is an instructional episode. Obviously, so is the teaching of identifying main ideas in narrative text. Any instructional episode entails a dynamic process comprised of at least three general components: 1) the teacher's activities in presenting the information, 2) the characteristics of the learner, and 3) the information or content. When a child fails to perform a task, each of these components must be examined. In the case of low performing children, examining the context of failure becomes especially important and uniquely complex. How the classroom teacher goes about accounting for failure and buttressing against the context of failure is crucial.

Before explaining why a learner is failing or before taking measures to prevent that failure, teachers first must critically examine their assumptions about each component interacting in the instructional episode. For example, what assumptions am I, the teacher, making about the learner's ability to learn? What assumptions am I making about the teaching presentation? Finally, what assumptions am I making about the design of the curriculum? The assumptions the classroom teacher makes about each of these components will determine the teacher's behavior in accounting for *why* the learner is failing and what must be done to prevent that failure. If the teacher operates under the assumption that a child's failure to produce a correct response is largely a result of physiological predisposition (e.g., the child was born lazy, or the child is learning disabled so you can't expect much), the teacher is not likely to adjust any aspect of teaching behavior or the curriculum. In fact, such an assumption requires no action at all since it views the learner as a hopeless victim with a fixed and unalterable problem. Nothing is likely to help this particular learner—not the best possible teaching strategies nor a faultless teaching sequence. Under this assumption, the teacher is basically an irrelevant and trivial component, as is the content or curriculum. Fortunately, such an assumption is not one that is likely to be embraced by teachers.

In contrast, suppose the teacher assumes that the learner is indeed capable of learning any concept that is taught. This assumption requires that the teacher look elsewhere, that is, not at the learner but at the other two components (i.e., the content and the method of instruction) to account for failure in the instructional episode. This means the teacher must scrutinize the teaching presentation *and* the design and nature of the content. This assumption unflinchingly places the full burden of failure in the instructional episode on the teacher. Only the teacher can change the teaching presentations and the content. Unless the classroom teacher strictly scrutinizes these components and exhausts all possible instructional strategies for breaking the cycle of failure, no other assumption is logically, professionally, or even ethically acceptable. The Direct Instruction Model is predicated on the presumption that all children are capable of learning any concept that is communicated. More important, it approaches the context of failure by presuming that if the learner fails, the failure is not with the learner but with the instructional episode.

Design of Instruction Analysis

Apart from the assumptions it makes about the learner, the Direct Instruction Model also provides an analysis for conceptualizing and designing the knowledge, content, or curriculum. This analysis is based on a set of empirically derived design of instruction principles formulated by Engelmann and Carnine (1982). A design of instruction analysis of a cognitive operation is a complex process that involves 1) identifying component discriminations that make up a cognitive operation, 2) selecting and sequencing examples of the component discrimination, 3) constructing and testing procedures for teaching the component discriminations separately (either successively or cumulatively) and, finally, 4) linking the teaching procedures of the component discriminations into a systematically integrated and sequenced teaching routine. That routine must also incorporate sufficient practice and review of component discriminations and of the complete operation. This analysis results in teaching the entire operation in a series of component instructional stages: the teaching of necessary preskills, teaching separate component discriminations, and the chaining of component discriminations into a complete teaching routine.

Engelmann and Carnine's design of instruction analysis of cognitive tasks contains two very central principles. One principle involves the organization of knowledge; the other involves the distinction between physical nonsymbolic operations (e.g., throwing a ball) and cognitive symbolic operations (e.g., comprehending main idea).

Organizing the Universe of Knowledge

The first principle is that the universe of knowledge (i.e., information labeled as a skill, cognitive operation, rule, discrimination, or task) can be grouped into specific categories of knowledge. Engelmann and Carnine (1982) break down the universe of knowledge into three major categories: basic forms, joining forms, and complex forms. *Basic forms* are typically sensory based concepts that are best taught through concrete examples. For instance, the concept of *over* could be taught through a definition meaning "when an object is in the upper projectile of another object, it is over." However, a child who does not know the concept of over is unlikely to understand a definition consisting of many other concepts (e.g., object, upper, projectile, another). Concepts like over are best taught through the presentation of positive and negative examples that communicate the quality of *over* and *not over*. In contrast, *joining forms* involve relationships between basic form concepts. Joining forms involve combining two unrelated basic concepts and demonstrating how they can be related in some way. Unrelated basic form concepts such as *over* and *table* can be combined by presenting objects in different positions of over, such as over a table or over a chair. Finally, *complex forms* involve multiple concepts and responses that are related in some way. Examples of concepts within each of these three categories are presented in Table 1. The details for designing instructional sequences for tasks within each major category are specified in Engelmann and Carnine (1982).

Table 1

ORGANIZATION OF KNOWLEDGE

Basic Forms (sensory feature concepts)

A. Noncomparative single dimension concepts. For example: *under, over, between, gradual, at the bottom of the hill, full.*

B. Comparative single dimension concepts. For example: *deeper, more gradual, fuller, wider, heavier, more precariously balanced, hotter, more permeable.*

C. Noun multidimensional concepts. For example: *chairs, dogs, shoes, tools, trucks, trees, vehicles, furniture.*

Joining Forms (relationships between sensory feature concepts)

A. Single transformations. For example: rhyming with the word *at*, identifying the subjects of statements, simplifying passive voice constructions, constructing fractions that equal one.

B. Correlated features relationships (rule relationships). For example: the steeper the grade of the stream the faster the water flows, all insects have six legs, products that are readier to use cost more, hotter air rises.

Complex Forms (chains of Joining Forms)

A. Cognitive problem solving routines. For example: locating a word in a dictionary, the angle of reflection equals the angle of incidence, column addition, concept of specific gravity.

B. Communications about events (fact systems taught through visual spatial maps). For example: animals with backbones, the human circulatory system, the workings of an internal combustion engine, different types of teeth, different types of metals.

In the Engelmann and Carnine analysis, knowledge is examined and placed in a group on the basis of the physical features and physical structure of the concept, discrimination, or rule being taught. This analysis suggests that we can sort and classify knowledge in pretty much the same way we classify physical objects, be they trees (gymnosperms, angiosperms, oak, sandlewood), clothing (winter clothes, summer clothes, skirt, shirt), or animals with backbones (mammals, amphibians, reptiles, whales, newts, snakes). The classification analysis, as in the case of physical objects, requires a close examination of the structural features of the concept, rule, operation, or discrimination being presented. For example, in order to determine to what specific class of trees a particular example of a tree belongs, we must critically examine the structural features of the leaf or leaves of the tree. By closely studying the physical features of the vein pattern of the leaf and the configuration of the lobes of the leaf, we can determine if a tree is a white oak, a black oak, a sycamore, a maple, or some other tree. By studying many examples of leaves we can determine the qualitative sameness and differences of these examples and place examples that have the same features into the same group. Examples with only a minimal difference are placed in another group.

The universe of knowledge can benefit from a similar analysis of features applied to the universe of physical objects. Cognitive concepts, rules, operations, and discriminations have specific physical features that can serve as a basis for separating them into different groups. However, the purpose for placing types of knowledge into different categories is not exercised merely for the purpose of creating manageable taxonomies that are hierarchically neat and uniform. By classifying knowledge into different categories, we assume that the instructional procedures used to teach or communicate one concept or skill could also be used to teach all of the concepts within the same category, since they all share the same structural features. For example, by specifying a detailed instructional sequence for teaching the concept of "getting farther apart," I would also be able to conceptualize and design other instructional sequences that would allow me to teach the concepts of getting fuller, getting hotter, getting greener, getting steeper, getting wider, and getting faster. Engelmann and Carnine (1982) consider this type of concept to be a comparative single dimension concept. Comparative concepts have only one structural dimension and that one dimension or quality of the concept is what the teacher must present to the learner.

The teacher has the burden of engineering the instructional sequence in such a way that the learner, by simply observing the teacher's physical and verbal actions and sequence of examples, will be able to extract what specific feature is the same in all of the examples. As Engelmann and Carnine (1982) point out, "If the examples treated in the same way share quality A and if the learner has the capacity to abstract this sameness, the learner will generalize to examples that have quality A" (p. 9). The teacher, by treating successive examples the same way, is not guaranteeing that the examples are the same. Instead, the teacher is signaling to the learner that something in the instructional sequence is the same. However, the instructional sequence is engineered in such a way that everythng in the presentation is held constant except for the one structural feature that is unique to the specific concept being presented. For example, in teaching the comparative concept of "farther apart," the teacher could design the sequence by arranging examples so that the learner could observe the constant feature *and* the one quality that differs in all examples.

An example of an instructional sequence for teaching the concept of "farther apart" is given in Figure 1. This example illustrates various elements of a successful instructional sequence.

Set Up   The teacher will use his or her hands as the physical set up to teach the concept of "farther apart." The teacher will face the learner(s), placing his or hands in front of the chest in a vertical position so that the fingertips are directly in line with the ceiling.

For each example of the concept "farther apart," the teacher will either move hands closer to or farther away from each other. The position of the teacher's hands will not change from example to example. The teacher will pause between each successive example of "farther apart" to tell the learner whether the hands are "farther apart" or "not farther apart." All of the examples will be presented successively within one teaching presentation that will take no more than two to three minutes.

Example of Concept	Actions of Teacher	Teacher Wording	Learner Response
MODELED EXAMPLES			
Starting Point	Holds hands 12" apart from each other and at same vertical orientation and height.	"Watch my hands. I will tell if they get farther apart."	Observes teacher
		"What are you going to watch?"	"Your hands."
		"What will I tell you about my hands?"	"If they get farther apart."
Example 1	Holds hands 16" apart from each other at same vertical orientation and height.	"My hands got farther apart."	Observes teacher
Example 2	Holds hands 28" apart from each other.	"My hands got farther apart."	Observes teacher
Example 3	Holds hands 36" from each other.	"My hands got farther apart."	Observes teacher
Example 4	Holds hands 34" apart from each other.	"My hands did not get farther apart."	Observes teacher
Example 5	Holds hands 28" apart from each other.	"My hands did not get farther apart. (pause) Now, watch my hands and tell me if they get farther apart."	Observes teacher

| *Example 6* | Holds hands 30″ apart from each other. | "Tell me, did my hands get farther apart?" | "Yes." |

| *Correction Procedure* | If the child responds incorrectly, the teacher should stop and return to the starting point of the teaching sequence and present the teaching sequence again (Examples 1-5) before testing the learner on Example 6. |

| *Example 7* | Holds hands 36″ apart from each other. | "Did my hands get farther apart?" | "Yes." |

| *Example 8* | Holds hands 12″ apart from each other. | "Did my hands get farther apart?" | "No." |

| *Example 9* | Holds hands 18″ apart from each other. | "Did my hands get farther apart?" | "Yes." |

| *Example 10* | Holds hands 24″ apart from each other. | "Did my hands get farther apart?" | "Yes." |

| *Example 11* | Holds hands 38″ apart from each other. | "Did my hands get farther apart?" | "Yes." |

| *Example 12* | Holds hands 10″ apart from each other. | "Did my hands get farther apart?" | "No." |

Figure 1. Format for teaching farther apart.

Every teaching sequence is comprised of a set up (i.e., the physical materials the teacher will use to demonstrate the concept to the learner), a sequence and range of examples that the teacher models (i.e., specific instances of visual and verbal representations of what the salient feature or features of the concept are and what they are not), teacher wording (i.e., the verbal label the teacher uses to signal the quality of the example that is being taught), and a sequence of examples that tests the learner on the adequacy of the teacher's presentation. While these are the major components of a teaching sequence, the coordination and arrangement of these components is what makes the design of teaching sequences difficult. More important, the critical aspect in the design of a teaching sequence is the juxtaposition of examples the teacher has selected to present within the designated set up. As Figure 1 illustrates, the positive instances of the concept "farther apart" (i.e., when the teacher's hands are indeed further apart) and the negative instances (i.e., Examples 4, 5, 7, 10, and 11 that show not farther apart) are placed in a very specific order (see Engelmann & Carnine, 1982, pp. 68-78 for details). An examination of the teaching sequence in Figure 1 reveals how the deliberate arrangement of examples makes obvious to the learner the *one* quality that makes an example either "farther apart" or "not farther apart." As the examples in the sequence indicate, everything in the set up remains constant with the exception of the physical position of the teacher's hands. Therefore, the learner is required to focus only on that dimension or quality and no other feature. The learner's memory load is reduced significantly because everything in the instructional episode is held constant except for the one feature that changes the concept from "farther apart" to "not farther apart." That one feature is clearly presented in Figure 1 from Example 3 to Example 4 and Example 5 to Example 6. These minimally different examples communicate to the learner that there is only one feature that changes the concept from "farther apart" to "not farther apart," and that feature is the proximity of the teacher's hands to each other.

One instructional sequence of the concept farther apart is obviously not sufficient. Many other sequences for teaching the concept of farther apart with different set ups are needed. A learner who received only the instructional sequence given in Figure 1 might infer that the concept farther apart can occur only within the context of the teacher's hands. If the teacher were to test the child by manipulating two blocks and asking, "Are the blocks farther apart?" the child may either not respond at all or respond in a puzzled and bewildered manner. To break this generalization problem, the teacher must design and present a variety of other teaching sequences using different set ups (e.g., two rectangular blocks of the same color placed on a table or two chairs of the same make and color). These features of an instructional sequence (i.e., the set up, the selected examples to demonstrate the concept, the teacher wording) will be necessary in constructing a teaching sequence for teaching the identification of main idea in text.

Physical Nonsymbolic Operations
Versus Cognitive Symbolic Operations

The second principle central to the Engelmann and Carnine (1982) analysis (see pp. 22-25) is the distinction between physical nonsymbolic operations (e.g., throwing a ball) and cognitive symbolic operations (e.g., making text based inferences in a narrative passage). The distinction between physical and cognitive operations is important because it implies how a teacher must analyze and teach a skill in order to communicate it unambiguously to the learner.

The properties of physical operations, which make them easier to learn, are absent in cognitive operations. Physical operations have the following important properties: 1) all component behaviors are overt and remain overt (try opening a door without performing the overt behaviors, such as turning the knob and pushing); 2) the goal is achieved only when the overt behaviors are carried out in the proper sequence; and 3) the physical environment provides feedback on every trial as long as the learner understands the goal of the operation. The physical environment effectively tells the learner either "Your behavior was okay on the trial." or "Your behavior was inadequate on that trial. Change it." The feedback comes about because the physical environment prevents the learner from achieving the goal unless the physically overt behaviors are produced correctly.

Cognitive operations are different because only the final response, rather than the component responses, needs to be overt. Because the component responses are not overt, we cannot easily identify necessary components. For cognitive operations, furthermore, the physical environment does not prevent the learner from producing an inaccurate response, and it provides no feedback whatsoever. For example, the learner can answer a comprehension question incorrectly, and the physical environment would not prevent this response from occurring.

The distinction between physical operations and cognitive operations suggests that a covert process can be made more understandable to the learner if the teaching of such a process were modeled after a physical operation so that: 1) the steps for teaching component discriminations that make up a cognitive operation are made overt, 2) the learner overtly responds to each step, and 3) the teacher provides consistent feedback regarding learner success.

Responding to a teacher directed routine in which steps are made overt is not the ultimate goal of instruction, however. If the learner is not weaned from extensive teacher guidance, the instruction would not be effective: It would provide undesirable dependence, preempting the learner from independent practice and exploration. Consequently, as soon as the learner has demonstrated some proficiency with a highly structured routine, less structured and more independent work is presented. As teachers fade their guidance, the routines become internalized, or covert, and serve as frameworks for mediating new examples (Baer, 1979; Homme, 1965; Luria, 1961; Vygotsky, 1962).

Making the cognitive processes in reading comprehension skills instructionally overt is only one part of the design of instruction that is necessary in specifying the intricate requirements of teaching complex tasks (Gage, 1978). Yet, if this part is not analyzed correctly, any efforts to specify the details of the instructional episode will be impeded.

Direct Instruction of Main Idea

The evaluation of basal reading programs (e.g., Durkin, 1981; Hare & Milligan, 1984; Steely & Engelmann, 1979) suggests that main idea instruction does not appear to conform with the design of instruction principles as previously described. More important, requiring teachers to use these basal materials with low performers may be inappropriate. An analysis of main idea instruction explicitly designed with the low performer in mind is needed.

The skill of identifying the main idea is essentially a summarization skill that allows learners to reduce the amount of information in a text to a manageable piece that can be retained in memory. As Carnine and Silbert (1979) point out, "Since students cannot remember everything they hear or read, acquiring summarization skills ensures that they will remember major events rather than random details" (p. 250). The very identification of this summarization skill as a main idea skill provides the teacher with a clue to this skill's critical and unique structural feature. As noted in the earlier section on the design of instruction analysis, before designing a teaching sequence for main idea instruction, the teacher must look closely at the structural features of the skill or concept. An examination of the structural features of main idea suggests that it is a basic form, single dimension concept in the Engelmann and Carnine (1982) classification of knowledge (see Table 1). As a basic form, single dimension concept, the skill of identifying main ideas is a concept that has a clear and precise boundary line. In other words, a main idea in a text has one clear and precise dimension — it is either *the* main idea in a text, or it is not the main idea. The concept "farther apart" in Figure 1 is also a single dimension concept; that is, there is a clear and precise boundary to the teacher's hands being farther apart or not being farther apart. As in the concept of farther apart in which the learner is required only to attend to one dimension (i.e., the proximity of the teacher's hands to each other), a teaching sequence for main idea must be designed to make obvious to the learner the one dimension of a main idea. Singling out this one dimension in a text can be difficult because the one dimension of main ideaness is typically embedded among many other ideas. The burden on the teacher in designing an instructional sequence is to make it clear to the learner the idea (either in a text or derived from a text) that summarizes elements central to the text.

Classifying the identification of main idea as a single dimension concept specifies for the practitioner the complexity of the concept to be taught. A single dimension concept is not a complex concept. As noted earlier, the practitioner must only communicate to the learner the structural feature that is unique to the concept. Furthermore, within the Engelmann and Carnine (1982) design of instruction analysis, knowing that a particular concept is a single dimension concept also specifies for the practitioner how to go about designing an instructional sequence to teach that concept.

The same components used to design the teaching sequence for farther apart (see Figure 1) will be used to design the teaching sequence for main idea. Therefore, teaching main idea as a single dimension concept requires that the practitioner specify 1) a set up, 2) a set of examples, 3) teacher wording, and 4) a sequence of test examples. Each of these components will be discussed in detail.

Phase I: Main Idea Instruction Using Pictures

Set up. The set up refers to the materials the practitioner will use to teach the concept. In main idea instruction, the materials must be based on the academic or skill level of the learners. For example, during the early part of the beginning stage, brief passages (approximately fifty words and four to five sentences) could be used. The passages would be accompanied by a series of statements. The statements would vary in their summary of the passage. One statement would focus on one aspect of the passage while another statement would focus on another aspect of the passage. The teacher would model the skill of identifying main idea by reading each statement and indicating whether the statement best summarizes the main idea of the passage.

For low performing children who may require a less ambiguous presentation of main idea instruction, the set up could include the use of pictures (see Figure 2). Because of the absence of a verbal text, pictures reduce the memory demands placed on the learner. The picture allows the learner to examine a stimulus continuously and to determine what the critical and noncritical features of the picture are when examples and nonexamples of main idea statements are presented. Figure 2 presents a detailed teaching format for main idea instruction using pictures.

The unique aspect about this teaching sequence for main idea is that each set up presents only one positive example of a main idea within a single context. Obviously this is inadequate since the learner might infer that main idea can occur only within one specific set of examples. For example, in Modeled Example 1 in Figure 2, the learner could decide that main ideas occur only in a text about a hunter getting caught in a trap. To prevent this, several positive examples of main idea must be designed. More specifically, the same format described in Modeled Example 1 in Figure 2 must be presented with additional sets of examples. Modeled Examples 2 through 5 in Figure 2 present added instances of main idea in differing contexts. With the presentation of each successive set of examples, the learner identifies a qualitative sameness about all the different sets of examples. The learner observes the examples and extracts the one feature or dimension repeated in each set of examples. In detecting main ideas in pictures, the learner is prompted by a rule announcing the critical feature of main idea (the main idea tells about the whole picture; one sentence for each picture tells about the whole picture; the others do not) which is coupled with a series of positive and negative examples of the rule. The learner thus has two sources of information (positive and negative examples and the rule) to use to discern the one dimension critical to identifying main idea. With repeated examples of the picture, the rule, and the accompanying verbal text (i.e., the individual sentences), the learner retains the rule in memory and uses it to make decisions about each of the successive examples presented.

In another set up, the teacher could present a series of pictures depicting specific events and actions instead of only one picture. The picture series as presented in Figure 3 would be an appropriate follow up for this phase of instruction. Unlike the single frame picture used in Figure 2, a series

The man was scared.
The dog looked surprised.
The trap snapped the hunter's foot.
The hunter got caught in a trap.
The hunter found a trap.

Teacher Wording	*Learner Response*
1. "Today we're going to learn about main ideas."	Observes teacher.
2. "Look at the picture." (Monitor children to make sure they are looking at the picture.) "I'll read all of the sentences below the picture; you follow along." (Teacher reads all five sentences with children following along.)	Observes teacher then looks at picture. Looks at picture then reads sentences below picture.
3. "Now let's look at the sentences below the picture again. I'll read the first sentence; you follow with your finger." (Check children to see if their fingers are on the right sentence.)	Reads sentences and follows along with finger.
4. " 'The man was scared.' Is that the main idea of the picture? No. How do I know? Because it doesn't tell about the whole picture."	Reads sentences and follows along with finger.
5. "Put your finger on the next sentence. I'll read it; you follow along."	Reads sentences and follows along with finger.
6. " 'The dog looked surprised.' Is that the main idea of the picture? No. How do I know? Because it doesn't tell about the whole picture."	Reads sentences and follows along with finger.

7. "Put your finger on the next sentence. I'll read it; you follow along."	Reads sentences and follows along with finger.
8. " 'The trap snapped the hunter's foot.' Is that the main idea of the picture? No. How do I know? Because it doesn't tell about the whole picture."	Reads sentences and follows along with finger.
9. "I'll read the next sentence. 'The hunter got caught in a trap.' Is that the main idea of the picture? Yes. How do I know? Because it tells about the whole picture.	Reads sentences and follows along with finger.
10. "Next sentence. 'The hunter found a trap.' Is that the main idea of the picture? No. How do I know? Because it doesn't tell about the whole picture."	Reads sentences and follows along with finger.

Set Up: Modeled Example 2 (new set of examples)

The cowboy ran into a snake.
The cowboy wore a hat.
The snake hissed at the horse.
The cowboy looked scared.

11. "Now let's look at another picture." (Teacher presents the above picture and set of statements.) "I'll read all the sentences below the picture; you follow along." (Teacher reads all sentences while children follow along.)
12. Teacher repeats steps 3-10 with the above picture and set of statements.

Set Up: Modeled Example 3 (new set of examples)

A boy had a striped shirt on.
The boys were fighting.
The boys were on the floor.

13. Teacher repeats steps 3-11 with the new picture and set of statements.

Set Up: Modeled Example 4 (new set of examples)

The creature was funny looking.
The spacecraft was broken.
The man was a farmer.
The man and the creature were working together.
The man and the creature were fixing the spacecraft.
The creature did not wear clothes.

14. Repeat step 13.

Set Up: Modeled Example 5 (new set of examples)

The man lost his canteen.
The man was thirsty.

Set Up: Testing Example 1

The frog sat on the river bank.
The frog had big eyes.
The frog had a long tongue.
The frog caught the dragonfly.

Teacher Wording	*Learner Response*
15. "Look at this picture." (Monitor children's attention to picture.) "I'll read all of the sentences below the picture. You follow along." (Teacher reads all four sentences with children following along.)	Observes teacher.

16. "Now let's decide which sentence tells us the main idea of the picture. I'll read the first sentence, and you tell me if that's the main idea."	Observes teacher.
17. (Teacher reads the first sentence.) "The frog sat on the river bank." (Pauses and looks at children.) "Listen, is that the main idea of the picture?" (Teacher calls on a volunteer for a response.)	"No."
18. "How do you know that is not the main idea of the picture?"	"Because it doesn't tell about the whole picture."

Correction Procedure   If the child responds incorrectly, the teacher models the answer: "Listen, that's not the main idea of the picture. How do I know? Because it doesn't tell about the whole picture. Now it is your turn again. Listen, 'The frog sat on the river bank.' Is that the main idea of the picture? (Child responds.) How do you know?" (Child responds.) The teacher may want to model a new set of examples for the learner before continuing with the testing sequence.

19. "I'll read the next sentence; you follow along. 'The frog had big eyes.' " (Pauses and looks at children.) "Is that the main idea of the picture?" (Teacher calls on a volunteer for a response.)	"No."
20. "How do you know that's not the main idea?"	"Because it doesn't tell about the whole picture."
21. "I'll read the next sentence. 'The frog had a long tongue.' " (Pauses and looks at children.) "Is that the main idea of the picture?" (Teacher calls on a volunteer for a response.)	"No."
22. "How do you know?"	"Because it doesn't tell about the whole picture."
23. "I'll read the next sentence. 'The frog caught the dragonfly.' " (Pauses and looks at children.) "Is that the main idea of the picture?" (Teacher calls on a volunteer for a response.)	"Yes."
24. "How do you know?"	"Because it tells about the whole picture."

Set Up: Testing Example 2 (new set of examples)

25. "Now let's look at another picture." (Teacher selects another picture and set of statements.)

26. Teacher repeats steps 15-24 with new set up. The teacher may now require children to read the statements out loud or to themselves.

(The teacher should test children on a total of at least three new pictures before terminating the instruction.)

Figure 2. Format for main idea instruction: Phase I, pictures.

*The pictures used in Figures 2 and 3 were taken from *Action Express Paragraph and Story Writers* by David E. Howe and Edward J. Kameenui. Copyright 1983 by Stoelting Company. Used by permission of publisher.

of pictures more closely approximates the requirements of identifying the main idea in a text or passage. As in reading a passage, the series of pictures set up requires that the learner progress from one context (i.e., one picture frame) to another context in determining the main idea of the entire series of pictures. The set up provided in Figure 3 would communicate to the learner that the skill of identifying main idea requires identifying, remembering and integrating information that is repeated from one context (picture, sentence, or paragraph) to the next.

Modeled set of examples. The picture examples used in Figure 2 for teaching main idea are peculiar from a design of instruction perspective. Each set of examples includes only one picture and a range of statements about features of the picture. Since each example has only one picture, each picture can represent only one main idea. This is unlike the set of examples used to teach farther apart presented in Figure 1. In that particular sequence, there are three modeled examples of the concept "farther apart." The learner received repeated examples of what the concept was within one sequence of examples. The farther apart sequence is ultimately more efficient than the main idea sequence since it presents in one sequence of examples what is typically presented in three to four main idea instructional sequences (see Figure 2). The main idea instructional sequence is by design a more ambitious sequence (i.e., it requires more teaching time to communicate the concept or skill) simply because it is text based. In other words, main idea can be taught only within a text and it will require numerous examples of text — each one different in length, content, and main idea — to convey to the learner the concept of main idea.

The girl called for help.
A lifeguard was on duty at the beach.
A lifeguard rescues swimmers in trouble.
A swimmer was rescued by the lifeguard.
A lifeguard was running on the beach.

Each added picture in Figure 2 (i.e., Modeled Examples 2-5) is different, and the number of statements from which the learner must select the main idea is also varied. By varying these features of the set up, we communicate to the learner that content and number of statements is not relevant to determining main idea. The learner is taught through a range of examples of pictures and statements that in order to identify the main idea of a text, one must examine the features of pictures. Later the learner will be taught to examine the linguistic features of a text, instead of the visual features of a picture, to determine main idea.

In order to teach main idea with the use of pictures, at least six to eight different sets of examples should be prepared (see Figures 2 and 3). Each set of examples should include one picture and a series of statements (minimum of two) that describe aspects of the picture. After presenting or modeling two to three sets of examples (see Figure 2), the teacher then uses the remaining sets of examples for testing; that is, the teacher uses the instructional sequences to assess whether children can adequately identify main idea (see Testing Examples 1 and 2 in Figure 2) by requiring the learner to read the statements and asking, "Is that the main idea of the picture?"

Presenting minimally different examples which are juxtaposed to one another (e.g., see Examples 3, 4, 5, and 6 in Figure 1) is a critical feature in designing teaching sequences for single dimension concepts. These examples convey to the learner the one quality that is responsible for the change in label from a positive example of the concept to a negative example of the concept. The selection and inclusion of minimally different examples for main idea instruction is also important. When teaching main idea using pictures, minimally different examples are included in each picture set up. For example, in Modeled Example 1 of Figure 2, the two statements, "The hunter got caught in a trap" and "The trap snapped the hunter's foot," are minimally different examples of the main idea statement for that picture (the former statement being the positive example, while the latter is a negative example of main idea). Both statements are minimally different in their meaning and interpretation of the features of the picture. Both statements refer to the hunter and the trap. However, only one statement specifies a higher order classification of what the entire picture is about. The other statement specifies a specific detail of the picture. These minimally different examples require the learner to examine each statement carefully when discriminating specific details of a picture from the more general classification of features, actions, and events depicted in the picture. These minimally different examples of main idea statements are systematically sequenced within each set of main idea statements that follow each picture (see Figures 2 and 3).

Teacher wording. The teacher wording in the instructional sequence is straightforward. For each example (see Figure 2), the teacher reads each statement then models the question form (e.g., "Is that the main idea of the picture?") before answering the question. The extensive verbal modeling of the question and the subsequent answer followed by the announcement of the rule for main idea demonstrates to the low performer the relationship between the statements, the question, the answer, and the rule. This kind of teacher wording may appear to be awkward and cumbersome. However, with each successive statement, the low performer receives a clear model of the required response form, as well as the sequence in which the information will typically unfold within each set of examples.

Note that the teacher wording is as tightly controlled as the examples selected to convey the notion of main idea. What the teacher says is not open ended nor left to chance. What the teacher says and how it is said is critical to a clear and unambiguous communication of the concept. By keeping the teacher wording to a few selected words and sentences, the learner is given a consistent statement about what needs to be attended to and what can be ignored. The teacher who includes noncritical or even irrelevant and trivial statements in the instructional episode runs the risk of muddying up the communication about main idea.

The wording specified in Figure 2 is by no means the only possible teacher wording available, but the teacher wording must be as precise and concise as possible. In the instuctional sequence in Figure 2, the teacher wording is prescribed in a specific order. A statement describing the picture is read followed by a question that explicitly requires the learner to make a determination about main idea. In the modeled examples of the instructional sequence, the teacher models a "yes" or "no" response to the question for the learner. Finally, the rule about main idea is given. The rule verbally specifies for the learner the salient feature about main ideaness (i.e., the statement must tell about the "whole picture").

Test examples. The examples used to assess whether the student has learned to identify the main idea are similar to the modeled examples. Nothing in the set up of the initial instructional episode is changed. The only differences between the set of examples modeled in Figure 2 and the test examples are the examples and the teacher wording. In the testing sequence of examples, the learner reads each statement followed by the teacher asking the question, "Is that the main idea of the picture?" The learner must simply answer yes or no, an easy response for a low performer. Memory demands placed on the learner are minimized by the continued presence of the picture and statements and by the teacher's asking of the question. Finally, the teacher may ask the learner to verify the yes or no response by applying the rule. As indicated in Figure 2, after determining whether the statement is the main idea, the teacher asks "How do you know?" Such a question requires the learner to apply the rule by answering "It tells about the whole picture." This response is more difficult than the yes/no choice response because the learner must retain the rule in memory, discriminate how to apply it correctly, and verbally produce it when appropriate. This kind of response may be difficult for some low performers and should be used only if the teacher is confident the learner can produce such complex responses.

The order in which positive and negative examples of main idea occur within a particular set of examples must also be systematically varied, that is, the positive example of main idea should not consistently be the first, second, or last example in every set of examples. Obviously, the position of the positive examples within and across instructional sequences must be varied to prevent the learner from attending to the placement of main idea within a text instead of the features that make up the concept of main idea. Oftentimes, the low performer will extract a feature from the teaching presentation that is irrelevant to the nature of the concept simply because the feature happens to occur in more than one example.

Table 2

FIRMING CYCLE SCHEDULE FOR THE FIRST DAY OF MAIN IDEA INSTRUCTION

8:30-9:00	Initial teaching sequence for main idea instruction
9:00-9:15	Independent worksheet activity on main idea
10:00-10:02	Firming of main idea
1:00-1:02	Firming of main idea
2:30 or before end of school day	Firming of main idea

Schedule of instruction. Perhaps one of the most important elements of instruction that is typically overlooked in designing instructional sequences for the low performer is that of the schedule of instruction. The traditional schedule of instruction involves teaching a new skill once a day with little or no review of the skill at any other time on the day it was first taught. Furthermore, the traditional scheduling of instruction is less likely to provide the systematic, cumulative review of a skill over time that a low performer requires in order to retain and apply the skill accurately and consistently.

Main Idea Instruction for Low Performers   263

A low performer will require more teaching and more practice on a skill once it is introduced than the average learner. More important, the amount of instruction and practice must be scheduled to give the learner opportunities to review the skill during the day and week in which the skill was first introduced. Furthermore, the skill must be reviewed periodically throughout the school year even though levels of mastery have been reached; that is, the low performer must be placed in a kind of *firming cycle*. The firming cycle refers to a process in which the teacher structures and schedules a specified number of brief one to three minute review sessions. These review sessions must be scheduled beginning with the very first day of main idea instruction. In fact several firming sessions should be scheduled during the first day of instruction. The firming cycle schedule for the first day of main idea instruction is presented in Table 2.

The firming cycle schedule reflects the opportunities the learner will have to review the skill of identifying main idea. During each of these brief sessions, the teacher will simply present one or two instructional sequences to the learner and ask the learner to identify the main idea. For example, the teacher would approach the child at 10:00 and say, "I see you just finished your spelling. I want to quickly review the main idea skill we learned this morning in reading group. Look at this picture. (Teacher presents a picture.) Now, read each statement to yourself and tell me which sentence tells the main idea of the picture." The task that the teacher prepares and presents to the learner during the firming cycle is no different from the instructional sequences prepared for the initial teaching sequence used to first introduce and teach main idea (see Figure 2).

The firming cycle accomplishes two important things. First, the learner realizes the information taught earlier is important and must be remembered; second, the learner receives several opportunities to review the skill. The amount of firming required for main idea instruction will vary depending on the learner. A minimum of two instructional days of an intensive firming schedule is recommended. Following this intensive schedule, review of main idea need not be as frequent. A schedule of instruction for main idea during the first week of introduction is in Table 3. The numbers in the schedule represent the number of times each activity should occur each day of instruction. The second week of main idea instruction should offer daily review of the skill. How frequently the skill of main idea is reviewed after the second week should be determined by a learner's performance during the previous weeks of main idea instruction.

Table 3

FIRMING CYCLE SCHEDULE FOR THE FIRST WEEK
OF MAIN IDEA INSTRUCTION

Type of Instruction	Day of Instruction				
	First	Second	Third	Fourth	Fifth
Initial Teaching	1-2	1	1	1	1
Firming Cycle	3	3	2	2	2

Phase II: Main Idea Instruction Using Text

Set Up. This particular phase of main idea instruction uses various forms of text as its set up. Instruction for most children appropriately begins with the identification of main idea in text. (However, for low performing children, the use of pictures as presented in the previous phase of main idea instruction is necessary as an initial introduction. Once a learner clearly understands the concept of main idea as presented through the use of a decontextualized form such as pictures, transition to a text based identification of main idea should be easier.)

Set Up: Modeled Example, Passage 1

Ann was excited. She always wanted a puppy. She first heard it bark. Then she heard a scratch on her door. She jumped up from her bed and ran to open the door. Ann smiled and picked up her new puppy from out of the basket.
Underline the statement that tells the main idea.

1. Ann heard a scratch at her door.
2. Ann was excited.
3. The puppy lived in a basket.
4. Ann got a new puppy.
5. Ann got what she wanted.

Teacher Wording	*Student Response*
1. "Today we're going to learn about main ideas. This time when we learn about the main idea we're not going to use pictures. From now on we're going to find the main idea of a passage."	Each student has a passage and statements as in the set up.

2. "What are we going to find the main idea of?" "A passage."
3. "Yes, we're going to find the main idea of a passage. Everyone, put your finger on the first word of the passage." (Monitor children to see if they've located the first word of the passage.)

   Place finger on first word of passage.

4. "I'll read the passage; you follow along with your finger." (Teacher reads the passage and monitors children.)

   Child follows along.

5. "Now I'll read all of the statements below the passage. You follow along with your finger." (Teacher reads all of the statements.)
6. "Now let's go back and decide which statement tells us the main idea of the passage. I'll read the first statement; you follow along." (Teacher reads the first statement.) "Ann heard a scratch at her door."
7. "Listen, that's not the main idea of the passage. How do I know? Because it doesn't tell about the whole passage. So, am I going to underline it? No."
8. "I'll read the next statement. You follow along." (Teacher reads the next statement.) "Ann was excited."
9. "That's not the main idea of the passage. How do I know? Because it doesn't tell about the whole passage. So, am I going to underline it? No."
10. "I'll read the next statement, you follow along." (Teacher reads the next statement.) "The puppy lived in a basket."
11. "That's not the main idea of the passage. How do I know? Because it doesn't tell about the whole passage. So, am I going to underline it? No."

12. "I'll read the next statement."
    (Teacher reads the next statement.)
    "Ann got a new puppy."
13. "That's the main idea of the passage.
    How do I know? Because it tells
    about the whole passage. So, am I
    going to underline it? Yes."
14. "Listen to the next statement."
    (Teacher reads the last statement.)
    "Ann got what she wanted."
15. "That's not the main idea of the
    passage. How do I know? Because it
    doesn't tell about the whole
    passage. So, am I going to underline
    it? No."
16. "Look at all of the statements. Let's
    review the main idea of the passage
    again. Who can read the statement
    that tells the main idea of the
    passage?"
17. (Teacher calls on a volunteer who is   Child reads the statement. "Ann
    raising a hand.)   got a new puppy."
18. (Teacher directs question to a
    child). "How do you know that is   "Because it tells about the
    the main idea?"   whole passage."
19. (Teacher directs question to group.)
    "If that's the main idea of the
    passage, what are you going to do
    to that statement?"   "Underline it."

Set Up: Modeled Example, Passage 2

20. "Now let's read another passage and
    find the main idea." (Teacher selects
    another passage and a set of state-
    ments.)
21. Teacher repeats steps 4-19 with the
    new passage.

Set Up: Modeled Example, Passage 3

22. Teacher repeats steps 20-21 with a
    new passage and set of statements.

Set Up: Modeled Example, Passage 4

23. Same as step 22.

Set Up: Test Example, Passage 1

Whales are like human beings in many ways. They are mammals like us. They have hair, they breathe air, they are born alive, and their babies take milk from their mothers. Whales are also warm-blooded animals like us.

Underline the statement that tells the main idea.

1. Whales are mammals like us.
2. Whales and human beings have many things in common.
3. Whales and human beings are common animals.

Teacher Wording	*Learner Response*
24. "Will someone please read the passage out loud?" (Teacher calls on a volunteer.)	Child reads passage orally while others follow along.
25. "Will someone please read the three statements below the passage?" (Teacher calls on a volunteer.)	Child reads passage orally while others follow along.
26. "Now let's go back and look at each statement. I'll read the first statement again; you follow along. Whales are mammals like us." (Pauses and looks at children.) "Listen, is that the main idea of the passage?" (Teacher calls on a volunteer for a response.)	"No."

Correction Procedure   If the child responds incorrectly, the teacher models the answer: "Listen, that's not the main idea of the passage. How do I know? Because it doesn't tell about the whole passage. Now it's your turn again. Read the first sentence again." (Child reads, "Whales are mammals like us.") "Is that the main idea of the passage?" (Child responds.) "How do you know?" (Child responds.) The teacher may want to model a new set of examples for the learner before continuing in the testing sequence.

27. "How do you know?"	"Because it doesn't tell about the whole passage."

28. "So, will you underline it?"	"No."
29. "I'll read the next sentence. 'Whales and human beings have many things in common.' " (Pauses and looks at children.) "Is that the main idea of the passage?" (Teacher calls on a volunteer for a response.)	"Yes."
30. "How do you know?"	"Because it tells about the whole passage."
31. "So will you underline it?"	"Yes."
32. "Look at the next sentence. 'Whales and human beings are common animals'." (Pauses and looks at children.) "Is that the main idea of the passage?" (Teacher calls on a volunteer for a response.)	"No."
33. "How do you know?"	"Because it doesn't tell about the whole passage."
34. "So, will you underline it?"	"No."

Set Up Test Example 2

35. "Now let's read another passage." (Teacher selects another passage and set of statements and presents it.)
36. Teacher repeats steps 24-34 with the new set up.

(The teacher should test children on a minimum of three new passages before terminating the instruction.)

Figure 4. Format for main idea instruction: Phase II, text.

The initial set up for main idea instruction (see Figure 4) would involve brief passages that consist of a series of four to six sentences (approximately 25 to 50 words in length) written in a paragraph form. Each set up consists of one paragraph followed by a series of correct and incorrect statements of the main idea for the given paragraph. As in the picture set up in Phase I of instruction, the number of possible main idea statements that follow a paragraph should be varied. The number of statements could range from two to six with the incorrect main idea statements describing either one or two details of the text only and not the entire text.

Main Idea Instruction for Low Performers   269

The explicitness of the main idea statement within the text should be varied. A passage could contain a topic sentence that specifies for the learner that the main idea is right there in the passage. Passages could also require children to infer the main idea of a passage from the supporting details in a passage that does not have a topic sentence.

The variation in the explicitness of the main idea in passages selected in a set up should not present a problem. The instructional set up includes not only a passage but also a series of correct and incorrect statements of the main idea which allow the learner merely to choose a main idea statement. The choice response format reduces the complexity of the task by allowing the child to select a main idea from a prescribed list instead of verbally producing one. The production response is significantly more difficult than the choice response since it requires the student to formulate a main idea statement based on information the learner is able to extract from the text passage. In a more advanced and subsequent phase of instruction, such a production response is not only appropriate but necessary to the learner's individual development of independent reading comprehension skills. In the set up for an advanced application of main idea instruction, the learner would be required to read a passage or multiple passages and independently generate a main idea statement based on his or her comprehension of the text. This application would be more in keeping with the requirements of main idea tasks typically found in basal reading series and other mainstream reading programs.

Modeled set of examples. As in Phase I of main idea instruction using pictures, only one modeled example of the main idea can be presented within each set up in Phase II of instruction using text. Since one modeled example is inadequate for teaching main idea, the teacher must include more modeled examples of main idea, at least four passages in the initial teaching. The teaching format presented in Figure 4 specifies four modeled examples, each presented one after the other. Since the set up in this phase of instruction involves passages of varying length, the instructional time required for this initial teaching will be greater than that required for Phase I using pictures.

Before modeling the first passage, the teacher alerts the learner to the transition from the use of pictures to text in learning about main ideas. The teacher begins the Modeled Example with a brief discrimination activity inserted into the teaching format as a way of checking and prompting the learner's attention to the task (see steps 1 and 2 in Figure 4). By simply asking "What are we going to find the main idea of?" the teacher receives instant feedback as to whether or not the learner attended to the transition

Kameenui

from pictures to text. In the first modeled passage (steps 4 to 15), the teacher models every aspect of the instruction while the learner observes. The teacher reads the passage out loud (see step 4); the teacher reads all of the main idea statements (see step 6); and then the teacher reads each statement again when applying the given rule (see steps 6 to 15). Individual learners can read most, if not all, of Modeled Examples 2 to 4. However, the teacher should continue to model the application of the rule to each of the possible main idea statements.

The rule application used to determine the main idea statement in steps 6 to 15 is highly structured and overt. The teacher models all of the features of the entire response requirement. First, each statement that serves as a possible instance of the main idea of the passage is read followed by the teacher specifying whether the statement is the main idea of the passage. Next the teacher models a verification response. By asking "How do I know?" and subsequently applying the rule to the selected statement, the teacher identifies for the learner the one dimension that must be evident in the selected statement in order for it to be the main idea of the passage — it must tell about the whole passage. By modeling each part of the rule application, the teacher provides the learner with an example of the relatedness of the passage and statements to the concept of main idea and to the responses required of the learner. Before proceeding to the next modeled example, the teacher quickly reviews the main idea statement for the passage (see steps 16 to 18).

Test examples. The procedures for testing the learner's knowledge of main idea in this phase of instruction are similar to the procedures described for Phase I of main idea instruction using pictures. The rationale for the testing procedures in this phase of instruction also have been previously described.

If the learner incorrectly identifies two or more main idea statements across the four separate testing passages, several features of the entire instructional episode must be examined immediately. First, the teacher may want to select a shorter and more readable passage as an example to model. In modeling the passage, the teacher should be careful to attend to the wording used and to the pacing of its presentation (e.g., is it too fast or too slow?). Second, the teacher may want to examine the type of passages selected as modeled examples. If the passages selected to be modeled vary greatly in text features such as length, topic, syntactic complexity, frequency and proximity of irrelevant information, density of new information, occurrence of low frequency vocabulary, and so on, the type of passages to be modeled may need to be limited to a particular subtype (e.g., brief narrative prose passage with a minimal load of new information). This kind of remediation will require more instructional time overall and more carefully designed instructional set ups.

The schedule of instruction described for Phase I of main idea instruction using pictures can also be followed with this phase of instruction. More specifically, the lower the student's performance is in basic skill areas, the more likely that learner will require placement in a firming cycle that provides extensive review as well as a cumulative review of all skills previously taught in main idea instruction.

Phase III: Advanced Strategies for Main Idea Instruction

This phase of instruction is to be initiated after Phases I and II of main idea instruction have been mastered. A set of instructional procedures for teaching main idea when the set up involves extensive or multiple passages will be described briefly since the format of Phase III is similar to that presented in Phases I and II. Figure 5 presents a Phase III lesson.

The first steamboat that worked was built in the United States in 1787. It had many paddles on the sides. The next year two men in Scotland made a steamboat and it used wheels to move the paddles. This steamboat had a paddle wheel on each side. It could travel about five miles per hour. Soon other steamboats were built. One of these had a single paddle wheel at the back of the boat.

An American named Robert Fulton saw a paddle wheel steamboat in Scotland and decided to make one. He built a successful steamboat in France. When he went back home, he planned a bigger and better one than any that had been built. He thought such a steamboat would soon pay for itself. So he set about carrying out his plan. People told him the plan would not work. But he kept on trying.

At last Fulton's steamboat was finished. It was named the Clermont. It was ready for a trial on the Hudson River in New York State. The people who gathered on the banks of the Hudson made fun of it. They called it "Fulton's Folly." Soon the great paddle wheels on each side of the boat began to turn. The steamboat moved slowly up the Hudson River. The people on the river banks stopped laughing. They stared in wonder. The day of the steamboat had begun.

Step 1. *Teacher*   "I need a volunteer to begin reading." (Teacher calls on a volunteer.) "Why don't you start reading the passage and I'll tell you when to stop."

       Learner   (Reads the first three sentences out loud.)

| Step 2. *Teacher* | "Stop. Thank you. Can anyone tell me what those sentences were about? (Teacher calls on a volunteer.) |
| *Learner* | "They were about steamboats." |

| *Correction Procedure* | If the response is incorrect, the teacher may want to have a learner reread each sentence. After reading the first sentence the teacher would stop the child and ask, "What does that whole sentence tell about?" The child should respond, "It tells about the first steamboat." If the child responds incorrectly, the teacher may want to model the correct response. After reading the first sentence and identifying the main topic, the teacher should have a learner read the second sentence. After reading the second sentence, the teacher should prompt the learners about the main topic of the first sentence. For example, "Listen, what did the first sentence tell about?" (Child responds, "The first steamboat.") "Now, does the next sentence also tell about the first steamboat or something else?" (Child responds, "The first steamboat.") "So, what do the first two sentences tell about?" (Child responds, "The first steamboat.") After the third sentence is read, the teacher would continue prompting by asking, "Does the next sentence also tell about the first steamboat or about something else?" (Child responds, "Something else.") "Listen, the first sentence tells about a steamboat, the second sentence tells about a steamboat, and the third sentence tells about steamboats. What do all of those sentences tell about?" (Child responds, "Steamboats.") |

| Step 3. *Teacher* | "Yes, they tell about steamboats. Now let's read the next three sentences and see if they continue to tell about steamboats." (Teacher calls on a volunteer to read.) |
| *Learner* | (Reads the next three sentences out loud.) |

| Step 4. *Teacher* | "Stop. Thank you. Now let's see if those sentences still tell about steamboats." |

(Steps 1 to 4 are repeated with remaining text.)

Figure 5. Format for main idea instruction: Phase III, advanced strategies.

The set up for this phase of instruction would consist of passages selected from a text the learner is using in reading, language, or a content area. The set up for this phase of instruction would *not* include a set of statements representing instances and noninstances of main idea statements for the entire set of passages. In other words, in this phase of instruction instead of choosing a correct main idea statement from a list, the learner will be required to produce a main idea statement based on comprehension of the passage.

The initial teaching in this phase of instruction can begin with a set up consisting of only one passage or of multiple passages depending upon the teacher's assessment of the learner's skill level. The strategy to be used for low performing learners in this phase of instruction is a facilitative questioning strategy. In this strategy, the teacher requires the learner to read small chunks orally (i.e., either one, two, or three sentences) of the passage at a time and then asks questions to lead the learner to identify the main idea of the passage(s). Through the questioning strategy, the learner is guided and prompted to examine information in the text being read and to determine whether the main idea identified in the first chunk of the passage is again repeated in subsequent chunks of the passage. Steps 1 to 4 in Figure 5 present an example of the facilitative questioning strategy.

The four step facilitative questioning strategy requires the teacher to lead the learner through each small chunk of text. This highly teacher directed strategy allows the teacher to monitor the learner's comprehension of the text. The strategy also allows the teacher to provide the learner with immediate feedback about the text. The strategy for identifying the main idea consists of the teacher guiding the learner to identify the main topic for the first chunk of sentences. Once the main topic for the first chunk of sentences is identified, the teacher again guides and prompts the learner to determine whether the main topic stays the same or changes from chunk to chunk until the entire text is completed. At the end of the text, the teacher informs the learner that the topic is in fact the main idea of the entire text.

As children progress through this phase of instruction, the teacher should require the learner to read (perhaps silently) longer chunks of the selected text. The teacher should also provide less facilitative questions and require the child to examine the text and identify the main idea independently.

Summary

Main idea instruction for low performers based on the Direct Instruction Model have these general characteristics:
1. Prerequisite skills and component discriminations of a strategy are taught, and mastery of them is demonstrated before strategy instruction.

2. Initial teaching sequences for all instructional presentations are completely demonstrated and directed by the teacher.
3. All steps in the instruction during the initial teaching sequences are overt and highly prompted. Feedback is immediate, frequent, and specific.
4. Instruction progresses in phases in which later phases require demonstrated mastery of earlier phases. During instruction in later phases, steps in the strategy are combined and made less overt. Application of the strategy is less teacher directed and more automatic.
5. In the final phase of instruction, teacher direction is minimal and the learner practices the strategy covertly and independently.
6. Skills and strategies previously mastered are cummulatively reviewed. Systematic firming of skills is also scheduled.
7. The skill of identifying main ideas is viewed as a single dimension concept. The teacher must design a teaching sequence that presents that one dimension.
8. Teaching sequence of main idea must consist of modeled positive and negative examples of main idea.
9. Teaching sequences must also consist of a test set of examples that immediately follow the modeled teacher demonstration.
10. Correction procedures and a schedule of instruction should be included in the design of an instructional sequence for main idea.

References

Alexander, C.F., Strategies for finding the main idea. *Journal of Reading*, 1976, *19*, 299-301.

Axelrod, J. Getting the main idea is still the main idea. *Journal of Reading*, 1975, *18*, 383-387.

Baer, D. *Is attribution the square root of modification?* Paper presented at the annual meeting of the Association for the Advancement of Behavior Therapy, San Francisco, California, December 1979.

Baumann, J.F. A generic comprehension instructional strategy. *Reading World*, 1983, *23*, 284-294.

Baumann, J.F. The effectiveness of a direct instruction paradigm for teaching main idea comprehension. *Reading Research Quarterly*, 1984, *20*, 93-115.

Becker, W.C. Teaching reading and language to the disadvantaged: What we have learned from field research. *Harvard Educational Review*, 1977, *47*, 518-543.

Becker, W.C., and Carnine, D.W. Direct instruction: An effective approach to education intervention with disadvantaged and low performers. In B. Lahey and A. Kazkin (Eds.), *Advances in child clinical psychology, vol. 3,* New York: Plenum, 1980, 429-447.

Bereiter, C., and Kurland, M.A. A constructive look at follow through results. *Interchange*, 1981-1983, *12*, 1-22.

Carnine, D., and Silbert, J. *Direct instruction reading.* Columbus, OH: Merrill, 1979.

Dishner, E.K., and Readence, J.E. A systematic procedure for teaching main idea. *Reading World,* 1977, *16,* 292-298.

Donlan, D. Locating main ideas in history textbooks. *Journal of Reading,* 1980, *24,* 135-140.

Duffy, G.G., and Roehler, L.F. Direct instruction of comprehension: What does it really mean? *Reading Horizons,* 1982, *23,* 35-40.

Durkin, D. D. Reading comprehension instruction in five basal reader series. *Reading Research Quarterly,* 1981, *16,* 515-544.

Engelmann, S., and Carnine, D. *Theory of instruction: Principles and applications.* New York: Irvington Publishers, 1982.

Gage, N.L. *The scientific basis of the art of teaching.* New York: Teachers College Press, 1978.

Gersten, R., and Carnine, D. Direct instruction mathematics: A longitudinal evaluation of low income elementary school students. *Elementary School Journal,* 1984, *84,* 395-407.

Guthrie, J.T. Research views — follow through: A compensatory education experiment. *The Reading Teacher,* 1977, *3,* 240-244.

Hare, V.C., and Milligan, B. Main idea identification: Instructional explanations in four basal reader series. *Journal of Reading Behavior,* 1984, *16,* 189-200.

Homme, L. Perspectives in psychology: Control of covenants, the operants of the mind. *Psychological Record,* 1965, *15,* 501-511.

House, E.R., Glass, G.V., McLean, L.D., and Walker, D.E. No simple answer: Critique of the "Follow Through" evaluation. *Harvard Educational Review,* 1978, *48,* 128-160.

Isakson, R.L., Miller, J.W., and O'Hara, J.J. Finding the main idea: Can your students do it? *Reading World,* 1979, *19,* 28-35.

Kennedy, M. Findings from the Follow Through Planned Variation Study. *Educational Researcher,* 1978, *7,* 3-11.

Luria, A. *A role of speech in regulations of normal and abnormal behaviors.* New York: Liveright, 1961.

Rosenshine, B. Classroom instruction. In N.L. Gage (Ed.), *The psychology of teaching methods.* Seventy-fifth yearbook of the National Society for the Study of Education, Part 1. Chicago: University of Chicago Press, 1976, 335-371.

Singer, H., and Balow, I.H. Overcoming educational disadvantageness. In J.L. Tzeng and H. Singer (Eds.), *Perception of print: Reading research in experimental psychology.* Hillsdale, NJ: Erlbaum, 1981, 274-312.

Stebbins, L. (Ed.). *Education as experimentation: A planned variation model, vol. 3A.* Cambridge, MA: ABT Associates, 1976.

Stebbins, L., St. Pierre, R.G., Proper, E.L., Anderson, R.B., and Cerva, T.R. *Education as experimentation: A planned variation model, vol. 4A-D.* Cambridge, MA: ABT Associates, 1976.

Steely, D., and Engelmann, S.E. *Implementation of basal reading in grades 4-6.* Final Report. Eugene, OR: Engelmann-Becker, 1979.

Vygotsky, L. *Thought and language.* New York: Wiley, 1962.

Williams, J.P., Taylor, M.B., and Jarin, D.C. *Research on text structure and instructional development: Determining the main idea of expository paragraphs.* Paper presented at the meeting of the AERA, Montreal, Canada, 1983.

Zohorik, J.A. and Kritek, W.J. *Using direct instruction.* Paper presented at the meeting of the AERA, Montreal, Canada, April 1983.